An Invitation to **Social**
Construction

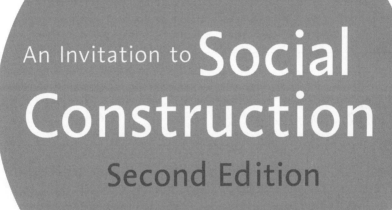

An Invitation to **Social Construction**

Second Edition

Kenneth J. Gergen

Los Angeles • London • New Delhi • Singapore • Washington DC

© Kenneth J. Gergen 2009

First edition published 1999
Reprinted 2000, 2001, 2002, 2003, 2005, 2008
This second edition published 2009

SAGE Publications Ltd
1 Oliver's Yard
55 City Road
London EC1Y 1SP

SAGE Publications Inc.
2455 Teller Road
Thousand Oaks, California 91320

SAGE Publications India Pvt Ltd
B 1/I 1 Mohan Cooperative Industrial Area
Mathura Road
New Delhi 110 044

SAGE Publications Asia-Pacific Pte Ltd
33 Pekin Street #02-01
Far East Square
Singapore 048763

Library of Congress Control Number: 2008932854

British Library Cataloguing in Publication data

A catalogue record for this book is available from
the British Library

ISBN 978-1-4129-2300-2
ISBN 978-1-4129-2301-9 (pbk)

Typeset by C&M Digitals (P) Ltd, Chennai, India
Printed and bound in Great Britain by TJ International Ltd, Padstow, Cornwall
Printed on paper from sustainable resources

CONTENTS

PREFACE

My aspirations for this book are not meager. My dearest hope is that these pages can provide the reader with an entry into a range of exciting dialogues occurring across the academic disciplines, within sectors of the culture at large, and around the globe. The dialogues most often fall under the label, *social construction*. Others speak more narrowly of "constructivism", or more broadly in terms of "postmodernism". For all participants these discussions are momentous in implication. They seem equivalent to the radical changes in thinking and societal practices taking place in sixteenth- and seventeenth-century European culture. This, we have come to see, is a period in which the culture moved from the "Dark Ages" into the "Enlightenment". As I see the present dialogues, they not only unsettle the grounds for the investments of the Enlightenment – in reason, the individual mind, objective truth, and moral princi- ples. More importantly, they offer unparalleled opportunities for creative delibera- tion and action. They invite us into new spaces of understanding from which a more promising world can emerge. The ideas in this book have changed my life; they have done the same for so many of my colleagues and acquaintances. At the same time, these dialogues are provocative and even irritating to many. Controversy abounds. If this book is successful, however, you should be able to join these discussions, appreciate their significance, sample their potentials, worry about shortcomings – and most hopefully, take away inspiration for action. This book is not intended as "the last word", but as a beginning.

The present volume is a revision of my 1999 work, *An invitation to social construc- tion*. The reasons for bringing the new work into being are twofold. First, there is a steadily increasing demand for writing on social construction to meet classroom needs. The initial volume did speak to these needs, but primarily for an advanced readership. Required was a work that spelled out the essential reasoning with more accessible clarity. The present work is thus shorter and more directly "to the point". Moreover, I have added two features to increase the educational impact of the work: you will find a series of boxed inserts for the purposes of expanding the implications of the unfold- ing arguments. These will give readers more opportunity to pause and reflect. I have also added numerous visual supplements that may bring further life to the text.

The second reason for the revised work was the fact that contributions to social con- struction have multiplied at a rapid rate since 1999. New issues and applications are everywhere apparent. One of the most important features of social constructionist thought is its relevance to the times. Although the basic ideas of social construction are highly general, the chief focus is on practice. Can the ideas be put to use in practical ways? The past decade represents a formidable tribute to the potential of these ideas. In the academic arena we find a virtual renaissance in approaches to research, forms of expression, and theoretical exploration. Almost all of these efforts are ultimately concerned with social change. Outside the academic world, constructionist ideas have stimulated an enormous expansion in forms of practice. For example, educators, therapists, social workers, organizational change specialists, peace workers, and community builders – among others – have all contributed impressively to new and effective forms of practice. My hope is that this work will not only reflect these exciting developments, but will encourage readers to extend the possibilities.

A personal word to my readers will also be helpful. We both bring important limitations to these pages now uniting us. I am limited by the fact that I have lived the better part of my life as a scholar. My habits of expression are acceptable enough in professional circles, but they are not necessarily congenial to those outside the professions. I do attempt to break free from the worst of the "academic habits", but you will find that I am not always successful. My life experiences are also bounded. It is not only that my words will inevitably carry the traces of nationality, gender, age and sexual preference, but my life experiences are also limiting. I have lived a life of some privilege: I have had a steady job, never fought on a field of battle, and never lived in poverty. I have had my share of suffering, but I cannot write out of the depth of fear and pain that has affected so many of the world's people during my lifetime. You as reader also bring to these pages a unique background, special enthusiasms, and particular dreams for the future. I can only hope that your approach to this text will enable you to find provocative ideas, useful insights, and possibly inspiring potentials.

As I write I try to imagine you as the reader sitting and talking with me as an interested friend. Yet, these words will be more or less significant to you depending on how you imagine me. In these pages you will get to know me through the rhythms and melodies of relationships I have shared with others across time and circumstance. However, you can do as you wish with these words – work, play, invent, fantasize, devour, spit. Perhaps we shall best make meaning together if you can imagine me as someone who can be educated by your reactions to the text. It is not my aim here to persuade, to win, or to educate you in "the right way". It is you who must breathe life into these words. And if we are successful in this author–reader relationship, perhaps new paths will open. As we relate together so do we construct our future.

PUBLISHER'S ACKNOWLEDGEMENTS

The authors and publishers wish to thank the following for permission to use copyright material:

We thank A. P. Watt Ltd and Simon & Schuster for permission to use an extract from Yeats, W. B. 'Death':
Reprinted by permission of A. P. Watt Ltd on behalf of Gráinne Yeats.
Reprinted with the permission of Scribner, a Division of Simon & Schuster, Inc., from *THE COLLECTED WORKS OF W.B. YEATS, VOLUME I: THE POEMS, REVISED* edited by Richard J. Finneran. Copyright © 1933 by The Macmillan Company. Copyright renewed © 1961 by Bertha Georgie Yeats. All rights reserved.

We thank Georges Borchardt Inc and Taylor and Francis for permission to use an extract from Foucault, Michel (1965):
Madness and Civilization by Michel Foucault. English translation copyright © 1965 by Random House, Inc. Originally published in French as *Histoire de la Folie* Copyright © 1961 by Librairie Plon. Reprinted by permission of Georges Borchardt, Inc., for Librairie Plon.

We thank Hackett Publishing Company for permission to use an extract from *Ways of Worldmaking* by Nelson Goodman (Indianapolis: Hackett Publishing Company, Inc., 1978). All rights reserved.

We thank Heini Schneebeli and Bridgeman Art for granting permission to use Torso of a Naked Youth (marble by Roman (1st century BC). Photo © Heini Schneebeli / Bridgeman Art.

We thank Indiana University Press for permission to use an extract from Minh-Ha, Trinh T. (1989) *Woman Native Other.* Reprinted with permission of the Publisher.

We thank Monte Isom for permission to use a photo image of Tiger Woods. Reprinted with permission of the photographer.

We thank Polity Press for permission to use an extract from Kappeler, S. (1986). *The Pornography of Representation*, Polity Press. Reprinted with permission of the Publisher.

We thank Robert Grudin for permission to use an extract from Grudin, R. (1997) *On Dialogue: An Essay in Free Thought*, Mariner Books. Reprinted with permission of the author.

We thank Simon & Schuster and Continuum International Publishing Group for permission to use an extract from Buber, M (1970) *I and Thou*. Reprinted with the permission of Scribner, a division of Simon & Schuster, Inc., from *I and Thou* by Martin Buber, translated by Walter Kaufman. Copyright © 1970 by Charles Scribner's Sons. Introduction copyright © 1970 by Walter Kaufman. All rights reserved. Reproduced by kind permission of Continuum International Publishing Group.

We thank Springer for permission to use an extract from Flux, J. (1993) 'Multiples: On The Contemporary Politics of Subjectivity', *Human Studies*, Vol 16, Numbers 1-2, pp. 33–49. Reprinted with permission of the Publisher.

We thank the University of Minnesota Press for permission to use an extract from Smith, P (1988) *Discerning the Subject*, University of Minnesota Press. Reprinted with permission of the Publisher.

We thank the University of Notre Dame Press for permission to use an extract from *Beyond Virtue: A Study in Moral Theory* by MacIntyre (1981), University of Notre Dame Press.

We thank the University of Texas Press for permission to use an extract from *Speech Genres and Other Late Essays* by M.M. Bakhtin, translated by Vern W. McGee, edited by Caryl Emerson and Michael Holquist, copyright © 1986. By permission of the University of Texas Press.

We thank the University of Toronto Press for permission to use "Pure unstoried action, pure unstoried existence in the present, is impossible" from Randall, W.L. (1995) *The Stories We Are: An Essay on Self-Creation*, p. 93, University of Toronto Press. Reprinted with permission of the Publisher.

We thank W.W. Norton for permission to use an extract from "Poetics". Copyright © 1969 by A. R. Ammons, "The Confirmers", from *Collected Poems* 1951-1971 by A. R. Ammons. Used by permission of W. W. Norton & Company, Inc.

We thank SAGE Publications for permission to use extracts from:

Brinkmsnn, S. (2006) 'Questioning Constructionism: Towards an Ethics of Finitude' *Journal of Humanistic Psychology*, p. 94.

Denzin, N.K. and Lincoln, Y.S. (2000) *Handbook of Qualitative Research*.

We thank Taylor and Francis for permission to use extracts from:

Bohm, D. (2004) *On Dialogue*, Routledge, p. 43.

Holzman, L. (1997) *Schools for Growth*, Lawrence Erlbaum Associates, Inc.

Wittgenstein, L. (2001) *Tractatus Logico Philosophicus*, p. 68, Routledge Classics.

We thank Wiley-Blackwell for permission to use extracts from:

Eagleton, T. (1996). *The Illusions of Post-Modernism*, Wiley-Blackwell.

Wittgenstein, L. (1973) *Philosophical Investigations*, Wiley-Blackwell.

1

SOCIAL CONSTRUCTION: REVOLUTION
IN THE MAKING

Recently I had a diagnostic test in which needles were stuck into my arm, and the doctor delivered a series of electrical shocks. The test is known to be a bit painful and I was not looking forward to it. However, as the doctor began to insert the needles into my skin, I decided to try an experiment. Each time I was jolted by a shock I would respond not with an anguished grunt, but with laughter. The procedure began, along with my experiment in hilarity. Possibly the doctor thought that it was really my sanity that was in question. But for me the little experiment was paying off. Sure, there were sensations I would call painful, but somehow the laughter had a transformative power. I wasn't in agony; in fact, I found myself light-hearted, and smiling as I left the examination room.

But why did I attempt this little experiment? It is largely because I have been deeply involved in the drama – both intellectual and practical – that will unfold in the pages that follow. Consider the longstanding tradition that teaches us that we must know the world for what it is. We must study the world carefully and objectively; with such knowledge we can predict and control what takes place. But what is this objective world? Surely, we would count pain as something worthy of study. But if my laughter can change my experience of pain, then clearly, pain does not exist "out there", independent of me. Pain depends, at least in part, on how one approaches it. In effect, pain is not pain is not pain. And if this is the case with pain, what else should we include? Do racial differences exist "out there", independent of how we approach the world, or differences in intelligence or gender? And if one's approach is important in these cases, then what are the limits? Are the mountains the same for a young child, an athlete and an old man? Is a tree the same object for a botanist, a forester, and a landscaper? What indeed is "the objective world?"

Herein lies the opening chapter of this drama called *social construction*: what we take to be the world importantly depends on how we approach it, and how we approach it depends on the social relationships of which we are a part. When fully understood, you will find that constructionist ideas will challenge long honoured words like "truth", "objectivity", "reason", and "knowledge". Your understanding of yourself – your thoughts, emotions, and desires – will also be transformed. Your relations with others will come to have an entirely new meaning. You will see world conflict in a different light. Constructionist ideas and practices are now explored in all corners of the world. You may travel from Buenos Aires to Helsinki, from London to Hong Kong, from New Delhi to Moscow and find lively discussions of these issues. As many believe, these ideas may be vital to the world's future. To be sure, there is controversy; with change there is inevitably resistance. You may also find yourself resisting. All the better. This should sharpen the edge of your reading.

You should also realize that the ideas generally called social constructionist, do not belong to any one individual. There is no single book or school of philosophy that defines social construction. Rather, social constructionist ideas emerge from a process of dialogue, a dialogue that is ongoing, and to which anyone – even you as reader – may contribute. As a result, however, there is no one, authoritative account that represents all the participants. There are many different views, and some tensions among them. However, in this chapter I will first outline a number of major proposals as shared by many. To appreciate these proposals in greater depth, I will then fill out some of the historical background. How did people – scholars or otherwise – come into this orientation? This discussion will also give you some insight as to why these ideas are so revolutionary and so controversial. Later chapters will be devoted to implications and applications.

Together We Construct Our Worlds

If I ask about the world, you can offer to tell me how it is under one or more frames of reference; but if I insist that you tell me how it is apart from all frames, what can you say?

Nelson Goodman, *Ways of Worldmaking*

The pivotal idea in social construction is simple and straightforward. However, as you unpack the implications and consequences, this simplicity rapidly dissolves. The basic idea asks us to rethink virtually everything we have been taught about the world and ourselves. And with this rethinking we are invited into new and challenging forms of action. To appreciate the possibilities, consider the world of common sense knowledge. What is more obvious than the fact that the world is simply out there for us to observe and understand? There are trees, buildings, automobiles, women, men, dogs and cats, and so on. If we observe carefully enough, we can learn how to save the forests, build strong buildings, and improve the health of children. Now, let's stand these trusted assumptions on their head.

What if I proposed that there are no trees, buildings, women, men, and so on until you and I agree that there are? "Absurd", you may say, "Just look around you; the trees were here long before we came along". That sounds reasonable, but let's take little Julie, a one-year-old, out for a walk. Her gaze seems to move past trees, buildings and cars without notice; she does not seem to distinguish men from women. William James once said that the world of a child is a "booming, buzzing confusion". Whether you agree with him or not, Julie's world doesn't seem to be the kind we live in as adults. Unlike Julie, we notice the buds on the trees turn to leaves as Spring approaches. We see the leaves fall from the trees when Autumn comes. We read the advertisement on the passing bus, and pay attention when the policeman tells us to stop. In Julie's world there are no men and women, no budding trees, no advertisements, and no police. What reaches our eyeballs may not be different from Julie's, but what this world *means to us* is different. In this sense, we approach the world in a different way. This difference is rooted in our social relationships. It is within these relationships that we construct the world in this way or that. In relationships the world comes to be what it is for us. And, as Julie's relationships with her family and friends are extended, she will come to construct the world in much the same way we do.

Different You's from Different Views

To the:	You may be:
Biologist	"a mammal"
Hairdresser	"needing a cut"
Teacher	"college material"
Gay man	"possibly straight"
Christian	"a sinner"
Parent	"surprisingly successful"
Artist	"an excellent model"
Psychologist	"slightly neurotic"
Physicist	"an atomic composition"

(Cont'd)

Banker	"a future customer"
Doctor	"a hypochondriac"
Hindu	"in an imperfect state of Atman"
Lover	"a wonderful person"
Ifalukian	"filled with liget"

Could you ever be described in terms that were not shared by others? And if there is something there prior to description, how would we identify it? Whose terms would we use to describe it?

The basic idea of social construction may seem simple enough. But consider the consequences: if everything we consider real is socially constructed, then *nothing* is real unless people agree that it is. You may now be skeptical. Does this mean that death is not real, or the body, or the sun, or this chair on which I am seated … and the list goes on. It is important to be clear on this point. Social constructionists do not say, "There is nothing", or "There is no reality". The important point is that whenever people define reality – that death is real, or the body, the sun, and the chair on which they are sitting – they are speaking from a particular standpoint. To be sure, something happens, but in describing it you will inevitably rely on some tradition of sense making.

To illustrate, if someone says, "My grandfather is dead", he or she is usually speaking from a biological standpoint. The event is defined as the termination of certain bodily functioning. From other traditions we might also say, "He has gone to heaven", "He will live forever in her heart", "This is the beginning of a new cycle of his reincarnation", "His burden has been eased", "He lives in his legacy of good works", "In his three children, his life goes on", or "The atomic composition of this object has changed". Each of these descriptions is legitimate in the traditions in which they were created. But, for little Julie, the event might indeed be unremarkable. In her world "grandfather's death" doesn't exist as an event. For the constructionist, it is not that "There is nothing", but "*nothing for us*". In other words, it is from our relationships with others that the world becomes filled with what we take to be "death", "the sun", "chairs", and so on.

In a broader sense, we may say that as we communicate with each other we construct the world in which we live. In one conversation, we may find much that is wrong with the world. There are the daily pressures, the lack of money, the lack of opportunity, and so on. In other conversations there are excitements, enthusiasms, and hopes. The realities we live in are outcomes of the conversations in which we are engaged. As long as we make the familiar distinctions, for example, between men and women, day and night, good and bad, life remains relatively predictable. Yet, all that we take for granted can also be challenged. For example, "problems" don't exist in the world as independent facts; rather we construct worlds of good and bad, and define anything standing in the way of achieving what we value as "a problem". If the conversation could be changed, all that we construct as "problems" could be reconstructed as "opportunities". As we speak together, we can also bring new worlds into being. We could construct a world in which there are three genders, the "mentally ill" are "spiritual healers", or where "the power" in all organizations lies not within individual leaders but in the lowly worker.

It is at this point that you can begin to appreciate the enormous potential of constructionist ideas. For the constructionist, our actions are not constrained by anything traditionally accepted as true, rational, or right. Standing before us is a vast spectrum of possibility, an endless invitation to innovation. This is not to say that we must abandon all that we take to be real and good. Not at all. But it is to say that we are not bound by the chains of either history or tradition. As we speak together, listen to new voices, raise questions, ponder alternatives, and play at the edges of common sense, we cross the threshold into new worlds of meaning. The future is ours – together – to create.

With this fundamental vision at hand, we can now explore more deeply some of the central assumptions at play here. These five assumptions form the backbone for the remainder of the book.

1. The way in which we understand the world is not required by "what there is".

> Man has created death.
>
> William Butler Yeats, *Death*

You might readily agree there is nothing about your particular body that required your receiving the name you live by. If your name is James, you could have been named Jordan, Julia, or Jerome. In effect, you owe your name to others. It is a matter of social convention. But now expand the implications: given whatever exists, we may say that there is no arrangement of syllables, words or phrases that must be used to describe or explain it. For any state of affairs a potentially unlimited number of descriptions and explanations should be possible. If this is so, then it also follows that everything we have learned about our world and ourselves – that gravity holds us to the earth, planes and birds both fly, cancer kills, or that the earth revolves around the sun – could be otherwise. There is nothing about "what there is" that demands these particular accounts; we could use our language to construct alternative worlds in which there is no gravity or cancer, or in which persons and birds are equivalent, and the sun revolves around the world. For many people this supposition is deeply threatening. Not only does it suggest that there is no truth – words that truly map the world – but it also suggests there is nothing we can hold on to, nothing solid on which we can rest our beliefs, nothing secure. Isn't this nihilistic?

Perhaps this state of insecurity is not as bad as it might appear. In daily life, many of our categories lead to untold suffering. Consider the distress and death that have resulted from such phrases as:

"This is mine".
"He is to blame".

5

"They are evil".
"This is a superior race".
"This group is more intelligent than that".
"The fertilized egg is a human being".
"There is only one God".

From the constructionist standpoint none of these phrases is demanded by "the way things are". Other ways of talking are possible, and with far more promising outcomes. This is not to abandon our various traditions of truth, but simply to see them as optional.

2. The ways in which we describe and explain the world are the outcomes of relationship.

The meaning of a word is its use in the language.

Ludwig Wittgenstein, *Philosophical Investigations*

In Western culture we have long placed a value on personal experience. As commonly held, we each have our own private and personal experience of the world. It is through such experience that we come to know the world, to appreciate, to fear, to see its potentials, and so on. And, on this account, when we meet together, we try to communicate our experiences to each other. Coupled with the idea that we first experience the world, and then try to put the experience into words, is the view of *language as a picture*. That is, if our experience mirrors the world – thus providing us with a mental picture – then effective language should communicate to others the picture in our minds. In effect, the language could then give you a picture of the world – at least the way I experience it. If you have never been to Marrakech, I could return from a visit and my descriptions would give you a picture of what I saw. The picture theory of language is also important to our traditional understanding of truth. As often put, truth exists when our language accurately *depicts* the world. Thus, if I told you that at the centre of Marrakech you would find "The Square of the Dead", you could go there and see if this were true. As philosophers of science, have phrased it, a true statement *corresponds with* actual fact.

Now recall the proposition that the world does not drive our understanding. Whatever there is makes no demands on our descriptions. As the philosopher, Immanuel Kant, pointed out, we could stare at the world for years and never come up with concepts of number or causality. But for that matter, returning to Julie, at what point would her private observations stimulate her to talk about men as opposed to women, autumn leaves, policemen and so on? All these terms have their origins in human communities. What we take to be true about the world is not then born of the pictures in our minds, but of relationships. Understandings of the world are achieved through coordinations among persons – negotiations, agreements, comparing views, and so on. From this standpoint, relationships stand prior to all that is intelligible. Nothing exists for us as an intelligible world of objects and persons until there are relationships. This suggests that any words, phrases or sentences that are perfectly sensible to us now could, under certain conditions of relationship, be reduced to nonsense.

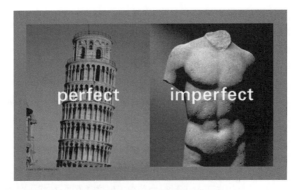

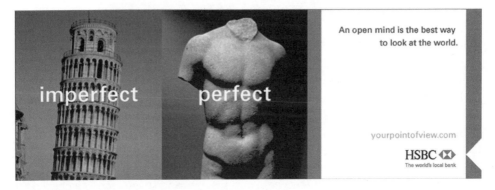

An open mind is the best way
to look at the world.

yourpointofview.com

HSBC ◆X◆
The world's local bank

Figure 1.1

Or conversely, in the right conversation even a muffled grunt can be endowed with deepest significance. If we do quest for certainty, something to count on, a sense of grounded reality, it can only be achieved through supportive relationships.

Let me be more concrete: we generally prize the natural sciences – physics, chemistry, biology, astronomy, and the like – for their advances in knowledge. They tell us about the world as it is. As also claimed, scientific knowledge begins with careful observation. In effect, high value is placed on the individual scientist who observes carefully, thinks rigorously, and tests his/her conclusions against the world. This seems reasonable on the face of it. But consider this configuration that I call "my desk". In my world the desk is solid, mahogany coloured, weighs some 180 lbs, and is odourless. Yet, the atomic physicist approaches this configuration and tells me that it is not solid after all (but primarily constituted by empty space); the psychologist informs me that it has no colour (as the experience of colour is produced by light waves reflected on the retina); the rocket scientist announces that it only appears to weigh 180 lbs (as weight depends on the surrounding gravitational field), and the biologist proposes that my sense of smell is inferior to that of my dog for whom the desk is rich in olfactory information. As carefully as I might observe, I would never reach any of these conclusions.

7

Consider further: each of these scientists employs a different vocabulary for understanding what I call my desk. Physicists speak of it in terms of atoms, biologists of cellulose, and engineers of static properties. None of these vocabularies is simply derived from individual observation. I could not read them from nature. Rather, the vocabularies spring from the professional disciplines; they are the forms of description and explanation particular to these traditions of practice. A physicist as such will never "observe" cellulose, nor a biologist a static property, and so on. If this seems reasonable, then scientific truths can be viewed as outgrowths of communities, and not observing minds. Likewise, to extend the logic, objectivity and truth are not byproducts of individual minds but of community traditions. And also, science cannot make claims to universal truth, as all truth claims are specific to particular traditions – lodged in culture and history.

This view of reality as emerging from relationships is importantly wedded to a major shift in the way we have understood language. If the picture theory of language is flawed, what is an effective replacement? Here the work of the twentieth-century philosopher, Ludwig Wittgenstein, has been central to constructionism. In his pivotal writing, *Philosophical Investigations*, Wittgenstein replaces the *picture metaphor* of language with that of *the game*. "What is a word really?" asks Wittgenstein. It is equivalent to asking "What is a piece in chess?"(Wittgenstein, 1978, section 7). How are we to make sense of this metaphor? Consider first the game of chess, in which two opponents take turns in moving pieces of various sizes and shapes across a checkered board. There are explicit rules about when and how each piece can be played, along with implicit rules of proper social conduct (for example, you may not curse or spit at your opponent). Here it is possible to say that each piece in the chess set acquires its meaning from the game as a whole. The small wooden chess pieces would mean nothing outside the game; however, once in the game, even the smallest pieces can topple "kings" and "queens".

Words acquire their meaning in the same way, proposes Wittgenstein. To say "good morning" gains its meaning from a game-like relationship called a greeting. There are implicit rules for carrying out greetings: each participant takes a turn, typically there is an exchange of mutual glances, and there are only a limited number of moves that one can legitimately make after the other has said "hi, how are you?" You may respond with "great, how are you?" for example, but you would be considered "out of the game" if you responded by screaming or cuffing the other in the head. Further, the words "hi, how are you?" are generally meaningless outside the game of greeting. If we are in the midst of a heated argument on unemployment, and I suddenly say, "hi, how are you?" you would be puzzled. Have I lost my mind? Wittgenstein termed the language and the actions into which it is woven, the *language game* (1978, section 20e). Words, then, gain their meaning through the requirements of the game. In the game of baseball, "home run" is an important term. In the same way, "atoms" feature importantly in the game of physics, and "economic class" in the game of sociology.

3. Constructions gain their significance from their social utility.

As the game metaphor suggests, as we relate together we come to develop reasonably reliable patterns of coordination. These patterns have a rule-like character; they follow a rough set of conventions about what is acceptable and what is not. It is not that our relationships *are* games; rather, they are similar in that together we have created a way of going on together. These ways of going on together not only include our words and actions, but the various objects, spaces, and environments around us as well. Thus, for example, the vocabulary of tennis (e.g. serve, volley, love three) is related not only to the movements of the players, but to the fact that they have racquets, balls, a tennis court, and available light. Wittgenstein called the entire array of relationships – words, actions, objects – a *form of life*. We might otherwise call them cultural traditions. To see our constructions as embedded in forms of life is very helpful. At the outset, we can appreciate why the terms in which we construct the world come into being. Why, for example, do Eskimos have more words for snow than people who live in warmer climes? It is because these distinctions are useful for those who live in the Arctic. They can adjust their behaviour more carefully to the surrounding conditions; the distinctions could even be life saving. For the most part, world construction and social utility are interdependent.

The phrase	is useful	when you are:
"Today's specials ..."		eating at a restaurant
"Strike three"		playing baseball
"I want a trim"		at the hairdresser's
"I need two tickets"		going to the movies
"Atomic accelerator"		smashing atoms

This view of language as gaining its meaning from its use in relationships also helps us to solve a significant problem remaining from the preceding discussion. Recall the problems confronted by the traditional view of language as a picture or reflection of the world. As pointed out, this view is wedded to the assumption that truth can be carried by language, and that some languages are closer to the truth than others. As we found, however, there is no privileged relationship between world and word. For any situation multiple constructions are possible, and there is no means outside social convention of declaring one as corresponding more "truly" to the nature of reality than another. However, these puzzlements left us in a poor position, without answers to some very important questions. If language does not describe or explain the world as it is, then what is the status of travel guides, news reports, weather reports or scientific findings? If words don't correspond or picture the world, then how can we meaningfully warn each other that drinking and driving are a dangerous combination, or that there is an acute danger of forest fires? If we become ill, surely we would prefer the account of the trained physician to that of a child or a witch doctor. All descriptions are not equal; some seem accurate and informative while others are fanciful or absurd. If language doesn't give us a map or a picture, then how do we explain these differences in accuracy?

If we view language as gaining its meaning from its utility in our various forms of life, we have an answer to this question. When we say that a certain description is "accurate" (as opposed to "inaccurate") or "true" (as opposed to "false") we are not judging it according to how well it pictures the world. Rather, we are saying that the words have come to function as "truth telling" within the rules of a particular game – or more generally, according to certain conventions of certain groups. In the game of soccer, we talk about "penalty kicks", and there is no question about when a penalty kick is occurring. The term is very useful to carry out the game in a fair manner, and it can be used with complete accuracy within the conventions of the game. In the same way, the proposition that "the world is round and not flat" is neither true nor false in terms of pictorial value, that is, correspondence with "what there is". However, by current standards, it is more acceptable to play the game of "round-world-truth" when flying from Kansas to Korea; and more useful to "play it flat" when touring the state of Kansas itself. Nor is it true beyond any game that the world is composed of atoms; however, "atom talk" is extremely useful if you are carrying out experiments on nuclear energy. In the same way, we can properly say that people do indeed have souls, so long as we are participating in a form of life that we call religion. The existence of atoms is no more or less true than the existence of souls in any universal sense; each exists within a particular form of life.

Let me illustrate the social process of "achieving truth" with an example from my adolescence. I was serving as a summer assistant to an ill-tempered, foul-mouthed wall plasterer named Marvin. Despite his personal shortcomings, Marvin was very good at his job. And when he climbed to the top of a ladder, his arms working the plaster to perfection on the ceiling overhead, it was crucial that I serve up mixtures of water and plastering compound exactly to his specification. At times the mixture had to be moist, so it could be subtly worked and reworked; at others it had to be dry, so that it could rapidly seal the contours. Thus, depending on his progress, he would bellow, "skosh" (for a wet mixture) and "dry-un" (for a drier compound). Of course these words meant nothing to me when I began my servitude, but within a few days I became proficient in producing the desired mixtures. In effect, "skosh" and "dry-un" became part of the form of life in which we were engaged.

Yet, consider what has been achieved as a byproduct of this primitive dance of words, actions, and objects. After two weeks of practice in this procedure, Marvin and I could have observed a series of plaster mixtures, and with very little error, we could have agreed on which were "skosh" and which were "dry-uns". And, if I said "dry-un cumin' up" this would also inform Marvin of what he might predict on that occasion. This prediction could have been confirmed or disconfirmed by what I delivered. In effect, by virtue of their function within the relational game, such terms as "skosh" and "dry-un" began to function as descriptions that could tell the truth. No, the words themselves do not describe the world; but because of their successful functioning within the relational ritual, they became truth telling.

In this context we can come to see why the term "truth" is both useful and potentially dangerous. It is useful within any given form of life, because it affirms that something is the case according to the rules or conventions of the participants. It helps the participants coordinate their actions in ways that are valuable to them. In this way, to say, "it is true that … " is an invitation for others to place their trust in you. Thus, if a biochemist reports the results of an experiment on amino acids, he or she is contributing to what biochemists take to be knowledge of the world – according to the rules of biochemistry. And, the researcher presumes that other biochemists will trust the results. If they repeat the experiment, they will find the same results. Within a tradition, the word "truth" is most valuable. However, when the term leaps from its grounding in a specific tradition we confront the possibilities for constriction, conflict and oppression. As we saw, in accepting the biological definition of death, we radically reduce the possibilities of understanding and action. To declare that a fertilized egg is a human being runs directly against the truth that it is not. And, to pronounce that one religion worships the only true god is a signal of conflict and oppression to come. In the name of universal truth the world has witnessed oppression, torture, murder, and genocide.

4. As we describe and explain, so do we fashion our future.

As constructionists propose, our practices of language are bound within relationships, and our relationships are bound within broader patterns of practice. Thus, for example, words like "crime", "plaintiff", "witness", and "law" are essential to carrying out the traditional practice of law; our tradition of higher education depends on a discourse of "students", "professors", "curricula", and "learning". Without these shared languages of description and explanation these institutions would fail to exist in their present form. More informally, it would be difficult to carry out a recognizable love affair without such words as "love", "need", "care", and "hope". In a broad sense, language is a major ingredient of our worlds of action; it constitutes social life itself.

Consider the implications. If we do not continue to speak the way we do, then our long-standing traditions of cultural life are under threat. If we abandon our languages of the real and the good, so do we destroy forms of life. This is easy enough to see in the case of religion. As the language of Holy Spirit, sin, soul, saviour, and everlasting life are no longer used in certain sectors of society, religious institutions die out. Churches are empty, or they are turned into theatres or community centres. Sustaining one's traditions requires a continuous process of regenerating meaning together. This challenge is especially difficult in a world of rapid global change, a world in which new meanings are continuously being circulated, and new forms of action are constantly evolving. Consider the mushrooming of social networks on the internet, and the way in which YouTube sends images of novel behaviour to millions every moment. As many believe, if institutions such as government, law, religion, education, and so on, are to survive, they must continuously modify and rework the meaning of their languages. For example, given the costs of higher education, the tradition faces a threatened future. Yet, to redefine "college education" as a goal attainable through distance learning programmes, new life is injected into the institution. In order to ensure that young people do not drop away from religion, many churches have replaced the formal and solemn services of yore with guitar and drum sing-alongs. Paradoxically, to sustain the tradition means transforming it.

Yet, constructionism is relevant not only to maintaining traditions. Rather, many are drawn to constructionist ideas because they offer a bold invitation to build new futures. Transforming ourselves, our relationships, or our culture need not await the intervention of some expert, a set of laws, force of arms, bold leaders, public policies or the like. As we speak together *right now*, we participate in creating the future – for good or ill. If we long for change, we should shake up our traditional ways of constructing the world and set out to generate new ways of making sense. Constructionism invites us to become *poetic activists*. New ways of living are not secured simply by refusing or rejecting the meanings as given, for example, avoiding sexist or racist language. Rather, the strong invitation is for the emergence of new forms of language and ways of interpreting the world. Invited are *generative discourses*, that is, ways of talking and writing or representing (as in photography, film, art, theatre, and the like) that simultaneously challenge existing traditions of understanding, and offer new possibilities for action. We shall take up the challenge of generative discourse again in Chapter 4.

5. Reflection on our taken-for-granted worlds is vital to our future well-being.
The challenge of sustaining valued traditions is one challenge; the creation of alternative futures another. Every tradition closes the doors to the new; every bold creation undermines a tradition. What shall we save; what shall we resist and destroy; what worlds should we create? These are not only complex questions, but in a world of multiple and competing constructions of the good we also see that there can be no universal answers. There is a strong tendency under these conditions to resort to "good reasons, good evidence, and good values". That is, if we simply think about a given tradition, evaluate the evidence, consider its moral and political implications, we can arrive at an acceptable conclusion. However, from a constructionist standpoint, there is reason for critical pause. The generation of good reasons, good evidence and good values is always *from within a tradition*; already accepted are certain constructions of the real and the good, and implicit rejections of alternatives. Whether we should ban smoking from public buildings, allow child pornography, oppose land mines, or support feminist liberation in Arab countries are questions that can only be treated from within some tradition of discourse. Thus, our "considered judgements" typically suppress those alternatives lying outside our tradition.

For constructionists, such considerations lead to a celebration of *critical reflexivity*; that is, the attempt to place one's premises into question, to suspend the "obvious", to listen to alternative framings of reality, and to grapple with the comparative outcomes of multiple standpoints. For the constructionist this means an unrelenting concern with the blinding potential of the "taken-for-granted". If we are to build together toward a more viable future then we must be prepared to doubt everything we have accepted as real, true, right, necessary or essential. This kind of critical reflection is not necessarily a prelude to rejecting our major traditions. It is simply to recognize them as traditions – historically and culturally situated; it is to recognize the legitimacy of other traditions within their own terms. And it is to invite the kind of dialogue that might lead to common ground.

As you can see, these five assumptions are revolutionary in their implications. We shall explore many of these implications in the remaining chapters. However, you can also imagine that because they challenge many traditional beliefs, such assumptions are highly controversial. I will take up the most important criticisms in the final chapter.

Origins of Social Construction

If my writing has been successful, the preceding arguments should seem reasonable enough. However, they have not always been regarded as reasonable. And they did not suddenly spring from nowhere. In fact, it is only within recent decades that social constructionist ideas have evolved and flowered in the form I have described. In the remainder of the chapter, I wish to discuss these developments as they have emerged in scholarly circles. Not only will this discussion help you to appreciate the deeper dimensions of constructionist ideas, but also you will begin to see more fully its revolutionary implications. Further, you will see more clearly why controversy continues. However, two cautionary notes may be helpful. First, although the arguments in this section have been enormously stimulating for many scholars, they are also more complex than the broad outline I have just sketched. Second, a full mastery of these arguments is not essential to appreciating the subsequent chapters of the book.

In my view, social construction today represents an amalgam of three major lines of dialogue. Each of these dialogues began in a separate domain of study. They were "hot ideas" within these circles. However, over time, scholars in one area began to learn of developments in another. And, as it became increasingly clear, the hot ideas in one area could be wedded to those in another. This did not mean that all agreed; tensions among these areas of study remain today. However, the force of the combinations has been so powerful that many see in them a major transformation – both in the scholarly community and Western culture more generally. This transformation has many names. The most common is *postmodernism*, where the word, "modernism" generally refers to developments in Western culture following the Enlightenment. As mentioned earlier, somewhere toward the sixteenth century, Western culture shifted from the Dark Ages of religious control, to a belief in the powers of individual reason, informed by empirical fact. (Many see science as at the centre of "modernism" in this respect.) Often equated with the modernist worldview are the values of reason, objectivity, scientific truth, order, prediction, and control. In this sense, postmodernism represents a challenge to these values, as they have been realized in the past, and a search for more promising possibilities. Although the term postmodernism is a highly general term, social constructionism may be viewed as a specific outcome. As you will see in the following discussion, the three major movements are all critical of central modernist ideas. The social constructionist dialogues grow from this soil of critique, but shift the balance from critique to creativity. As later chapters will illustrate, the central hope of social constructionist practitioners is to bring forth new and more promising ways of life.

Objectivity: The Crisis of Value Neutrality

Each year I receive numerous requests from my students for recommendations. These students usually have good reason to expect my letters to be positive. But what does "positive" mean in this case? Without any sense of misrepresentation I could describe the same student as "a good worker", "an able performer", "intelligent", or "intellectually a delight". Each of these descriptions is positive; each recommends the student. But most important, I cannot select one over the other on the basis of objective accuracy. So, how do I select? As you will quickly realize, what is distinctive about these differing descriptors is what they suggest about my enthusiasm for the student. If I really care about the student's success, I will not describe him or her as "a good worker" or an "able performer". To be sure, the words are positive, but they convey no enthusiasm. Even "intelligent" does not carry the intensity of "intellectually a delight". Depending on my investment in the student, then, I can – without being unfair – tip the balance in one direction or another.

Now, consider the broader implications: I am a news correspondent. I am trying to write as objectively and accurately as possible about what is taking place in Afghanistan. I can describe the figures lying on the road before me as "casualties", or as "promising young men whose bodies have been ripped apart by an explosion". Neither of the descriptions is inaccurate by common standards. However, the value implications are dramatically different. In effect, when you read a newspaper, you are not receiving a value neutral, "just the news" description of what is taking place. You are absorbing a world of values. What seems to be an objective report is a cloak that masks the implicit values. If you do not recognize the implicit values, it is because you and the reporter typically share the same values.

The significance of this argument was made particularly apparent by early Marxist writings. As proposed, capitalist economic theory offers itself as an accurate reading of the world of economics. However, because the theory favours a system in which its proponents are benefited, it is suspicious. The theory rationalizes a condition in which the "haves" continue to profit through the exploited labour of the "have nots". Or in Marxist terms, although seemingly neutral and objective, the theory *mystifies* the public, leading them to believe a falsehood that keeps them enslaved. Marx mounted the same argument against religious authority. Religious teachings, as Marx proposed, do not illuminate the world of the spirit; rather religion serves as an "opiate of the masses", diminishing the consciousness of suppression and exploitation.

Yet, this kind of critique is scarcely limited to Marxists. As social theorist Jürgen Habermas proposed in his influential volume *Knowledge and Human Interests*

(1971), any search for knowledge favours certain political and economic goals over others. In this sense, virtually all authoritative accounts of the world contain implicit values. All carry an ideology, that is, implicit ideas of what the political and social order *should* be like. Whether a scientist, scholar, supreme court judge, or news commentator, all are subject to *ideological critique*, that is, critique aimed at revealing the interests, values, doctrines, or myths that underlie seemingly neutral claims to truth. As ideological critique suggests, no matter how trustworthy the source, one's values inevitably lead one to select certain ways of putting things and not others. The critic asks, what has been left out, what descriptions are they suppressing? Who gains by the account? Who is being silenced, exploited, or erased?

One of the most important lines of ideological critique has been directed toward the sciences. Because the gains of science are clear to all, they seem immune to such critiques. Scientists don't seem to be ideologically invested; and their findings are open to public scrutiny. Yet, for the ideological critic, it is this seeming neutrality of science that is most misleading, most mystifying. Critical scrutiny is essential. In this light, consider Emily Martin's analysis of the ways in which a biological science text, in both the classroom and laboratory, characterises the female body. She concludes from her analysis that a woman's body is largely portrayed as a "factory" whose primary purpose is to reproduce the species. It follows that the processes of menstruation and menopause are characterized as wasteful if not dysfunctional, for they are periods of "nonproduction". To illustrate, note the negative terms in which standard biology texts describe menstruation (italics mine): "the fall in blood progesterone and estrogen *deprives* the highly developed endometrial lining of its hormonal support"; "*constriction*" of blood vessels leads to a "*diminished* supply of oxygen and nutrients"; and when "*disintegration* starts, the entire lining begins to *slough*, and the menstrual flow begins". "The loss of hormonal stimulation causes *decrosis*" (death of tissue). Another text says that menstruation is like "the uterus crying for lack of a baby" (Martin, 1987).

Martin makes two essential points. First, these scientific descriptions are anything but neutral. In subtle ways they inform the reader that menstruation and the menopause are forms of breakdown or failure. These negative implications have broad social consequences. For the woman, to accept such accounts is to alienate herself from her body. Such descriptions furnish grounds for judging herself negatively – both on a monthly basis during most of her adult years and then permanently after the years of fertility have passed. Women who are childless are condemned, by implication, for their *unproductivity*. Of equal importance, these characterizations could be otherwise. Such negative descriptions are not required by "the way things are", but reflect masculine interests, an ideology that reduces the woman to "baby maker".

To secure the case, Martin points out that there are other bodily processes – exclusive to men – that could be described in the same manner but are not. For example, in the case of ejaculation, seminal fluid picks up cells that have been shed as it flows through the male ducts. However, biological texts make no mention of males "losing" or "wasting" in describing ejaculation. In effect, many different descriptions are possible, and the dominant choice in the biological sciences reflects male interests to the detriment of women.

SOCIAL CONSTRUCTION

Martin's analysis is but one illustration of an ideological critique. It is also but a single manifestation of an enormous body of feminist critique – sophisticated and sharply pointed scholarship that spans the humanities, social sciences, and natural sciences. Nor are Marxists and feminists the only groups to make use of ideological critique. Currently such critique is used by virtually all groups that find themselves marginalized, oppressed, misrepresented, or "unheard" by society at large; by African Americans, Native Americans, Asian Americans, gays and lesbians, Chicanos, religious fundamentalists, and Arab activists, to name but a few. In all cases, the critique calls into question the taken-for-granted logics or realities of the dominant culture, and shows how these logics both support the self-interest of the dominant groups and perpetuate injustice.

The Critical Movement

The critiques of the values saturating all our descriptions of reality give minorities a new and powerful voice in the contemporary world. Among the liveliest movements today are carried the banners of critical race theory and post-colonial critique. The critical race movement pays special attention to the way race is constructed in society, and the way these constructions are used for the purposes of sustaining power and privilege. Such attention is particularly useful in matters of law, where court rulings often seem to favour those in power as opposed to minorities. For example, in matters of hate speech, court rulings often favour the dominant or white classes. Whites who burn crosses – symbolizing white supremacy – are protected by Supreme Court justices on the grounds of protecting freedom of speech. Yet, black rappers are penalized for using lyrics that express anger at whites.

The critical race movement usually focuses on people oppressed by a particular racial category (for example, black, Asian). In contrast, post-colonial critique is concerned with peoples from around the world whose cultures have been invaded by outsiders. The colonialist expansion of England, France, and Spain provides some of the most obvious cases. But cultural invasion is now subtler, and may take the form of tourism and global business expansion. The central concern is with the way in which the invaded cultures are typically discounted – viewed as somehow inferior, less developed, or backward. Their voices go unheard; their cultural traditions are either destroyed or viewed as quaint. Much post-colonial critique is embedded in novels emerging within the post-colonial populations. However, scholars have increasingly pinpointed the subtle ways in which colonial attitudes continue to pervade the way in which people in first world countries discredit the cultures of the "less developed" nations.

Nor is it an easy matter for the targets of such criticism to defend themselves. Any defence of what appears to be a self-serving statement will itself give rise to the same suspicion. The target can make no recourse to "the facts", because these are already described in ways that seem to represent the same, self-serving investments. And, because ideological critique is typically directed against those in power – who have wealth, position, privileges, security, and the like – their defences seem especially flimsy. Would "the haves" say anything that wasn't designed, in the end, to protect their own interests? Some see ideological critique as a great new defender of democracy, because everyone is subject to critique, and everyone has a right to a voice. No one can be pushed out of the conversation because others claim Truth. Let us now turn to a second major line of postmodern argument.

Reason on the Run: The Literary Assault

A second slide into skepticism began quietly in a small corner of the scholarly world; but its once tiny voice now bellows. The beginnings can be traced to the writings of the Swiss linguist Ferdinand de Saussure (1857–1913). In his influential volume *A course in general linguistics* ([1916], 1974) Saussure laid out the rationale for what became the discipline of *semiotics,* that is, a science focused on the systems by which we communicate. Two of Saussure's ideas are particularly important to our discussion: first, a distinction is made between the *signifier* and the *signified,* with the signifier referring to a word (or some other signal), and the signified to that which we believe is signalled by the word (that for which it stands). Thus, we have here an object (the signified), and a word we use to name it (the signifier). As Saussure proposed, *the relationship between signifiers and signifieds is ultimately arbitrary.* The point here is similar to the first constructionist proposition above: the world makes no demands as to how we talk about it. We can, in principle, use any signifier to refer to any signified. Saussure's second significant proposal was that *sign systems are governed by their own internal logics.* Put simply, our language can be described in terms of various rules, such as rules of grammar or syntax. When we speak or write we must approximate these rules (or internal logics); otherwise we will fail to make sense. You will recall here Wittgenstein's concept of the language game and the demands it makes on how we talk. Making sense is a matter of following the rules of language.

Truth as Style

A lively illustration of the extent to which "truth in language" depends on convention is given in Raymond Queneau's little volume *Exercises in Style* (1981). In this work Queneau generates 195 different descriptions of a single occasion. Variously he relies on metaphor, verse, scientific notation, and other genres of writing, to give the reader a heady sense of the many ways we could describe a given situation. Consider first one of the more colourful descriptions:

In the centre of the day, tossed among the shoals of traveling sardines in a coleopter with a big white carapace, a chicken with a long, featureless neck suddenly harangued one, a peace-abiding one, of their number, and its parlance, moist with protest, was unfolded upon the airs. Then, attracted by a void, the fledgling precipitated itself thereunto.

(Cont'd)

17

> In a bleak, urban desert, I saw it again the self-same day, drinking the cup of humiliation offered by a lowly button. (p. 26)

For most of us, this account doesn't seem to be objective – true to the facts. It seems whimsical and poetic, a play with words. Let's turn to a second account:

> In the S bus, in the rush hour, a chap of about 26, felt hat with a cord instead of a ribbon, neck too long, as if someone's been having a tug-of-war with it. People getting off. The chap in question gets annoyed with one of the men standing next to him. He accuses him of jostling him every time anyone goes past. A sniveling tone which is meant to be aggressive. When he sees a vacant seat he throws himself on to it.
>
> Two hours later, I meet him in the Cour de Rome, in front of the gare Saint-Lazare. He's with a friend who's saying: "You ought to get an extra button put on your overcoat". He shows him where (at the lapels) and why. (p. 29)

Here we breathe a sigh of relief. Now we have a glimpse of what's really going on. But why do we draw such a conclusion? Is it because the language is more precise? Consider, then, good scientifically acceptable prose:

> In a bus of the S-line, 10 meters long, 3 wide, 6 high, at 3 km. 600 m. from its starting point, loaded with 48 people, at 12.17 p.m., a person of the masculine sex aged 27 years, 3 months and 8 days, 1 m. 72 cm. tall and weighing 65 kg. and wearing a hat 3.5 cm. in height around the crown of which was a ribbon 60 cm. long, interpellated a man aged 48 years 4 months and 3 days, 1 m. 68 cm. tall and weighing 77 kg., by means of 14 words whose enunciation lasted 5 seconds and which alluded to some involuntary displacements of from 15 to 20 mm. Then he went and sat down about 1 m. 10 cm. away.
>
> 57 minutes later he was 10 meters away from the suburban entrance to the gare Saint-Lazare and was walking up and down over a distance of 30 m. with a friend aged 28, 1 m. 70 cm. tall and weighing 71 kg. who advised him in 15 words to move by 5 cm. in the direction of the zenith a button which was 3 cm. in diameter. (p. 41)

Now we have precise details, without colour or passion, but again we aren't certain about "what truly happened". What is it, then, that makes one language "objectively accurate" and another "aesthetic" or "obscuring?" It does not appear to be the correspondence of the words to the world; nowhere in these accounts have we confronted "the world" to which they refer. Rather we have confronted only variations in styles of writing. Truth is a matter of "being in style".

For literary theorists this focus on language took a second significant turn We have already seen how traditional ideals of truth, objectivity, and impartiality have been challenged. Literary theorists also thrust reason itself into question. Reason has long been prized in Western culture; it is perhaps the chief virtue of the modernist world-view. As we are lead to believe it is the power to reason that sets humans above the remainder of the animal kingdom, and contributes most importantly to the capacities for human survival. Literary study suggests otherwise. Among the most important objections are those of the French literary theorist Jacques Derrida (see especially Derrida, 1997). Derrida's writings, often identified as *deconstructionist*, are highly ambiguous in themselves, and scholars have drawn from them in many different ways. One of these interpretations significantly undermines the value placed on human reason. First consider two major premises. On the one hand, suggests Derrida, rational arguments bring about a *massive suppression of meaning*. When we absorb a rational argument we do not know more, but less. Second, if closely examined, the *sense of reason will collapse*. Rationality, then, is not a foundation for anything – for our institutions of government and science, for example, or for a way of deciding on what is moral or worthwhile. Rather, Derrida suggests, our "good reasons" are in the end both suppressive and empty. These are strong, even outrageous, conclusions. How can they be defended?

First, how can one conclude that rationality invites suppression, or narrows our views? Drawing from early semiotic theory, Derrida views language as a system of *differences*, a system in which each word is distinct from all others. Simply put, language is made of separate words, each distinct from all others. A formal way of talking about these differences is in terms of *binaries* (the division into two). That is, the distinctiveness of words depends on a simple split between "the word" and "not the word" (or all other words). The meaning of "white", then, depends on differentiating it from what is "non-white" (or "black" for instance). Word meaning depends, then, on differentiating between a *presence* (the word you have used) and an *absence* (those to which it is contrasted). To make sense in language is to speak in terms of presences, what is designated, against a backdrop of absences. As you can see, the presences are privileged; they are brought into focus by the words themselves; the absences are only there by implication. Or, we may simply forget them altogether. But take careful note: these presences would not make sense without the absences. Without the binary distinction they would mean nothing.

Let us put this argument into action: consider the widely accepted view of science, that the cosmos is made up of material. We as humans, then, are essentially material beings – whether we speak of this material in terms of neurons, chemical elements, or atoms. Take away the material and there is nothing left over to call a person. Humanists and spiritualists are deeply troubled by this view; it seems to repudiate everything we hold valuable about people. We want to believe there is something that gives human life more value than an automobile or a new television. Yet, materialism as a world-view seems so obviously true! Look around you; is there anything but material? But now consider the deconstructionist's arguments: the word "material" gains its meaning only by virtue of a binary, that is, in contrast to "non-material". Consider this binary in terms of material/spirit, for example. To say, "the cosmos is material" makes no sense unless you can distinguish it from what is spirit. Something identifiable as spirit must exist then, in order to say what material is. Yet, if spirit must exist in order to give material any meaning, then the cosmos cannot be altogether material. To put it another way, in the world-view of materialism, the spiritual world is *marginalized* (thrust into the unnoticed margins of the page). The spirit is an unspoken absence. However, without the presence of this absence, the very sense of "the cosmos is material" is destroyed. As one might say, the entire world-view of materialism rests on a suppression of the spirit.

As Derrida also proposes, in the Western tradition there are many binaries for which there is a strong tendency to privilege or value one side over the other. In Western culture we generally prize the rational over the emotional, mind over body, order over disorder, and leaders over followers. As many social critics have pointed out, there is also a tendency for the dominant groups in society to lay claim to the privileged pole, while viewing "others" as the opposite. Consider, for example, the ways in which masculinity is commonly associated with rationality, mental control, order, and leadership, while femininity is often characterized as emotional, bodily oriented, disorganized and dependent. Because of the oppressive implications of our common distinctions, deconstructionist critics are drawn to upsetting the binaries or blurring the boundaries. These issues will occupy us later in the book.

The assault on rationality does not terminate with its suppressive character. Rather, from a deconstructionist perspective we find that when rational arguments are placed under close scrutiny, reason gives way to chaos. When closely examined, reason lies empty. How is this so? Return again to the idea of language as a self-contained system, where the meaning of each term depends on its relationship to other terms. As Derrida proposes, we might see this relationship as made up of two components, *difference* and *deferral*. As we have already seen, a word first gains its meaning by virtue of differing from other words. The word "bat" has no meaning in itself, but begins to acquire meaning when it is contrasted with other terms, such as "hat" or "mat". This difference, however, is insufficient to give "bat" its meaning. Rather, the word "bat" is empty in itself; simply a syllable. In order to understand the term we must defer to other terms that will tell us what "bat" means. This possibility seems clear enough in the case of definitions. Every entry in the dictionary is defined in terms of other words. In effect, each word defers its meaning until you read its definition. But each word in the definition is also empty without deferring to still other definitions. In some cases this process of deferring is circular. For example, if you search the dictionary for the meaning of "reason", you will often find that it is a "justification". If you then look up "justification", it will be defined as "reason". Now ask yourself, what is reason outside of this circle of mutual definition?

Realize at this juncture that we have more than one choice in this process of deferring. We can, for example, say that a bat is a "flying mammal", or alternatively that a "bat" is a "wooden club used in the game of baseball". More formally, we may say that the term *bears traces* of meaning from various histories of use, in this case from biology and athletics. Realize as well that once you begin the process of trying to find the meaning of a flying mammal or a wooden club used in baseball, there is no moment at which you have final clarification. We search for traces, and we find only further traces. In Derrida's words, "Nothing ... is anywhere simply present or absent. There are only, everywhere, differences and traces of traces" (1981: 38).

To give these arguments a critical edge, consider a term such as democracy We speak about democracy as a form of government to be cherished, studied, theorized, and protected if necessary with human life. Yet, the meaning of the term "democracy" is not derived from our simply observing people moving about. The word is not a picture of people's actions. Rather, to use the term meaningfully depends on a literary distinction between "democracy" and, for example, contrasting terms such as "totalitarianism" and "monarchy". Yet, the difference alone is insufficient to understand the term. What is democracy other than "not being a monarchy"? To gain clarity we find ourselves deferring to other words, words such as "freedom" and "equality". Yet what do these latter terms mean? What exactly is "freedom" or "equality"? For clarity we defer to other terms. "Equality", we might say, is the opposite of "inequality"; it is reflected in societies that are "fair" and "just". But what precisely is "inequality", and what is it to be "fair" or "just?" The search continues, and there is no means of exiting the self-referring texts of democracy to encounter "the real thing". The meaning of democracy is fundamentally *undecidable*.

From this standpoint, whatever is put forth as a rational argument, even with clarity and confidence, masks a profound fragility – the fact that all the terms making up the argument are deeply ambiguous. Clarity and confidence can be maintained only as long as one does not ask too many questions, such as "what exactly is democracy ... justice ... warfare ... love ... depression?" and so on. When examined closely, all authoritative arguments begin to collapse ... including the one you are now reading.

Scientific Knowledge as Communal Construction

These two critical movements just discussed – the one pointing to the values implicit in all accounts of the world, and the other to the shortcomings of reason – were pivotal contributions to contemporary constructionism. However, a third movement was perhaps the most broad-sweeping in impact. This movement challenged the very foundations of scientific knowledge. It is also a movement that incorporates most fully the major proposals of the first two movements. Many people consider science to be the crowning jewel of Western civilization. Where others have mere *opinions*, scientists have the hard *facts*; where others have armchair ideas, scientists produce real-world effects: cures, rockets, and atomic power. Because of our trust in scientific knowledge, science plays a major role in educational curricula, national policy-making, news reporting, criminal investigation, military planning, and more. Unlike any other authority – religious, political, ethical – scientific authority has remained virtually unchallenged.

It is precisely for these reasons that the constructionist challenge to scientific truth has been the most powerful in its consequences. At the outset, many constructionists have been concerned with the negative effects of science on society. Consider, for example, the implications of science for social equality. Enlightenment thinking was vastly important in terms of its granting to each and every individual the right to a voice. The privilege of royalty and religion to speak for all, to rule on the nature of the real and the good, was removed. Over time science became the model for equal rights to reason. In the scientific world, everyone has the privilege of independent observation, reason, and reporting. If one follows rigorous methods of investigation he or she can demand an audience. But now consider, what do you as reader have to say about the "PE surface for polyatomic molecules", "the indeterminacy of cyclopentane-1,3-diyl", or "*Hox* genes"? Chances are you have no opinion; you know little about such matters. Moreover you may scarcely understand the phrases. So you are forced to accept these realities; and why not? Don't scientists simply "tell it like it is?" Ironically, then, this bastion of equality now functions to remove equality: all voices save its own are moved to silence. Are we witnessing here the emergence of a new breed of high priests, a subtle dictatorship for which we are merely docile bodies?

It is this possibility, this closing of the common dialogue, that spurs many scholars to open scientific knowledge to social constructionist analysis. The point of this discussion is not to undermine scientific efforts, but to remove their authority and to place them into the orbit of everyday scrutiny. The focus, then, is on scientific interpretations of the world – the choice of certain languages of description and explanation as opposed to others. Recall, no particular language is privileged in terms of its picturing the world for what it is; innumerable accounts are possible. Most importantly, because scientists do make claims to the truth, their accounts have a way of creeping out into society, of forming society's conceptions of what is the case. In response to headlines about the origins of the universe, genetic coding, and the greenhouse effect, we are not likely to say "well, that's one way of putting it". Rather, the news media report these as universal facts, and we are inclined to accept them as such – until they are corrected by other scientists. As scientific accounts enter society as "truth beyond tradition, beyond value, beyond question" so do they affect our ways of life – undermining, disrupting, and refashioning. And there is little critical questioning of these effects, not only because the common person is mystified by scientific language, but also because scientists have traditionally been unable to escape their premises to ask reflexive questions from alternative standpoints.

Are such effects significant? Consider the way in which moral and spiritual issues have been slowly excluded from academic curricula – both in secondary education and universities – while science studies have steadily expanded. Issues of morality and spirit are, after all, not subject to empirical study, and thus, "merely speculative". There are also the more subtle effects of a curriculum that defines human beings merely as material – just objects for scientific inspection and manipulation. It is science that has reduced the enormities in human variation to a handful of racial categories, informed society that there are hereditary differences in intelligence and certain races are more intelligent than others, and has supported the idea that one's fundamental motivation in life is to sustain his/her genes. By interpreting nature in just these ways, many believe society is ill served. By understanding scientific claims as human constructions, lodged in a cultural tradition as opposed to an objective unlocking of nature's secrets, we open spaces for dialogue in which *all people* can voice the truths and values of their traditions.

How are we to understand the evolution our understanding of science as social construction? We must turn the clock back to 1929, and the publication of Karl Mannheim's groundbreaking volume, *Ideology and Utopia* (1951). One finds four central proposals in the work, the first quite similar to the first two construction-ist principles set out above: (1) scientific theories do not spring from observation but from the scientist's social group. Then, as he proposed, (2) scientific groups are often organized around certain theories. This leads to the more interesting con-clusion that (3) theoretical disagreements are therefore issues of group conflict, and finally to the far-reaching conclusion that (4) what we assume to be scien-tific knowledge is therefore a byproduct of a social process. These suppositions reverberated widely. Ludwig Fleck's 1935 work, *Genesis and Development of a Scientific Fact*, proposed that in the scientific laboratory, "one must know before one can see". By this he meant that one must participate in the assumptions of a social group before he or she can know what to look for. In England, Peter Winch's influential volume *The Idea of a Social Science* (1946) demonstrated ways in which theoretical propositions are "constitutive of the phenomena" of the social science. By this he meant that when we single out a phenomenon and define it in a certain way, we create the world in which we live. This idea later became the basis for *labelling theory* in sociology.[1] In this case, scholars were con-cerned with the way in which the labels we give to phenomena come to be self-fulfilling. Thus, to call a given behaviour a "criminal act", creates what we take to be crime, and as well, a population of criminals.

An important milestone in these developments is represented in Peter Berger and Thomas Luckmann's 1966 volume, *The Social Construction of Reality*. They focused in particular on the scientist's private experience of the world – what is seen, heard, or distinguished by touch. As they proposed, these experiences can be traced to the social sphere. In their terms, we are socialized into *plausibility structures*, that is, conceptual understandings of the world and rational supports for these understandings. As we come to rely on these plausibility structures, so do we develop a *natural attitude*, that is, a sense of a natural, taken-for-granted reality. They write:

> I apprehend the reality of everyday life as an ordered reality ... Its phenomena are prearranged in patterns that seem to be independent of my apprehension of them ... The language used in everyday life continuously provides me with the necessary objecti-fication and posits the order within which these make sense and within which every-day life has meaning for me ... In this manner language marks the co-ordinates of my life in society and fills that life with meaningful objects. (1966, p. 21)

To illustrate, consider the way in which we seem to experience time, and the way in which the clock (an eighteenth-century invention) now orders our life. As Berger and Luckmann write,

All my existence in this world is continuously ordered by [clock time] … I have only a certain amount of time available for the realization of my projects, and the knowledge of this affects my attitude to these projects. Also, since I do not want to die, this knowledge injects an underlying anxiety into my projects. Thus I cannot endlessly repeat my participating in sports events. I know that I am getting older. It may be that this is the last occasion on which I have the chance to participate … (p. 26)

In effect, we construct the idea of clock time, and now it comes to dominate our everyday life.

These were all important developments in the constructionist view of scientific knowledge. However, it was in the social ferment of the late 1960s that the major explosion occurred, primarily revolving around Thomas Kuhn's *The structure of scientific revolutions* (1962). The title of the work was not only resonant with the revolutionary spirit of the time, but also fuelled the fires of those who criticized scientists for their complicity in the Vietnam war. Kuhn's work became, at one time, the most widely cited work in the English language – including the Bible. Most importantly, this work represented a frontal challenge to the longstanding presumption that scientific knowledge is progressive, that with continued research – testing hypotheses against reality – we come ever closer to the truth. Few can doubt, for example, that the shift from a Ptolemaic view of the earth as the centre of the universe to the Copernican account of the earth's revolutions around the sun is not progress; or that the shift from Newtonian mechanics to relativity theory in physics is not a gain in understanding. Kuhn did, and his reasoning sent shock waves across the intellectual world. As Kuhn proposed, our propositions about the world are embedded within *paradigms*, roughly a network of interrelated commitments to a particular theory, conception of a subject matter, and methodological practices (or "form of life" in Wittgenstein's terms). Thus, even our most exacting measurements are only sensible from within the paradigm. A look into a microscope tells you nothing unless you are already informed about the nature of the instrument and what you are supposed to be looking at. Here Kuhn is at one with his predecessors.

What we call progress in science, for Kuhn, is not then movement from a less to a more objectively accurate paradigm. Objective accuracy is only achieved from within the terms of the paradigm. Findings within an alternative paradigm are *incommensurable*, that is, beyond measurement from another perspective (for example, a neurologist cannot measure the depth of a soul because the soul is not a fact within neurology). Rather, new paradigms are generated by *anomalies*, data that fall outside the range of problems capable of solution within a given paradigm. As new problems are explored, so do they give rise to alternative paradigms – new conceptions, apparatus, and objects of study. Scientific revolution is not progressive, in the sense of arriving ever closer to the truth; rather, we shift horizontally, from one paradigm to another. For Kuhn, "the scientist with a new paradigm sees differently from the way he had seen before" (1970, p. 115) While Kuhn subsequently came to regret the radical implications of his arguments, others extended them with even greater force.[2] No longer was it possible to justify science as a quest for *the* truth.

Researching the Researcher

These early works on science as social construction now give rise to an enormous range of scholarship exploring the social processes responsible for what we accept as scientific knowledge. For example, many social scientists study scientific research practices much as they would the practices of a primitive tribe. They sit in on the research meetings, ask probing questions, and watch the researchers practise in the laboratory. In one pivotal study, Latour and Woolgar (1979) spent hundreds of hours studying the way scientists in the Jonas Salk laboratories negotiate with each other to determine what will count as a scientific fact as opposed to opinion. They were sensitive to the way a scientist's commitment to a theory or to a measuring device could influence what counted as good data. They could witness the way in which the availability of grant funds and journal publication policies influence what was considered important and how the research was described. Historians are also active in exploring the social history of science. For example, the historian Stephen Shapin (1995) has traced the history of the very idea of truth, and the way in which our contemporary views of truth in science have their origins in the polite exchanges among gentlemen of the seventeenth century. Lorraine Daston and Peter Galison (2007) have explored the way in which the concept of "objectivity" has shifted over time, and how various techniques have been used in making claims that one's account is "true to nature". Why do we presume, for example, that an atomic accelerator reveals secrets about the basic matter making up our cosmos, or that an MRI tells us about the neural basis of psychological dispositions? It is not obviously the case, and many other stories could be told.

Yet, in spite of the enormous significance of this work, it is also important not to draw the misleading conclusion that scientific knowledge is so much hot air. These arguments do remove the sanctity of science, that somehow the sciences reveal the secrets of nature, that they are value free, and that they progress toward the Truth. However, this is not at all to disregard the outcomes of science, nor such propositions as "smoking causes cancer" or "high blood pressure often leads to heart disease". Within certain groups of scientists such propositions may be fully verified. And, because the values shared within these groups are also common to large segments of the public, the findings of the sciences may be enormously valuable to others. To be sure, "cancer" is a social construction, just as is the biological construction of "death". However, vast sectors of the population are willing to share these definitions with scientists, and the underlying value placed on biological life as opposed to death. We are dealing here with agreements in practical value, not in matters of Truth. At the same time, constructionists recognize the multiplicity of values in the world, and the possibility that what is practically valuable for some may be oppressive for others. Cloning, stem cell production, and genetic programming are cases in point.

From Despair to New Directions

These three intellectual movements – the first illuminating the values inherent in all constructions of reality, the second the fragility of rational argument, and finally, the social basis of scientific knowledge – are all major contributions to contemporary dialogues in social construction. There are other contributions indeed worth exploring. For example, there are major critiques of the presumption of independent and autonomous selves, which we shall take up in Chapter 5. There is also the *constructivist* movement, which has been centrally concerned with the way in which the world is constructed or construed by individual minds.[3] The central message here is that our actions are based not on the way the world is, but on the meaning it has for this individual. Although resonant with constructionist views, constructivists tend to place meaning within the mind of the individual, while social constructionists locate the origin of meaning in relationships.[4] Buddhist thought has also come to play an important role in the constructionist dialogues. As Buddhism has long advocated, human suffering largely originates in the categories (or languages) with which we understand the world and ourselves. If we did not distinguish between success and failure, and place such value on being successful, for example, we would not suffer because of failure. Meditation is one way in which these categories of understanding can be suspended (deconstructed).[5] As we also find in the pages to follow, numerous practitioners – in education, therapy, organizational change, social work, and more – have also been active contributors to the constructionist dialogues.

As you can see, these various movements – when considered together – pose major challenges to longstanding assumptions and time-honoured goals. For many, this new transformation is catastrophic. It represents the erosion of beliefs central to our ways of life, including our sense of truth and morality, the value of the individual self, and the promise of a better future. Traditions of democracy, religion, education, and nationhood are all placed under threat. Of course, you may also reply that constructionist ideas do little more than raise questions about the foundations of otherwise robust traditions. So what if all that we have taken to be objectively true is socially constructed? Why not acknowledge this and get on with life as usual? We have "our beliefs" in reality and reason, and they support "our ways of life". They don't need foundations any more than our tradition of eating three as opposed to five meals a day. This is just the way we do it; full stop.

Yet, we must pause at this point to ask who is the "we" who rests satisfied with these traditions? First, it is clear that the family of suppositions and practices in question are all byproducts of Western culture, and chiefly byproducts of recent centuries. If we simply take them for granted, we stop asking questions. In particular, we fail to ask about the downside – what are the negative repercussions for the various peoples making up society? Further, we fail to address whether these Western beliefs and practices can successfully function within the new century. For example, with the development of globe-spanning technologies of communication and transportation – from telephone, radio, television and jet transportation to computers, satellite transmission, the internet, and world wide web – the world's peoples increasingly confront each other. Rather than the *global village* for which many had hoped (McLuhan & Powers, 1989), we are confronting increasing numbers of contentious factions, expansionist movements, exploitative practices, animosities and resistances. Under these conditions we must ask whether any culture, and particularly a powerful one, can afford commitment without question. Consider some of the implications of our traditional commitments to truth, reason and moral principles.

Cultural Imperialism

As elsewhere, we in the West typically presume the universality of our truths, reasons, and morals. Our scientific truths are not "ours" in particular, we hold, but candidates for universal truth. That the world is made up of atoms and individuals who possess emotions is not for us a matter of cultural belief. Any reasonable person would reach the same conclusion. Yet, as we presume the reality and truth of our own beliefs, so do we trample on the realities of others. We unwittingly become cultural imperialists, suppressing and antagonizing. For example, while a visiting professor in Japan, a senior professor confided in me his sense of loneliness and isolation. Bitterly he recounted the years after the Second World War, when the Americans re-organized the university. Before the Americans, he recounted, all the professors in his department shared the same large office. "We talked, shared, and laughed. The Americans thought this 'backward', and re-organized the university so that each professor was placed in a separate office. Each should do his or her independent work. 'As my friend confided', now we don't talk, share or laugh very much". Modernism at work. The reaction can be far more bitter. Consider the sentiments of a Maori from New Zealand:

> Psychology ... has created the mass abnormalization of Maori people by virtue of the fact that Maori people have been ... recipients of [English] defined labels and treatments ... Clinical psychology is a form of social control ... and offers no more "truth" about the realities of Maori people's lives than a regular reading of the horoscope page in the local newspaper. (Lawson-Te Ano, 1993)

Knowledge and the New Totalitarianism

Enlightenment ideas were highly successful in undermining the totalitarian rule of royalty and religion. We hold that each individual is endowed with powers of observation and reason, and thus an inalienable right to participate in the process of governance. While we continue to cherish this right, we have also seen this prizing of individual knowledge as contributing to the rise of science, objectivity and truth. As scientific communities have grown strong, so have they developed specialized vocabularies, methodologies, forms of analysis and practices of reason. Thus, as suggested earlier, we confront the emergence of a new "knowledge class", groups that claim superiority of voice over all others. Further, without initiation into the class (typically through an advanced degree) one cannot challenge these claims. Opinions based on anything other than the standards of the knowledge class – for example, on personal values, spiritual insights, commitments to another tradition – are largely discounted. In effect, where the Enlightenment initially functioned to democratize the society, it has now succeeded in generating a new form of totalitarianism.[6] As many now feel, "when the trumpets of truth begin to sound, run for cover!"

It is in this context that the constructionist dialogues offer enormous promise. They invite us to reflect on our assumptions and practices, and most importantly, to construct new forms of understanding and new ways of conducting our lives together. Especially important, they emphasize the importance of collaborative participation. We have succeeded in creating a world of massive division and conflict; we confront the catastrophic consequences of our constructions. Could we not together create new possibilities?

The Present Volume

In the present chapter I have tried to sketch out a set of proposals that are somewhere toward the centre of the contemporary dialogues on social construction. I have also tried to illuminate some of the major lines of scholarship giving rise to these dialogues. This chapter has also placed many traditional understandings and practices in peril. In that sense, it has emphasized criticism of the past as opposed to building toward new futures. In the remainder of the book, the emphasis will shift toward the positive potentials of a constructionist orientation. In Chapter 2 we shall explore the way in which our constructions of the real, the rational and the good come into being. We shall consider the pivotal place of these constructions in sustaining our ways of life, our values, and our relationships. At the same time, we shall confront the potentials of our constructions to imprison us. In Chapter 3 we take up the question of research in the social sciences. Although constructionism does raise significant questions regarding traditional empirical research, these research methods are not abandoned. At the same time, the constructionist dialogues open new and exciting possibilities for study. These will be the primary focus of the chapter. In Chapter 4, we turn to the social construction of the self. This chapter will sketch out the major critiques of the traditional view of the self as independent decision maker. It will then explore the attempt of constructionist scholars to generate an alternative conception, one that places major value on relationship as opposed to the self.

In Chapters 5 and 6, we move from these more scholarly concerns to fields of practice. In Chapter 5 the special concern is with forms of dialogue holding promise for reducing conflict and hostility. Of special concern will be practices of transformative dialogue, especially useful in their bridging alien constructions of the world. Chapter 6 explores the flowering of new practices favoured by social constructionism. Attention will be directed specifically to psychotherapy, organizational management, education, and forms of scholarly communication. In each case we locate new possibilities for coordinating relations to build new futures.

Throughout these discussions you will certainly experience reservations – possibly even strong criticisms. You could scarcely grow up in modern society without some doubts about what will unfold here. In the final chapter, Chapter 7, I shall consider some of the major criticisms of social constructionist ideas. Issues of truth, objectivity, science, moral relativism, political activism, and the like will all be treated. You are welcome to peek into this chapter if at any point you find yourself resisting.

For over 25 years I have been deeply involved with the development of constructionist ideas. They have entered my relations with academic colleagues and students, therapists, organizational managers, peace workers, friends, family, and more. Early in my career I was a committed "modernist". I conducted experiments, tested theories, and generally sensed that I was contributing to truth and progress for all. As I became increasingly secure in my profession as a psychologist, I slowly began to reflect on the premises and promises. Doubt emerged, then skepticism, and finally pointed critique. I was scarcely alone in this shift; it was everywhere in evidence. This should be obvious from the pages of this chapter. In recent years, however, I have become far more optimistic. I have come to see that in a constructionist frame, we can move beyond both traditionalism and skepticism. Social construction may grow from the soil of critique, but this does not mean abandoning the past. This is primarily because unlike any other world view that I know of, *constructionism does not seek to establish the truth of its own premises*. It recognises that constructionism is itself socially constructed. Constructionism is not, then, a candidate for the truth. Nor is it a belief system. Rather, the constructionist dialogues represent invitations to a way of understanding. As constructionist ideas enter our ways of talking, they may also transform our actions. The major question asked from a constructionist perspective is "what happens to our lives together" when we construct the world in various ways? Yes, reflective critique is invited, even of constructionist ideas themselves. But all criticism is from "some point of view" or perspective, with no more foundations than any other. Thus, criticism is to be viewed as an invitation to dialogue, as opposed to an attempt to eradicate. Most important, however, is the constructionist message: the moment we begin to speak together, we have the potential to create new ways of being.

Notes

1 For a more recent account, see Link, B.G. & Phelan, J.C. (1999) The labelling theory of mental disorder. In A.V. Horwitz & T.L. Scheid (Eds.). *Handbook for the study of mental health*. Cambridge: Cambridge University Press.

2 For Kuhn's regrets, see Kuhn, T.S. (1977). *The essential tension*. Chicago: University of Chicago Press. For a more extreme view of the social determination of science, see Barnes, B. (1974) *Scientific knowledge and sociological theory*. London: Routledge & Kegan Paul; Bloor, D. (1976) *Knowledge and social imagery*. London: Routledge & Kegan Paul.

3 See, for example, the *Journal of Constructivist Psychology*.

4 The compromise is represented in a position sometimes called *social constructivism*. This view may be contrasted with *radical constructivism*, in which everything outside the individual mind is placed in question – including other minds. Social constructionism also tends to be radical in this regard, placing individual minds in question. We shall take up this issue in Chapter 4.

5 An account of the relationship between social construction and Buddhism can be found in Gergen, K.J. & Hoskins, D.M. (2006) If you meet social construction along the road. A dialogue with Buddhism. In M. Kwee, K.J. Gergen, & F. Koshikawa (Eds.). *Horizons in buddhist psychology*. Chagrin Falls, OH: Taos Institute Publications.

6 See, for example, Willard, C.A. (1998) *Expert knowledge: liberalism and the problem of knowledge*. Chicago: University of Chicago Press.

Further Resources

On Social Construction

Anderson, W.T. (Ed.). (1995). *The truth about the truth.* New York: Putnam.

Burr, V. (2004). *Social constructionism.* London: Routledge.

Arbib, M.A. & Hesse, M.B. (1986) *The construction of reality.* Cambridge: Cambridge University Press.

Gergen, K.J. (1994). *Realities and relationships, soundings in social construction.* Cambridge, MA: Harvard University Press.

Holstein, J.A. & Gubrium, J.F. (2007). *Handbook of constructionist research.* Thousand Oaks, CA: Sage.

Potter, J. (1996). *Representing reality.* London: Sage.

Sarbin, T.R. & Kitsuse, J.I. (Eds.). (1994). *Constructing the social.* London: Sage.

Shotter, J. (2008). *Conversational realities revisited.* Chagrin Falls, OH: Taos Institute Publications

Sugiman, T., Gergen, K.J., Wagner, W., & Yamada, Y. (Eds.). (2007). *Meaning in action, constructions, narratives and representations.* New York: Springer.

Crisis in Value Neutrality

Crenshaw, K. (Ed.). (1995). *Critical race theory: the key writings that formed the movement.* New York: New Press.

Desai, G. D. & Nair, S. (Eds.). (2005). *Postcolonialisms: an anthology of cultural theory and criticism.* New Brunswick, NJ: Rutgers University Press.

Fox, D. & Prilleltensky, I. (Eds.). (2008). *Critical psychology, an introduction* (2nd ed.). Thousand Oaks, CA: Sage.

Gergen, M.M., & Davis, S.N. (Eds.). (1997). *Toward a new psychology of gender.* New York: Routledge.

Hepburn, A. (2002) *An introduction to critical social psychology.* London: Sage.

Ibanez, T. & Iniguez, L. (1997) *Critical social psychology.* London: Sage.

Literary Theory and Deconstruction

Culler, J. (1982). *On deconstruction, theory and criticism after structuralism.* Ithaca, NY: Cornell University Press.

Fish, S. (1982). *Is There a text in this class? the authority of interpretive communities.* Cambridge: Harvard University Press.

The Social Construction of Science

Barnes, B., Bloor, D., & Henry, J. (1996). *Scientific knowledge.* Chicago: University of Chicago Press.

Danziger, K. (1990). *Constructing the subject: historical origins of psychological research.* Cambridge: Cambridge University Press.

Latour, B. (1987). *Science in action.* Cambridge, MA: Harvard University Press.

Latour, B. (2007). *Reassembling the social, an introduction to actor-network-theory.* New York: Oxford University Press.

McCarthy, E.D. (1996). *Knowledge as culture.* New York: Routledge.

Pickering, A. (1995). *The mangle of practice.* Chicago: University of Chicago Press.

Poovey, M. (1998). *A history of the modern fact.* Chicago: University of Chicago Press.

2

CONSTRUCTING THE REAL
AND THE GOOD

THE LANGUAGE WE LIVE BY
Language Structure: The Nourishing Constraint
Metaphors: Borrowing and Building
Narrative: Reality as Story
Rhetoric and Reality
••••
EVERYDAY RELATIONS: THE POWER OF THE UNREMARKABLE
••••
INSTITUTIONAL REALITIES: FOUCAULT ON POWER
••••
IDENTITY POLITICS: TO BE OR NOT TO BE
••••
REFLECTION
••••
NOTES
••••
FURTHER RESOURCES

Several years ago, two students enrolled in my honours seminar recoiled at the constructionist readings I had assigned. "Without any truth, how can we ever be sure of anything?" they asked; "Without sound reasoning, how are we to survive; and without a firm view of moral good, what is worth doing?" Everything they believed worthwhile seemed destroyed by the seminar. So moved were they that they took their complaints to the provost: the seminar was both immoral and nihilistic in their view and should be stricken from the curriculum. Fortunately the tradition of academic freedom saved the seminar. I can fully understand the depth of their concerns, but in my view this dark night of doubt is but a transitional phase. It is not that social constructionist ideas annihilate self, truth, objectivity, science, and morality – rather, the constructionist dialogues ask us to move beyond simplistic commitments, and consider the pitfalls as well as the promises of our traditions. Most important, these dialogues open vast potentials for co-creating the future.

To appreciate the potentials before us, it is first essential to explore the ways in our taken for granted worlds have been brought into being. In daily life we take it for granted that we should be paid for our work, we must attend to our bodily needs, that rape is immoral, and so on. And we know that smoking causes cancer, that the world's water supply is dwindling, and that the earth moves about the sun. For the constructionist, however, these assumptions are not endings – summaries of what we know to be the case – but beginnings. That is, they invite us to ask, how did we come to hold these views; why do they seem so very obvious; what do they do for us; who is silenced by such assumptions, and are there reasons to explore alternatives? The present chapter is primarily concerned with the origins of the undeniable. The focus is on the processes by which our common realities, rationalities, and moralities take shape in our lives. I single out three major contributions to reality making: the languages through which we relate, the process of daily conversation, and the institutions in which we live. This discussion will be followed by an exploration of identity construction.

The Language We Live By

Central to any ongoing relationship is the existence of a shared reality. That is, we must have at least rudimentary agreement on what exists. If you live in a world in which there are divine powers, evil spirits, and holy men, and I live in a world composed of neurons, synapses, and endorphins, we may find it difficult to go on together. Ideally, we should employ similar words on similar occasions. It is essential that we agree on what it means to "turn right at the next corner", "meet at 7pm", and "have a beer". If you are a surgeon working with your team, it won't do if your assistant responds to your demand for a scalpel by handing you a 'stick of gum'. More formally, our relationship will require establishing an *ontology*, a shared understanding of "what there is". In developing an ontology, we also lay the groundwork for establishing a rudimentary *morality*. That is, as we coordinate our talk and actions within various contexts, so do we establish a right way to do things. And with these standards we begin to recognise disruptions, glitches, and failures. The establishment of "the good" creates the context for its violation. At the most basic level, the disruption of "the good" functions as a threat to the accepted reality and all those patterns of action into which this reality is woven. Married couples are often jarred when they disagree on a story of the past; academics are often shunned if they disagree with the assumptions of their peers; and many have been martyred for unconventional religious convictions. "Evil" lurks in the disruption of the accepted patterns. To explore the origins of the real and the good, let us first take up the languages we live by.

Language Structure: The Nourishing Constraint

> The limits of my language mean the limits of my world.
>
> Ludwig Wittgenstein (1978)

Recall from the preceding chapter the central place of language in the construction-ist movement. As reasoned, language is perhaps the central vehicle through which we negotiate agreements about the real and the good. But it is also here that we confront an interesting paradox. We inherit longstanding traditions of language. To converse with others in English, for example, requires nouns and adjectives, transitive and intransitive verbs, and so on. If you chose not to conform to any of these conventions, and just babbled away, you would communicate very little. In effect, we rely on these conventions to get along from day to day. They enable us to collaborate with others in fulfilling ways; they nurture us; they sustain our way of life. If you have ever spent time in a land in which you couldn't communicate with the people who lived there, you can appreciate how reliant we are on having a common language.

Yet, this same set of conventions also functions as a form of prison. We are nur-tured, yes, but we can scarcely step out of the tradition to speak in some other way. To appreciate these limits, consider the common use of nouns, parts of speech that designate persons, places, or things. Nouns are obviously very useful in our everyday relations; we could scarcely live very well without them. Yet, nouns are also like threshing machines. They take a field of wheat, and chop it into separate bits. In the same way, in using nouns we construct a world of separation. There is a tree, a house, a road, a man, a dog, and so on. Consider in contrast how we would understand the world if we communicated in musical melodies and harmonies. Nouns cannot create Beethoven's *Pastoral Symphany*, a portrayal of life in the countryside.

Let us consider, then, two prominent characteristics of the language conventions on which we must depend: metaphor and narrative.

Metaphors: Borrowing and Building

What, therefore, is truth? A mobile army of metaphors ...

Friedrich Nietzsche, *On Truth and Falsity in their Extramoral Sense*

Where reality counts metaphors have a bad reputation. Why? Because we tradition-ally define metaphors in terms of their contrast with "literal" words. Literal language is accepted as "true to fact", "not exaggerated", while metaphors are considered mere packaging or pretty words. As George Eliot once said, "We all of us, grave or light, get our thoughts entangled in metaphors, and act fatally on the strength of them". Yet, as the preceding pages make clear, this traditional distinction is flawed. Words do not map the world; there are no words that are in themselves better matches to the world than any others. As we found, words gain the sense of being true to fact through long-term usage within a community. What then is a metaphor? We usually have the sense of a word being a metaphor when we take it out of one context of usage and place it within another. The world is *his oyster*; life is a *bowl of cherries*. The difference between literal and metaphoric words, then, is *essentially the difference between the conventional and novel use of the word*. All our descriptions can be viewed as metaphoric if we were to trace them to their origins. For example, we identify our-selves with names – which we take to be literal and precise. I am Ken, you are Sally, and you are Harry. Yet we were not always so – names are all borrowed words, once literal descriptions of other persons, ripped out of context and deposited on our beings. In a sense, then, we are all metaphors of other people.

George Lakoff and Mark Johnson entitled their classic work, *Metaphors we live by* (1980). Thus they pointed to the way in which the common words by which we understand our worlds are typically appropriated from other contexts. Because these words also make up our forms of life, tracing their metaphoric roots becomes an exciting challenge. It is when we free ourselves from the sense of the literal – words as maps – that we are free to consider other options. Consider: disagreements between people are typically the grounds for argument. However, as most of us will have found, arguments can often be unpleasant. Voices are raised, insults are exchanged, and instead of resolution there is animosity. These outcomes may be traced to a network of metaphors that define what an argument is. Specifically, as Lakoff and Johnson propose, arguments are equated metaphorically with war. Consider our common ways of talking:

> Your claims are *indefensible*.
> He *attacked* every weak point in the argument.
> Her criticisms were *right on target*.
> He *demolished* her case.
> I've never *won* an argument with her.
> He *shot down* all my arguments.

By equating argument with war in this way, we enter as combatants – it is either win or lose, destroy or be destroyed. But when we realize the metaphor of argument as war, we may wish to think of other ways of going on. What if we looked at arguments, for example, as a game? Perhaps we could then exchange positions from time to time, with each of us taking the side of the other. Would we not come to a much better understanding between us? Consider as well what we call the war on drugs, the war on poverty, or the war on terrorism. If we changed the metaphors, would there be other, possibly better options available?

Metaphors dominate the scientific sphere. Consider, for example, the use of metaphor in the mental health professions, and particularly in Freud's psychoanalytic theory. To put it simply, Freud proposed that we are born with strong erotic desires; at an early age, for example, young boys wish to possess their mothers sexually. However, because these and related desires are unacceptable – subject to severe punishment – the child *represses* them. In effect, the desires are forced out of the realm of consciousness. Individuals then erect neurotic defences – compulsions, self-defeating actions, etc. – to ensure they are never released. We thus live with many neurotic defences, unable to gain consciousness of our true desires. On this view, therapy is an attempt to unearth the unconscious, to reveal the desires, and to help the person gain conscious control over them. For the psychoanalyst, hints of the unconscious process can be obtained through dream analysis, slips of the tongue, and peculiar word associations. In effect, psychoanalytic practice derives from this particular conception of the mind.

Perhaps you sense the metaphoric elements in the psychoanalytic view. One of the most prominent metaphors, as Donald Spence (1987) described it, is the *archeological*.

The archeologist is one who studies the distant past, and because these early events can never be known directly, makes use of various artifacts (shards of pottery, bones, stone formations) to interpret what must have been. Often this means digging through layers of earth deposits to locate evidence of past lives. This metaphor dominates the Freudian approach – with its emphasis on the hidden and unavailable dimensions of the unconscious, the early formation of repression, the use of small bits of evidence to draw inferences regarding the unknown. The psychoanalyst serves as the archeologist, whose professional success rests on revealing "new knowledge". This metaphor continues to dominate much therapeutic practice, in which therapists "probe" the client's mind, to "get to the bottom" of the problem.

Yet, as Spence proposes, to see the archeological metaphor more clearly does not reduce the theory and practice to triviality (as in saying 'Well, it's only a metaphor'). "Because metaphors are central aspects of our understanding we will always continue to use them; by the same token, we should not be used *by* them" (1987, p. 7). For Spence, as a practicing psychiatrist, to be used by the metaphor is to mistake it for the real, and thus to reduce clinical sensitivity and imagination. It is to "reduce our options to only one" (ibid, p. 8). To *use* metaphors is also to take advantage of their capacity to organize elements in new ways. Different forms of research were set in motion by viewing light in terms of *waves* as opposed to *particles*. By viewing DNA molecules as structured like a *double helix*, many research findings could be brought together in a new and productive way.

All very well about scientific theory, you may say, but what about my "experience", and "emotion?" Aren't they real, something beyond metaphor? In answer, recall that the constructionist does not pronounce on what is *really* real. Rather, it is in singling out something as real that we are engaging in a social process of constructing. In this sense, we can ask about the metaphors that are implicit in what we understand as our "private experience". If closely examined, we find that the idea of private experience relies on a central metaphor of the person in Western culture, one that defines the *mind as a form of mirror*, with the world "out there", and its contents reflected by experience "in here". You can begin to realize that the idea of experience as an "in here" is a metaphor when you stop to locate what precisely is in versus out. Where does the outside stop and the inside begin, on the skin or the surface of the retina, in the receptor nerves, or perhaps the cortex? Consider: if you removed everything we consider "outside" from experience (for example, everything "in the physical world"), would there be anything left over we could identify as experience; and if you removed everything we call inside, would there be any "objects of experience" still remaining? When we try to tease apart what is inner versus outer, we enter a thicket of ambiguity. As scholars point out, history has also deposited on our doorstep competing metaphors of "the nature of experience". In terms of the mirror metaphor, experience is passive – simply reflecting the passing world. However, there is also the metaphor of experience as *a searchlight*, actively searching and illuminating the world in order to achieve certain ends (Bruner & Feldman, 1990). In/out, active/passive – all are borrowed ideas that construct our sense of experience.

The way we understand our emotions also owes a debt to metaphor. There are several basic metaphors that guide much of what we can say about our emotions

CONSTRUCTING THE REAL AND THE GOOD

(Averill, 1990). Because we believe that emotions represent *the animal* in us, we can say, "he bellowed in anger", or "her feathers were ruffled". However, because the animal metaphor is prominent we cannot easily say, "his anger was robotic". We inherit a metaphor of emotions as *driving forces*, and thus we can say, "He was driven by fear", or "love makes the world go round". We would be talking nonsense if we said, "He was so joyous that he nodded off to sleep". There is also a prevalent metaphor of emotion as *biological*, which enables us to say "I have a gut feeling", or "his heart broke from grief". To a lesser degree we also have a tradition of emotions as a *disease of the mind*. Thus, we say, "he was blind with envy", or "she fell madly in love", but not, "his rage is a sign of his maturity". One might say that when we "speak our minds" we enter the world of poetry.

The Question of Sex

As constructionists propose, the ways we understand the world are often constrained and controlled by the structure of language. As you will recall from the preceding chapter, one of the major features of language is its dependence on binaries. The meaning of any word depends on its contrast with other words. Thus, we contrast black and white, up and down, in and out, good and evil, and so on. Why is this sexy? Consider the following binaries: man/woman, and hetero/homosexual. In Western culture we generally presume there are two genders – men and women – and two directions of attraction – toward the opposite or the same sex. And, cultural tradition generally places the greater value on men, and most certainly on heterosexuality. But, from the constructionist standpoint these distinctions are not required by the way things are; we could make other distinctions, or depending on our interests, none at all. And the values could be reversed. Yet, it is difficult to "think outside the box" in this case, because the binaries have come to serve as "the real".

If this proposal seems radical, consider the following: how do you know that someone is a male or female? You might say by virtue of the differences in genitalia. However, small children make gender distinctions without the knowledge of genital differences. And, for biologists, it is not the genitalia that count but the chromosomes. Thus, a "female" Olympic star may be disqualified because "her" chromosomes indicate that she is a male. Further, there are many people who feel they have been born in the wrong body; often they seek surgery to restore themselves to their real gender. Who is to serve as the authority in such matters? And could there be alternatives, for example, a unisex?

Much the same arguments hold for sexual preference. What counts as an objective indicator of sexual preference? If women like to spend more time with their women friends, is this an indication of sexual preference? When young boys play with each others' genitals, is this homosexuality? When teenage girls practise kissing with each other, are they lesbians? If one has a sexual experience with someone "of the opposite sex" and doesn't like it, does this indicate homosexuality? And if one periodically enjoys sex with someone of the "same sex", does this mean they are basically homosexual? In addition, how do we classify those who prefer to masturbate rather than have intercourse, or those who become monastic and abandon sexuality altogether? Again, who is to serve as the final authority on what constitutes sexual preference? Can we also generate alternatives to an either/or orientation? We might avoid much misery by doing so.

Narrative: Reality as Story

I can only answer the question, 'What am I to do?' if I can answer the prior question 'Of what story or stories do I find myself a part?'

Alasdair MacIntyre, *Beyond Virtue*

Imagine yourself a witness to a crime, and placed on the witness stand. You are asked to describe what happened on the night of 6 June. You reply, "blue … four … shoe … I … hair" and then go silent. You are questioned again, "No, no, no … listen carefully … tell me clearly what really happened". You repeat yourself, and do so again, as the lawyer grows increasingly exasperated. Finally, the judge bellows, "I hold you in contempt of court!" Based on earlier chapters, the judge's actions would seem unjustified. After all, you know that whatever happened on that night doesn't demand or require any particular formation of syllables; words aren't pictures. However, within the Western tradition of "reporting what happened", the judge is perfectly justified. Within this tradition one is required to tell a proper story. One is required to treat reality as a story.

What does telling a proper story mean by Western standards? In the more formal terms, this is to ask about the standards for *narrative construction*. What, by Western standards, are the conventions or rules for constructing an acceptable narrative? There appear to be at least five significant features of what we commonly take to be well-formed narratives. A narrative may be acceptable without meeting all five criteria, but as the ideal is approximated the narrative will ironically seem more "true to life". Among the most prominent criteria for a well-formed narrative by traditional standards are the following.

A valued end point

An acceptable story must first establish a goal, an event to be explained, a state to be reached or avoided, or more informally, a "point". This point is typically saturated with value; it is understood to be desirable or undesirable. For example, your criminal testimony should be built around the single point: the occurrence of a crime. How did this awful event occur? If you answered the question of what happened on the evening in question in terms of how you tied your shoe, again you would be chastised. The event has no value in this context.

Events relevant to the end point

Once an endpoint has been established it more or less dictates the kinds of events that can figure in the story. Specifically, an intelligible narrative is one in which events serve to make the goal more or less probable, accessible, or vivid. Thus, if the point of the story is "the crime", you are expected to tell of events that are relevant to this point. If you said, "I tied my shoe, the dog barked, the light was on, John lay dead on the floor, and my tooth ached", you would still fail as a witness. The "truth and nothing but the truth" is not what is wanted, but a proper story. This means relating events that had specifically to do with John's death. This is to say that "the dog barked" could figure in the account, but connectives would be necessary, such as, "The dog barked at the man I saw jump from John's window".

Ordering of events

Once a goal has been established and relevant events selected, the events are usually placed in an ordered arrangement. The most widely used convention of ordering is that of linear time. In an intelligible story, one understands the events as unfolding in clock time. Thus you would fail as a witness once again if you said, "The man jumped from the window; a scream occurred, John lay dead on the floor, a shot rang out".

Causal linkages

The ideal narrative provides a sense of explanation. As it is said, "The king died and then the queen died" is only a listing of events. But to say, "The king died and then the queen died of grief" is the beginning of a tale. As narrative theorist Paul Ricoeur puts it, "Explanation must ... be woven into the narrative tissue" (1981, p. 278). Thus, you would receive high marks as a witness if you could tell a tale of John and Harry's argument, causing Harry to become angry and pull out a pistol, which caused John to scream at him, at which point Harry pulled the trigger, which sent John sprawling to the floor, the sight of which caused Harry to then leap from the window. Each event is causally related to the preceding in a seamless tale.

To illustrate the importance of these criteria of good narration, researchers asked participants to either tell a story of an actual occurrence in their lives, or to make up an occurrence (Bennett & Feldman, 1981). When a group of evaluators was asked to distinguish between stories they suspected to be true as opposed to false, the results were interesting. Stories that seemed more genuine to the evaluators were those that more closely approximated the well-formed narrative as outlined here. Particularly important to the "sense of truth" was evidence of a valued endpoint and causal linkages among events. In telling the truth, life should copy art.

To appreciate the significance of narrative in daily life, consider the way in which you understand your own life. First, consider the way we understand our momentary daily lives in terms of "ups" and "downs", progress and setbacks, fulfillment and frustration. To see life in these ways is to participate in a storied world. To be "up", to progress, or to be fulfilled is to participate in a story. Similarly I understand my writing at this moment not as an isolated act, but as coming from somewhere in the past and leading to something I value in the future. Or as one commentator has put it, "We dream in narrative, daydream in narrative, remember, anticipate, hope, despair, believe, doubt, plan, revise, criticize, construct, gossip, learn, hate and love by narrative" (Hardy, 1968, p. 73). The same may be said about the way others respond to us – at least our long-term acquaintances. They typically treat us as characters in a story, with

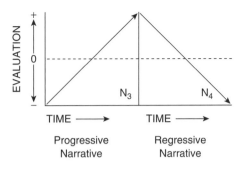

Figure 2.1   Rudimentary Forms of Narrative

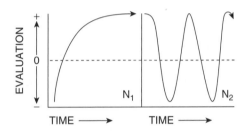

Figure 2.2   The Happily-ever-after Narrative and the Heroic Saga

issues of good and evil, success and failure, "ups" and "downs" prominent in the way they relate to us.

To gain a better grasp of the way in which narratives fashion our sense of identity, it is useful to consider major forms of narrative convention. Such forms can be understood best by returning again to the first essential ingredient of the good story, the valued endpoint. To make sense of our lives, we typically posit some kind of endpoint or goal ("how I came to be X", "achieve Y", or "believe in Z"). Given the endpoint, try to envision a two-dimensional space in which all events are arrayed over time in terms of whether they move toward or away from the valued goal. To illustrate, consider two rudimentary narrative forms: the *progressive narrative*, in which the endpoint is positive (a success, victory, etc.), and the story is all about the events that lead up to achieving this valued state; and a *regressive narrative*, in which the end-point is negative (a failure, loss, etc.), and the story tells about continuous decline. Although few of our stories about ourselves are pure examples of progressive and regressive narratives, they often approximate these cases. "How I won the match … came to this conclusion … achieved these results" and so on in the former case, and in the latter, "How my romance failed … I was cheated … ended up on drugs".

Fortunately these are not the only story forms available to us. Other popular variants of these more rudimentary forms include the *happily-ever-after narrative* ("How after many difficult years, I finally ended up in a profession that is rewarding"), and a narrative that is often very attractive to males, the *heroic saga narrative*. In this case one understands one's life as a series of ups and downs – a struggle, perhaps, to

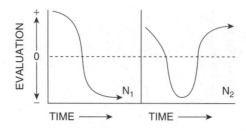

Figure 2.3   Tragic and Comedy-Romance Narratives

achieve a goal, misfortune sets in, I struggle again toward victory, but again set-backs occur, until finally I win out. Two other popular narratives deserve mention. The first is the *tragedy*, in which someone in a high position or at the point of success falls rapidly into despair or failure. If my computer crashes and takes my manuscript copy with it, and I shout a curse, I am giving expression to a tragic narrative – at the peak of production I am brought low. Finally, almost all prime-time television dramas take the form of what might be called a *comedy–romance*.[1] In this case a positive state of affairs is interrupted by a calamity (for example, a crime, an error of judgment, a *faux pas*), and the remainder of the story is occupied with a series of events that finally restore order and tranquility. Perhaps you are one of those many people who understand their daily lives in this way – constructing your world so that you begin strong in the morning, run into problems, snags, and glitches during the day, and then attempt to "dig out" so that by bedtime the day has come to a happy conclusion. Life approximates television.

Narrative Truth in Psychoanalysis

One of the most exciting application of these ideas was invited by Donald Spence's ground-breaking book *Narrative truth and historical truth* (1982). Most psychoanalysts attempt to locate the origin of people's problems. If someone has an uncontrollable fear, for example, it is natural for the analyst to ask why. Relief from distress, it is reasoned, requires that one grasps and overcomes the source of the problem. But how is one to ever accurately grasp the past? There are many problems in getting at historical truth: the fuzzy recollections of the patient, the incapacity of the verbal report of the patient to match the available images of the past, and the necessity for selecting events that will have meaning in the therapeutic relationship. But how can one be sure what events will have meaning? Here the therapist helps, typically by asking leading questions – for example, about the patient's relationship to his or her mother and father. In answering the questions, the analyst directs attention to certain things and not others. In effect, the analyst begins to help the patient create the past in a certain way. Most importantly, Spence reasoned, the analyst is guided by a theory of cause and cure. The theory presumes a regressive narrative – "I was fine, until some event brought me down" – and in addition, that analysis will constitute a progressive narrative.

The problem will be overcome. In effect, there is no free reporting of the past; the therapist and the patient work together to generate a narrative that will inevitably support the presumptions of psychoanalytic theory. This narrative truth then serves not only as the key to a cure, but for the patient it becomes "my life". As Spence concludes, "The construction not only shapes the past – it becomes the past" (ibid, p. 175).

Rhetoric and Reality

Rhetoric is the art of speaking well – with knowledge, skill and elegance.

Cicero, *De Oratore*

Interest in the ways language shapes our sense of the real soon brings us to the doorstep of an ancient tradition of study. The study of rhetoric dates to classical Greek civilization when rhetoric was an essential element in the education of promising young men. For centuries afterwards, the works of Aristotle, Cicero, and others were used to fashion skills in public speaking. Crudely put, rhetoric is the art of persuasion. In a more refined sense it is the art of using words in a way that invites others to participate in the worlds they create. Yet, with the growing influence of modernist beliefs in objectivity, science, and truth, rhetoric suffered the same fate as the concept of metaphor. To convince others by virtue of "pretty talk", cleverness, emotional appeals, and the like was illegitimate. For the modernist logic and factual evidence – expressed clearly and plainly – were the keys to progress.

In recent years the study of rhetoric – like metaphor – has undergone a renaissance. This rekindling of interest grows directly from the soil of social constructionism. Of particular interest is how rhetorical study can help us to understand the difference between effective and ineffective constructions. Or, to put it another way, if rhetoric is the art of persuasion, then the study of rhetoric can help us understand what kind of language convinces us that something is real. If we can appreciate how we are convinced, we are also freed from rhetoric's effects. Of course, in many situations we are already sensitized to the power of rhetoric. Not that we always resist, but we do understand advertisements, sales pitches, and political speeches in terms of rhetoric. More dangerous are communications that only "report the facts" – the world as it is, outside anyone's particular perspective. In these cases rhetorical analysis is especially useful. It attempts to question the authority of science, policy making, military decision making, economics. Too often, a resort to the facts functions to silence other voices. Too often, the language of objective reality is used as a means of generating hierarchies of inclusion and exclusion. This is so not only in science, where one of the chief aims of the scientist is to lift his or her own particular constructions into the status of "accepted fact" (Latour & Woolgar, 1979), but it is also the case more generally, where those who don't speak the rhetoric are scorned as "unrealistic", "deluded", "irrational", or "self-deceived". To illuminate these rhetorical manoeuvres is thus to challenge the conventions and thereby open a space for all to speak.

41

How is it that our discourse succeeds in generating the sense of the "really real" – the taken-for-granted world of atoms, chemical elements, neurons, cognitions, economic processes, social structure and the like? Although much has been written on this question (see, for example, Potter, 1996), central to the power of words to create "the real" is the widely shared image or construction of the person. More specifically, the rhetoric derived from the now familiar metaphor of the "mind as mirror", the belief in the mind is inside the head (subjective) and the world is outside (objective). Based on this metaphor, we hold that a person is objective when private experience is a perfect reflection of the natural world. One is objective when he/she "sees things for what they are", "is in touch with reality", or "takes a good look at things". As you will recall from the above discussion, it is very difficult to separate out what is "in the mirror" as opposed to "in the world". Thus, we find that objectivity cannot refer to a relationship between mind and world; rather, as the rhetorical scholar proposes, objectivity is achieved by speaking (or writing) in particular ways. Let's consider two significant ways in which rhetoric creates the real.

Distancing the object: the world "out there"

Because reality talk is supposed to be about a "world out there", it is important that the speaker employs *distancing devices*, that is, discursive means of ensuring that the object in question is not "in the mind" but exists at a distance. At the simplest level, words such as *the, that*, or *those*, call attention away from the observer and place the object(s) at a seeming distance. Distancing may be contrasted with personalization, terms calling attention to the object as a private possession of the mind. "My view", "my perception", "my sense of" are all personalizing. Thus, the scientist is likely to speak of "the apparatus", as opposed, for example, to "my sense of an apparatus", "the experimental chamber" as opposed to "my impression of an experimental chamber", or "those questionnaires", and not "my image of questionnaires". The former phrases create the real, while the latter create suspicion.

The distancing of object from observer can also be achieved through the use of metaphors. Consider, for example, the *metaphor of the hidden continent*, a land out there to be explored. In science one thus finds such phrases as "Smith first discovered the effect", "Jones found that ...", "Brown detected that ...", and so on. Terms such as "unearthed" and "brought to light" are similarly used, suggesting a companionate *metaphor of buried treasure*. Consider the unfortunate consequences of some personalized contrasts: "Smith first felt it was so", "Jones also shared this fantasy", and "Brown loved this image of the world".

Purifying the lens: the death of passion

The so-called "mirror of the mind" achieves objectivity when there is no interference, when it possesses no defect that might "distort", or "bias" the image produced by the world. One means of demonstrating that there are no "mirror effects" is to use phrases granting the world an *active power* to create the image (as opposed to characteristics of the mirror itself). Thus, such phrases as "the data tell us", or "The results are clear", contribute to the sense of the real. On the other hand, it is important to demonstrate the *absence of internal states* – such as

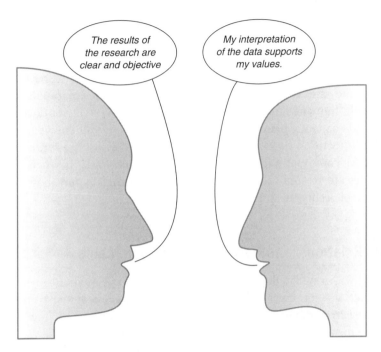

Figure 2.4   Who do you trust and why?

the emotions, motives, values, and desires – in creating the reflection. One can say, "We recorded a mean of 5.65 ...", "It was observed that the subjects were ill at ease ...", or "The results demonstrated ..". without generating doubt. However, should affective states be inserted into the same phrases, the effects would be off-putting. Consider: "My heart was set on finding a mean of over 5.00 and I was overjoyed when I got it ...", "Given that the research would not be published if we didn't get positive results, we looked for evidence that would support our hypothesis. It was great that it did so ...", or "I fell in love with this research subject and it is thus a pleasure to share her insights".

This purging of the mirror has an interesting side-effect on social science writing. Although such writing should be fascinating – as it attempts to "explore the depths" of human existence – it is typically dull, flat and antiseptic. One reason for this tendency is that emotional or colourful descriptions suggest biases in the mind's mirror. In contrast, passionless technical description suggests a neutral – and thus objective – standpoint. We learn, for example, that the research subjects were college males, or women aged 40–60, or elementary school children from the inner city. In contrast, there is no mention of such matters as sexual attractiveness, off-putting obesity, creative clothing styles, charming manners, stupefying ignorance, repulsive pimples, great hair styles, and so on. To write about such matters would destroy the sense of objectivity.

To demonstrate that objectivity is not a state of mind but of rhetoric allows us to pause, and ask, "who is this writing for; what purposes does it serve and for whom?" However, this is not to argue for abandoning the rhetoric of reality. Rather, the

CONSTRUCTING THE REAL AND THE GOOD

rhetoric of reality plays a very important role within communities. This rhetoric is often vital in achieving trust and achieving ends valuable to the community. For example, when space scientists use this rhetoric they ask their colleagues to trust that they are using the language in the same way and for the same purposes as the remainder of the community. They are "calling a spade a spade" in terms of the community's standards, and as a result, humans can walk on the moon. The same holds for doctors, military strategists and economic planners; and without such rhetoric there would be nothing we could call "truth" in courtroom testimony. The rhetoric of the real may be essential to effective community functioning; problems result primarily when the community's realities are treated as universal or "really real". Let us turn now to a second major source of reality making.

Everyday Relations: The Power of the Unremarkable

I just talked with my daughter on the phone, and we talked about many things – a family dinner, the summer vacation, her need for a new coat, car troubles, and so on. Nothing extraordinary here, simply everyday life. But in these few minutes we did far more than chat about the events of the day. We sustained a stable world of facts – dinners, vacations, coats, cars – and as well, affirmed the significance of our relationship. Our verbal constructions are glued to our life circumstances. We not only construct together, we also live out the implications of these constructions. The groundbreaking work on reality making in daily conversation was that of sociologist Harold Garfinkel. In his signal volume, *Studies in ethnomethodology* (1967), Garfinkel focused on the ways in which people work together to achieve a sense of order and understanding. Specifically, proposed Garfinkel, our interchanges are deeply reliant on *ethnomethods* – practices of talking and acting – that we use to achieve a rational or taken-for-granted order. Ethnomethods may be as simple as nodding one's head in agreement, not raising questions, or laughing at another's joke. They inject into everyday life the sense of a common, understandable, and reliable world.

Consistent with earlier discussions, Garfinkel points out that we treat words as if they were pictures of the objects to which they refer. At the same time, he proposes, we are always borrowing words and phrases from other contexts and simply "making do" with them in our present circumstances. For example, we treat a word like "car" as if it refers a specific object. Yet, we use the word to talk about large, gas guzzling vehicles, two-door vehicles; and tiny three-wheel vehicles. The word doesn't picture any of them exactly; we just make do with an inexact word and trust others to credit us with making sense. In Garfinkel's terms, we use words *indexically*, that is, to point or name *for all practical purposes*. In effect, our "natural", taken-for-granted world only remains so because we don't raise too many questions. When we don't ask too many questions, and agree to be imprecise, life goes on harmoniously. To illustrate, as a class exercise Garfinkel enlisted his students to break the unspoken rules of everyday life and report on the consequences. Specifically, they were to question the conventions we use to generate "common sense". Here is the account of a student's report on his interchange with a member of his car pool (A) who is telling him (B) about a flat tyre on the previous day:

A: I had a flat tire.

B: What do you mean, you "had a flat tire?"

A: [*Momentarily stunned, replies hostily*] What do you mean, "What do you mean?" A flat tire is a flat tire. That is what I meant. Nothing special. What a crazy question. (p.111)

In a second case, an acquaintance (A) of the student (B), waved his hand and said:

A: How are you?

B: How am I in regard to what? My health, my finances, my school work, my peace of mind, my ...?

A: [*Red in the face and out of control*] Look! I was just trying to be polite. Frankly, I don't give a damn how you are. (p.112)

Another student questioned his fiancée for approximately a minute and a half on the precise meaning of what she was saying. She then began to reject the questions, and finally became nervous and jittery, her face and hand movements uncontrolled. "She appeared bewildered and complained that I was making her nervous and demanded that I 'Stop it' ... She picked up a magazine and covered her face ... When asked why she was looking at the magazine she closed her mouth and refused any further talk" (1967, p. 42). As these vignettes suggest, if we challenge the taken-for-granted ways of indexing our world – even momentarily – the social fabric quickly unravels.

Now consider the issue of individual identity. We treat each other as "the same person" from day to day, even when our actions are never the same. We have an identity for practical purposes. To be sure we do create reliable worlds in this way. At the same time, however, these worlds can also be confining. There may be no escaping the self I have become. To illustrate, consider Paul Willis's (1977) analysis of how British adolescents come into their identity as working class. As Willis proposes, it is all too easy to look at economic betterment as a natural drive: everyone wants to make more money. And with this assumption in place it is typical to see the working class as oppressed, as people who have no choice but to remain in the lower economic ranks of society. However, through extensive field work in schools and the workplace, Willis challenges these common beliefs. As he finds, working-class boys join together to construct a world in which they are different from and better than the upper classes. Here, for example, they define their school teachers:

Joey: They're bigger than us, they stand for a bigger establishment than we do ... and [we] try to get [our] own back.

Eddie: The teachers think they're high and mighty 'cos they're teachers, but they're nobody really.·

(Willis, 1977, p. 11)

45

These dispositions also permeate the boys' classroom behaviour. Willis describes:

As the 'lads' enter the classroom or assembly, there are conspiratorial nods to each other ... [they] specialize in a caged resentment which always stops just short of outright confrontation ... During class a mouthed imaginary dialogue counterpoints the formal instruction: 'No, I don't understand, you c...'; 'What you on about, twit?'; 'Not f...... likely ...' At the vaguest sexual double meaning giggles and 'whaos' come from the back ... If the secret of the conspiracy is challenged, there are V signs behind the teacher's back, the gunfire of cracked knuckles from the side, and evasive innocence at the front. Attention is focused on ties, rings, shoes, fingers ... anything rather than the teacher's eyes. (ibid., p. 12–13).

This ontology of "us" versus "them" is also supported by implicit ethics: "we and our way of life our way of life are superior". It is a matter of pride to stick with the group:

Joey: ... when you're dossing on your own, it's no good, but when you're dossing with your mates, then you're all together, you're having a laff and it's a doss ...

Fred: We're as thick as thieves, that's what they say, stick together.

(ibid., p. 23–24)

The value placed on their way of life is revealed in the boys' characterisations of students who act in all the socially approved ways. These "ear'oles", as they were called (the ear being a symbol of someone who just passively listens) are the subject of continuous scorn. Consider:

Derek: [The ear'oles] are prats like, one got on his report he's got five As and one B ...

Spanksy: I mean, what will they remember of their school life? What will they have to look back on? Sitting in a classroom, sweating their bollocks off, you know, while we've been ... I mean look at the things we can look back on, fighting on the Pakis, fightin on the JAs [Jamaicans]. Some of the things we've done on teachers, it'll be a laff when we look back on it.

Joey: [The ear'oles] are still f...... childish, the way they talk, the way they act like ... they've got it all to come. I mean look at Tom Bradley, have you ever noticed him? I've always looked at him and I've thought, well ... we've been through all life's pleasures and all its f...... displeasures, we've been drinking, we've been fighting, we've known frustration, sex, f......, hatred, love and all this lark, yet he's known none of it. He's never been with a woman, he's never been in a pub. (ibid., p. 15–16)

It is in just such conversations as these that "the lads" help to create a world of differences, a world populated by different groups and individuals, and each laden with moral value. One must ask in this case – and perhaps all – whether these realities may not be imprisoning.

Constructing the Body

Critics often point out that the world exists prior to our constructing it. Constructionists agree that "something exists". However, once we go about trying to describe this something, we can do little else than fall back on traditions of construction. And these traditions are many. Consider the human body, for example. Something exists, but what is it? For example, Plato believed the body was a tomb, Paul the disciple that it is a temple of the Holy Spirit, Descartes that it is a machine, and the philosopher Jean Paul Sartre that it is the self. For contemporary marketers, the body – especially a woman's – is a vehicle for advertising. And for many young people today, the body is used as a cultural signal to one's identity. Both tattoos and body piercing are signs that others can read about "the kind of person I am". These differences in construction can be very important. In medicine, for example, a doctor may approach a patient's body as simply "an object to be repaired". From the patient's point of view, he or she is effectively reduced to a piece of meat. The result of this difference may be an insensitivity on the doctor's part to the full and important life situation of the patient. And if mistakes are made in treatment, the chances of a lawsuit are increased. Advanced forms of medical training attempt to help doctors take account of the multiple realities of the body.

Institutional Realities: Foucault on Power

Madness exists only within a society.

Michel Foucault, *Madness and Civilization*

Language structure and use are essential to the creation of our sense of the real and the good. However, our traditions of speech are often embedded in larger organizations. Such organizations come to have authority over matters of reality, reason, and right. Courts of law have authority over what is right or wrong in terms of the law; branches of science claim authority over what is true or false about their areas of study; religions serve as authorities on matters of the spirit; we rely on medical practitioners to be the authorities on matters of health, and so on. In effect, institutions such as these are enormously important in determining the constructions by which we live. It is for this reason that many view these institutions as centres of power. In these terms, a constructionist sensibility alerts us to issues of freedom and control.

Just such issues feature centrally in the works of one of the most catalytic social theorists of the past century, Michel Foucault. In the present context his concern is with the way in which people quite willingly subjugate themselves to subtle forms of power (see especially, Foucault, 1978; 1979). We are not speaking here of the obvious forms of power – control by law and arms – but rather, the insinuation of

CONSTRUCTING THE REAL AND THE GOOD

power into ordinary life. For the most part we live quite ordered lives; with few misgivings, we attend school, enter professions, pay for our purchases, go to doctors, and so on. For Foucault, in the very exercise of these taken-for-granted practices, we demonstrate our subjugation to power. For Foucault, "power is … an open, more or less coordinated … cluster of relations" (in Gordon, 1980, p. 199).

Language is a critical feature of such power relations, and in particular the discourse of knowledge. Foucault was centrally concerned with subjugation by various groups who claim "to know", or to be in possession of, "the truth" – especially about who we are as human selves. Consider, for example, the disciplines of medicine, psychiatry, sociology, anthropology, education, and the like. These *disciplinary regimes*, as Foucault called them, generate languages of description and explanation – classifications of selves as healthy or unhealthy, normal or abnormal, upper or lower class, intelligent or unintelligent – along with explanations as to why they are so. The regimes also employ various research procedures, whereby we are scrutinized and classified in their terms. In effect, when we offer ourselves for examinations of various sorts – from medical examinations to college board assessments – we are giving ourselves over to the disciplinary regimes, to be labelled and explained in their terms And when we carry these terminologies into our daily lives, speaking to others of our cholesterol level, our depression, or academic grades, we are engaging in power relations – in one way or another extending the control of the disciplinary regimes. As our disciplines of study begin to influence public policy and practices, we become further ordered in their terms. Ultimately we participate in our own subjugation.

To appreciate Foucault's argument consider an ordinary case: one day you are feeling down, a little blue, perhaps self-critical, and a friend asks "what's wrong …?" Chances are you might respond, "Oh, I'm just a little depressed". Although describing yourself as "depressed" is wholly unremarkable in today's culture, it was not always so. The first classification of mental disorders in the United States, occurring in 1840, contained only a handful of distinctions and was closely tied to organic dysfunction. In those days the term "depression" did not exist. It was only in the 1930s, with the emergence of psychiatry and clinical psychology, that "mental disorders" began to mushroom. By 1938, some 40 disturbances were recognized (including moral deficiency, misanthropy, and masturbation). Since that time the *Diagnostic and Statistical Manual of Mental Disorders*, the official handbook for diagnosis, has gone through four editions, and the number of deficit terms has now mounted to over 300 (which include such disorders as inhibition of orgasm, gambling, academic deficiency, bereavement, and negative attitudes toward medical treatment). Depression is not only a significant entry in the present manual, but there are several sub-types as well (for example, chronic, melancholic, bipolar). Mental health professionals now believe that more than 10% of the population suffers from depression. Anti-depressant drugs, virtually unknown a quarter of a century ago, are now a multi-billion dollar industry. And if you find yourself "feeling kind of blue" you may well expect to find yourself on medication.

Interestingly, this dramatic expansion of identified disorders roughly parallels the growing numbers of mental health professionals. For example, at the turn of the century the American Psychiatric Association numbered less than 400; today there are over 40,000 members – a hundred-fold increase. The costs of mental health have increased in similar magnitude. By 1980 mental illness was the third most expensive category of health disorder in the United States. In effect, we find ourselves facing what appears to be a *cycle of progressive infirmity*. Consider the phases: (1) as mental health professionals declare the truth of a discourse of dysfunction, and (2) as this truth is disseminated through education, public policy, and the media, so do we (3) come to understand ourselves in these terms. ("I'm depressed".) With such understandings in place, we will (4) seek out mental health professionals for a cure. As a cure is sought, (5) so is the need for mental health professionals expanded. And (6), as the professional ranks expand, so does the vocabulary of mental disorder prosper. The cycle is continuous and ever-expanding in its effects (for further elaboration see Gergen, 2006).

Is there a limit to the dysfunctional disciplining of the population? I recently received an announcement for a conference on the latest research and cure for addiction, called, "the number one health and social problem facing our country today". Among the addictions to be discussed were exercise, religion, eating, work, and sex. If all these activities – when pursued with intensity or gusto – can be defined as illnesses that require cure, there seems little in cultural life that can withstand the expansive power of the mental professions and pharmaceutical industry. Unless we can mount a collective refusal.[2]

A critique such as this is designed to mobilize resistance. Indeed, Foucault's own writings were focally concerned with ways of combating the expanding domains of *power/knowledge*, as he termed the process of cultural disciplining. Foucault urged his readers to fight against these forces through resistance, subversion, and self-transformation. Yet, while rousing the spirit of revolution, we must also realize the limits to the rebellious response to power/knowledge invasion. Consider, then, two substantial problems with the unrelenting posture of antagonism toward the dominant order.

First, there is the problem of freedom. To fight against the invasive influence of power, is to hold out a promise that we might one day become free – no one controlling or containing us with an alien knowledge. Yet, freedom from the ordering effects of language, from all traditions or conventions is not freedom: it is essentially a step into insignificance – a space where there is no freedom because there are no distinctions, and thus no choices. This is not at all to undermine the critical impulse; however, it is to place strong emphasis on visioning the alternative. We cannot step out of meaning or avoid ordering of any kind. If we wish to refuse one form of disciplining, what form of ordering do we suggest in its place? For example, there is good reason to put a lid on the expansion of psychiatric diagnosis. However, we do not therefore step into an arena of pure freedom. The invitation is to generate alternative understandings of greater promise.

Closely related is a second major problem with an unrelenting critical posture: it fails to take account of the positive effects of ordering. To reject all that Foucault might call "disciplining" or "ordering" would be to erase virtually all that we value. We cannot have another's love without participating in a social ordering of some kind; parents cannot give their children love without the regime we call "family"; we can scarcely achieve justice without an institution of law. Required, then, is *differentiating appraisal.* Given a range of disciplinary traditions, we may launch an enquiry into consequences, both negative and positive. In what ways does a tradition sustain that which we hold to be good, in what ways does it fail? How could it be otherwise? The professional practices of classifying and curing mental disease, for example, have the negative effects of inviting us to see the normal problems of daily life as "illnesses", diminishing our abilities to generate local solutions (believing these are problems for professionals), and providing us with multiple means of finding fault in others and ourselves (for example, "He is obese", "She is anorexic", "He is addicted to his work"). Yet, the classifications of "mental illness" do give many people the sense that they are not personally responsible for their problems ("I can't help it, I'm ill"), and that there are professionals who can alleviate their suffering. They are not alone, nor are they hopeless. In this kind of differentiating appraisal, then, we may bring forth alternatives that retain some of the virtues of our traditions while removing those we believe harmful.

Identity Politics: To Be or Not to Be

> Like any common living thing, I fear and reprove classification and the death it entails, and I will not allow its clutches to lock down on me ...
>
> Trin Minh-ha, *Woman Native Other*

In this chapter I have treated three major sources of our common constructions of the real and good. The discussion has centred on the structure of our language, on practices of everyday interchange, and on the institutions of authority. In many ways the discussion has emphasized the stability of our constructions. I have suggested the difficulty of escaping the structures of language, the way conversations draw us in to a common reality, and the power of institutions to sustain their authority. To be sure, I have also emphasized the importance of critical reflection and the potentials for resistance. However, in this final section I wish to balance the emphasis of the preceding sections on stability with a focus on fluidity in construction.

The process of world construction is taking place wherever people are in communication, and in every relationship there are multiple traditions coming into contact, creating new formations of expression. There are also conflicts among traditions that continuously threaten their existence. Thus, as you move from the context of the family, to a friendship group, to a classroom, to the athletic field, to a place of worship, and so on, you will continuously shift in the kinds of realities and values that are central. You will also import the realities and values central in one context into another, and this may yield creative combinations (e.g. teams engaging in prayer together before a game, families at dinner discussing a book you have read for class). There may also be conflicts, with the realities and values shared in a friendship group clashing with those of one's parents, or one's religious views scorned by a friendship group. Social life is thus a seesaw dynamic between forces for stability and for change.

To illustrate this dynamic in motion, let us return again to the construction of the self, and the way one's identity becomes subject to political movements. Consider first the way we are defined by others. In particular, much depends on the way we are represented in others' talk – their descriptions, explanations, criticisms, or congratulations. Such talk creates our social reputation. Yet, these are not the words we would necessarily choose; they are generated by others – our friends, family, neighbours, teachers and so on. It is our identity which is at stake, but we cannot fully control the way we are represented. For example, a child who grows into an adult may return home, only to find his parents treating him like a child. A woman who joins a company may find her male colleagues treating her more like a woman than a working partner.

Now consider the issue on a societal level: all of us are identified with one or more social groups – woman, man, Christian, Jew, black, white, German, Irish, Hispanic, and so on. Such groups are often the subject of media interest – films, novels, news reports, advertising, etc. When our group is represented to millions of people we confront helplessness writ large. When women are depicted as silly and emotional, Asians as obedient, Germans as menacing, Irish as aggressive and so on, we are implicated. It is not only a matter of public reputation, but as these reputations become shared so too do they come to be taken-for-granted realities. And it is these realities that inform public policies, educational practices, police actions, and so on. There is racial profiling of blacks, suspicion of Muslims, antipathy toward Germans, and so on. Further, these same public portrayals inform those depicted. Here one may learn what it is to be a woman, Asian, heterosexual, and so on. One's actions may begin to resemble the stereotype.

In terms of the present discussion we may say that our identities are importantly fashioned by the institutions of the media. And when the media create stereotypes of various groups, we now enter the arena of politics. Who is hurt by these practices; who is helped; how could things be different? The result of such questioning has set in motion several major movements, each of which deserves attention. The first movement is perhaps the most obvious: *resistance*. There were early critiques by Italian Americans for the media portrayals of them as gangsters, by African Americans for their caricatures as Uncle Toms and Aunt Jemimahs, and women for their one-dimensional depiction as sex objects. Now such resistance is multiplied. Native Americans reject the ways in which they are represented in museums, as savage and primitive; gays and lesbians show how Hollywood films enkindle homophobia; seniors resist the depiction of old people as incapacitated, and so on (see, for example, Naylor, 1982; 1991).

For many of those engaged in identity politics, these forms of resistance are only a beginning. More important is the challenge of gaining the capacity for depicting themselves. A second wave of identity politics is thus invested in *identity activism*. In the terms of social theorist Ernesto Lauclau, "The crucial question ... is not who the social agents are, but the extent to which they manage to constitute themselves" (1990, p. 36). Or as black feminist Patricia Hill Collins has put the case, "The insistence on Black female self-definition reframes the entire dialogue from one of protesting the technical accuracy of an image – namely refuting the Black matriarchy thesis – to one of stressing the power dynamics underlying the very process of definition itself ... the act of insisting on Black female self-definition validates Black women's power as human subjects" (1990, pp. 106–107). Put in this light, one's ethnic, racial or religious identity

CONSTRUCTING THE REAL AND THE GOOD

is a site of struggle, a contest between self-control versus being controlled by others. Thus we find television networks pressed to expand their fare to include and fairly present the experiences of under-represented groups. Oprah Winfrey, for example, has been singled out for the way in which she has transformed the public image of both women and black culture (Squire, 1994). We also find a proliferation of niche magazines by and about feminists, African Americans, the gay community, and so on; and a spate of films, plays and books revealing the lives of the marginalized in their own voices.

Yet, the movement toward identity activism is not without its problems. In the former case, if you write or make a film about "your people", *you* are representing *them* – and effectively, they continue to be without control. Further, many within such groups object to the way they are depicted "by their kind". For example, if an author wishes to reveal the miseries resulting from an oppressive society – emphasizing for example, suffering, drugs and violence – the identified group will often feel betrayed. They are appearing as abnormal, incapacitated victims. On the other hand, if the author wishes to stress the richness of a tradition, the joys, the communal bonds, and so on, antagonism again erupts. Here the work is faulted for the pretty picture it paints, a picture that provokes no political action but suggests the status quo is just fine. Consider the reaction of black feminist bell hooks to the way black film-maker Spike Lee portrays blacks and women:

The portraits of black men conform to popular stereotypes in the white racist imagination. Rather than threaten white audiences, they assuage their fear. [The film] excludes black women and their role in liberation struggle ... every black female in the film, whether she be mother, daughters or sisters is constructed at some point as sex object. (hooks, 1990, pp. 179–182)

We must ask then, can anyone be trusted to represent any group? Must the answer be "every person for him/herself?" Wouldn't this bring an end to the political power of group unity? At the same time, the issue of group unity has come under question. Many individuals who might otherwise be classified within a group will feel resentment at the classification. All too often they will be under pressure from others in their group to "be with and like us". They will be expected to "follow our traditions", marry within the group, "vote the way we do", and so on. Yet, not all those who can be identified with a group will wish to espouse its positions. There are many Jews who are committed Christians, Pakistanis who are gay activists, African Americans engaged in Muslim causes. Such individuals may be scorned and possibly ostracized. Similarly, if they are living outside the group, others may treat them as representatives of their group. They may be expected to speak for "their people". Their identity marker – skin colour, sexual preference, accent, or religious symbols – may come to stand for their entire identity. Others may be blind to their individuality.

Issues such as these have sparked yet another wave of identity politics, *category deconstruction*. Central to this wave is a growing critique of the ways in which all representations of a people, regardless of the author or content, tend to *essentialize* their object. To essentialize in this case is to treat a social category (for example, women, gays, Asians) as standing for an essence – a set of intrinsic qualities or characteristics residing within a people. This is a longstanding problem in the case of race, a category commonly used as

Figure 2.5   As the world's peoples increasingly converge, identity politics may well recede in importance. The golf impresario, Tiger Woods, symbolizes such a future. As a mixture of African American, Chinese, Native American, Thai and Caucasian, he challenges the very possibility of classification. Unless, of course, one accepts his suggestion for a new category, "Cablinasian".

if to mirror a specific set of essences that distinguish one group from another. Yet, there is no essence – no essential nature – lurking within people of which skin colour, height, facial hair, and so on are the "manifestations". As the cultural studies scholar Stuart Hall, puts it, "What is at issue here is the recognition ... that 'black' is a politically and culturally constructed category, which cannot be grounded in a set of fixed transcultural or transcendental racial categories and which therefore has no guarantees in nature" (Hall, 1996, p. 443). This tendency to essentialize people belonging to a group also fosters antagonism: avoidance, distrust, and hatred. For those inside a group, it suggests that "we are different, and you can neither understand nor fully participate in our community". For the outsider, every group thus becomes the Other: alien, self-seeking and ultimately antagonistic. So many and so politically active are the divisions within American society, that political theorist James Davison Hunter (1991) coined the phrase *culture wars* to characterize the condition.

Given these problems, how is political work to proceed? There is no single answer here; the dialogues are in motion. First there are those who feel betrayed by these critiques of essentialism. As they argue, just when women and minorities are beginning to gain a sense of autonomy and self-direction – taking charge of their own identities – the critics begin to fault their essentialism. To do this removes the grounds for social critique, and the rationale for changing society. For example, if there are no "women" (the category of "woman" is only a superficial label) how can we fight for equal rights for women?

CONSTRUCTING THE REAL AND THE GOOD

For feminist Naomi Weisstein those who see gender and other categories as socially constructed represent "a high cult of critique", and she has lamented, "Sometimes I think that, when the fashion passes, we will find many bodies, drowned in their own wordy words, like the Druids in the bogs" (Weisstein, 1993, p. 244).

There are more promising possibilities. For example, African American scholar Cornell West (1993) emphasizes the importance of developing within the black community a *love ethic*, which can enable people to work together in a context of heightened self-esteem. Such an ethic might enable better relations within the society more generally. Sociologist Tod Gitlin (1995) looks to popular movements and organizations that can cross the "identity trenches" to link otherwise disparate groups of minorities. Labour unions once served this purpose; new groups are now needed. Others believe we must radically expand the democratic process, so that people in all sectors of society can participate in dialogue. Supporting this view, others make strong arguments for civilizing our forms of public debate, finding less hostile ways of speaking together (see, for example, Hunker, 1994; Kingwell, 1995). More radical are the ideas of theorists such as Judith Butler (1990) who urges a wholesale dissolving of distinctions such as men and women, heterosexual and homosexual. Because being female, for example, is not a "natural fact" but a form of "cultural performance", we are free to perform in new ways. In revolutionary fashion, she opts for performances that blur the common distinctions; "gender bending" and "bisexuality" are illustrative. Others argue for a more fluid or nomadic conception of the self, one that is not fixed in any category but which moves with times and circumstances – taking political stands but not permanently so (see, for example, Flax, 1993; Deleuze & Guattari, 1986). Clearly, the challenge of political reconstruction remains very much with us; you as reader may well contribute to the next step.

Reflection

I have found so many of the ideas in this chapter intellectually exciting and personally useful. I have had to reconsider much in my life that I took for granted, I have changed many things about my life, and I find every day a creative challenge. It is my fond hope that as readers, some of this excitement and world-changing experience can be yours as well. But in looking over what I have written here, perhaps you feel as I do, that I have placed too much emphasis on spoken and written language. I have said almost nothing about what we might call the *material context*. After all, in common terms, how could we engage in conversation without an environment that sustains our lives? And certainly the way we construct the world must depend on matters of health, economy, politics, world conflict, and so on. Surely we don't go on constructing the real and the good, irrelevant of what is happening outside our verbal exchanges. And yet, as I consider this absence of the material world in these pages, I have also become aware of why so little has been written about its impact on social construction. Because once you enter the halls of social construction, there is no material world in itself. That is, what we call the material world is itself a construction. And this goes for matters of health, economy, politics, world peace, and so on.

This does not mean that we should no longer speak of these matters. Not at all. Rather, it means that when we do, we must be conscious that we are joining in the language games of our cultural traditions. My feeling is that it is the major challenge of this present book to stimulate this kind of consciousness. When this is fully in place, we can then talk more seriously about the significance of the material world – fully aware that this is but one way of understanding.

Notes

1 This term derives from Aristotle's classic theories of narrative, in which he distinguishes between the comedy and the romance on the grounds of their specific content. However, because both Aristotelian types share the same narrative form they are here allied.

2 For further steps toward refusal see
   http://www.swarthmore.edu/SocSci/Kgergen1/Psychodiagnostics/index.html

Further Resources

On the Narrative Construction of Reality

Bamberg, M. (Ed.). (2007). *Narrative – state of the art.* Philadelphia: John Benjamins.

Clandinen, D.J. (2006). *Handbook of narrative inquiry: mapping a methodology.* London: Sage.

Hinchman, L.P. & Hinchman, S.K. (Eds.). (1997). *Memory, identity, community: the idea of narrative in the human sciences.* Albany, NY: State University of New York Press.

Ruse, M. (2001). *Mystery of mysteries: is evolution a social construction?* Cambridge: Harvard University Press.

Sarbin, T.R. (1986). *Narrative Psychology, the storied nature of human conduct.* New York: Praeger.

Metaphors in Social Construction

Lakoff, G. & Johnson, M. (1980). *Metaphors we live by.* Chicago: University of Chicago Press.

Leary, D. (1990). *Metaphors in the history of psychology.* New York: Cambridge University Press.

Pickering, N. (2006). *The metaphor of mental illness.* New York: Oxford University Press.

Soyland, A.J. (1994). *Psychology as metaphor.* London: Sage.

Construction in Conversation

Antaki, C. & Widdicombe, S. (Eds.). (1998). *Identities and talk.* London: Sage.

Francis, D. & Hester, S. (2004). *An invitation to ethnomethodology: language, society and interaction.* London: Sage.

Shotter, J. (2008). *Conversational realities revisited.* Chagrin Falls, OH: Taos Institute Publications.

Edwards, D. & Potter, J. (1992). *Discursive psychology.* London: Sage.

Woofit, R. (2005). *Conversation analysis and discourse analysis: a comparative and critical introduction.* London: Sage.

The Rhetoric of the Real

Billig, M. (1996). *Arguing and thinking, a rhetorical approach to social psychology*. Cambridge: Cambridge University Press.

McClosky, D.N. (1985). *The rhetoric of economics*. Madison, WI: University of Wisconsin Press.

Myerson, G. (1994). *Rhetoric, reason and society*. London: Sage.

Potter, J. (1996). *Representing reality, discourse, rhetoric and social construction*. London: Sage.

Simons, H.W. (Ed.). (1990). *The rhetorical turn, invention and persuasion in the conduct of inquiry*. Chicago: University of Chicago Press.

Social Institutions, Power and Reality

Miller, L. (2007). Foucauldian constructionism. In J.A. Holstein & J.F. Gubrium (Eds.). *Handbook of constructionist research* (pp. 216–238). New York: Guilford.

Munoz, C. (2007). *Youth, identity, power: the Chicano movement*. London: Verso.

Pettenger, M.E. (2007). *The social construction of climate change: power, knowledge, norms, discourses*. London: Ashgate.

Identity and Cultural Dynamics

Butler, J. (2006). *Gender trouble: feminism and the subversion of identity* (2nd ed). New York: Routledge.

Castells, M. (2003). *The power of identity: the information age*. New York: Wiley-Blackwell.

Connolly, W.E. (2002). *Identity/difference: democratic negotiations of political paradox*, (expanded edition.). Minneapolis: University of Minnesota Press.

Gregg, G.S. (2007). *Culture and identity in a Muslim society*. New York: Oxford University Press.

3

HORIZONS OF HUMAN ENQUIRY

EMPIRICAL RESEARCH IN QUESTION
Fruits of Empirical Research
••••
RESEARCH TRADITIONS IN TRANSFORMATION
Ethnography and Cultural Understanding
New Histories
••••
DISCOURSE STUDY: EXPLORING CONSTRUCTED WORLDS
Narrative: Exploring Life Constructions
Discourse in Action: The Self as a Conversational Achievement
••••
IMAGINATION IN ACTION: QUALITATIVE ENQUIRY
Autoethnography
Collaborative Enquiry
Action Research: Social Change in Motion
Performance as Enquiry
••••
REFLECTION
••••
FURTHER RESOURCES

My colleagues tell me that social construction should not be taught to young students. Why? Because constructionist ideas place in question the cherished ideals of truth, objectivity, and knowledge. If the young absorb such doubts, they say, they will lose all interest in studying or entering fields of research. They will become skeptical of all claims to authority. If "it's all a social construction", they may come to feel that nothing is worth doing. Such fears are based on a flawed understanding of what constructionism is all about. If properly understood constructionist ideas can both increase admiration for existing knowledge-making endeavours, while simultaneously opening new and exciting vistas of possibility. In alerting us to the dangers in claiming truth, objectivity, or knowledge beyond human traditions of sense making, they invite us to be more selective in our choices. Rather than a growing negativity, constructionism invites us to appreciate multiple perspectives. Or, one might say, constructionism vastly expands the range of that which we can value, and the possibility for creating new worlds of living together.

In the present chapter I will focus on the way constructionist ideas are revolutionizing the practice of research in the human sciences. In the remaining chapters we shall explore the constructionist invitation to generate new and more useful accounts of self and world; we will explore the revolutionary changes taking place in therapy, education, and organizations; we will discuss developments in dialogue for reducing conflict. I chose to focus the present chapter on research practices in the human sciences for three reasons. First, recent developments in the sciences of human behaviour are both rich and abundant. Excitement abounds – in psychology, sociology, anthropology, history, political science, communication, social work, and more. Second, the human sciences are most closely connected with cultural life in general; the outcomes of such research are most likely to be communicated to the public, altering our lives for good or ill. Finally, given the title of this book, most readers are likely to be familiar with the traditions of human science research.

To appreciate the developments taking place in these areas, it is first important to take a closer look at the tradition of empirical research. What are its strengths? What are its failings? Why do most constructionist scholars seek alternatives to the empirical tradition? We can then take up the ways in which traditional approaches to research are being transformed.

Empirical Research in Question

Early in the twentieth-century, a broad movement began in the human sciences to model research methods on the natural sciences. The advances made by natural sciences such as physics, chemistry, and biology were impressive. Advances in human science knowledge could best be achieved, it was thought, by adopting their orientation to research. In general, we speak of this orientation as *empirical*, meaning literally, to be "guided by experience". You were introduced to this orientation in the Chapter 1 discussion of scientific knowledge. Here I will lay out some of the chief criteria of research excellence in the empiricist tradition, along with some of the problems that stimulate constructionist researchers to explore new directions.

Measure the phenomenon as accurately as possible. Empirical research more or less presumes the existence of the phenomena under study. It is the task of the researcher to illuminate the nature of these phenomena. Ideally one should develop rigorous methods of research, including accurate measures of the phenomena. Thus, for example, a researcher may begin with an interest in mental illness, crime, intelligence, or social class, and then develop methods and measures for studying them. *The constructionist replies*: When researchers select a phenomenon for study, they are giving voice to the cultural traditions of which they are a part. Mental illness, crime, and so on are not "there in nature", awaiting discovery. They are cultural constructions, but constructions that are so deeply embedded in the history of the culture that they are taken to be "really there" – independent of anyone's perspective. What we call "measures of the phenomenon" are not, then, reflections of an independent world. Rather, they construct the world in a particular way. For example, the concept of intelligence is a byproduct of Western culture at a particular time in its history. Intelligence tests essentially create a world in which people are judged along a continuum. While there is nothing inherently wrong with representing a tradition of beliefs in one's work, the constructionist holds, it is important to remain conscious of their local character. And it is important to reflect on who is helped or injured by the assumptions embedded in one's research. For example, measures of intelligence are highly injurious to those with low scores, and have been used to block their advancement in society.

Remove Personal Bias. The aim of good empirical research is to reflect the world as it is. Thus, the scientist must not allow personal biases to creep in and cloud his or her observations. Our predictions should not be coloured by what we hope to see; science focuses on what *is* the case, not *what* ought to occur from the researcher's standpoint. Scientists with emotional feelings toward the subjects under study, strong ethical or political motives, or deep religious interests are under suspicion. The scientist must keep a dispassionate distance between self and subject.

The constructionist replies: Scientists participate in social traditions, and whatever they do as scientists will reflect this participation. All social traditions carry with them certain values. Thus, whatever the scientist does in the way of research will reflect the values of the traditions in which he or she lives. These investments enter into the research at every point, from the words selected to frame the problem to the description of the people's actions. Scientists who study aggression, prejudice, or oppression, for example, do so because they participate in a culture in which these are undesirable actions. Those whose behaviour scientists single out as aggressive, prejudiced, or oppressive are thus morally condemned by the research. And, it should be noted, these same behaviours could be constructed in many other ways, and with far different moral implications. What many view as aggression could be seen as defence (consider the invasion of Iraq); those labelled as prejudiced may see themselves as discerning judges; and oppression is the flip side of maintaining social order. To claim that research is morally and politically unbiased is unjustified and misleading.

Predict and control. Most empirical research is based on the assumption that nature persists. That is, the objects of concern remain relatively stable across time. In this way, with increasing research we can know increasingly more about the object; knowledge will be increasingly accurate and refined. The result is that we can make increasingly better predictions about future events. By knowing "what leads to what", we can control events in ways that will benefit humankind. Thus, for example, with increasing our knowledge of smallpox or typhoid fever, we could reach the point of controlling these diseases. With an increased knowledge of global warming, we may be able to take steps that will stabilize its effects. As often reasoned, the experimental method is the only one that traces cause and effect relations. Experimental research enables one to test predictions.

The constructionist replies: Although the assumption of a persistent nature has some advantages in the case of natural science, its relevance to most human behaviour is questionable. This is most obvious in the fact that if informed of a research hypothesis in the human sciences, people can typically choose not to confirm it. If you tell people you predict that they will conform, be aggressive, or make prejudiced remarks, they very well may not do so. This is quite unlike the natural sciences, in which being told you will bleed when cut, or die if you take poison, will not allow you to choose not to bleed or die under these conditions. In effect, argues the constructionist, virtually all meaningful activity is constructed, and these constructions are highly malleable and continuously in motion.

Further, proposes the constructionist, research designed to predict and control demeans those under study. Such researchers place themselves in a superior position to those under study, essentially proclaiming, "we shall know about you". As critics point out, the human sciences have largely inherited a tradition of biological study in which specimens were collected, and animals were placed under observation. The attempt to predict and control was then carried over into the study of human beings. Researchers themselves do not intend to become specimens and placed under study. Only the subjects of their research qualify for this (Argyris, 1980).

Convert observations to numbers. Empirical researchers typically view verbal languages as clumsy devices for capturing precise differences. If accounts of the world can be converted to a system of numbers, high precision can be achieved. For example, we can move from rough concepts like "more" and "less" to fine gradients of change. Numbers also represent the most neutral language of description. Unlike many theoretical terms they do not carry subtle connotations of good and bad. And, most importantly, when observations are converted to numerals, we open the way for sophisticated statistical analysis. With a high degree of confidence we can estimate the strength and reliability of cause/effect relations. Fortified by statistical results we can begin to make reliable predictions of the future.

The constructionist replies: When our language of description is converted to numbers, we do not thereby become more precise. Numbers are no more adequate "pictures of the world" than words, music, or painting. They are simply a different way to represent the world. And, while useful in certain respects, this translation device also throws out most of what we hold to be valuable or significant about people. To learn of a friend who has been raped or robbed is important to us; we are moved and motivated to action; when such events are converted to crime statistics the suffering individual is removed from the scene, and we are distanced from those we care about. As one research participant remarked, "Statistics are human beings with the tears wiped off" (Linda B in Lather & Smithies, 1997, p. xxvi). Further, statistical language is an expert language, and those who speak it can use it in many subtle and ingenious ways. When the truth is announced to the public in this language, those without expertise are left voiceless. Because they cannot discern the manipulations necessary to produce a given result, they cannot raise questions. Statistics, then, often function to silence public opposition and obscure understanding.

Search for *the* answer. Because of its realist commitment to one objective world, empirical research strives to reveal the one true answer to any question. Good science will replace mixed opinions with the single, clear solution. It is the researcher's task to empirically test the competing claims to determine what is truly the case.

The constructionist replies: Whatever the nature of the world, there is no single array of words, graphs, or pictures that is uniquely suited to its portrayal. Further, each construction has both potentials and limits, both scientifically and in terms of societal values. Thus, in its efforts to abandon all voices save one, there is an enormous suppression of potential. And when it is the investigator's voice that finally reigns supreme, the voices of those under study are silenced. Increasingly, those who are treated as deficient in some way – called mentally ill, learning impaired, blind, deaf, autistic, and so on – are clamouring to be heard on their own terms. In the commonly shared phrase, they proclaim "Nothing about us without us!"

Fruits of Empirical Research

Given these critiques of the empirical research tradition, what are we to conclude? Is this to argue for a wholesale abandonment of all experimentation, data collection, statistics, and the like? Should we simply cast away the vast domain of empirical literature – journals, hand-books, and monographs on human behaviour? Not at all. Recall that it is not the aim of constructionism to establish a truth, against which all competitors – such as empiricism – are silenced. Constructionism makes no claims for its own truth, and all traditions or ways of life sustain certain values and useful forms of practice. The empiricist tradition is no exception. In this light, consider the following potentials of empirical research in the social sciences.

Empirical findings can generate vivid illustrations of a perspective

While not themselves proving (or disproving) a theory, empirical results can provide powerful illustrations. They can inject life into an idea in a way that helps us to appreciate its significance and plausibility. In this sense good research in the social sciences can function like photographs in journalism or eye-witness accounts on television news. We are moved and absorbed. My introduction to the Skinnerian theory of reinforcement was precisely of this sort. Although prepared to resist the theory on intellectual and political grounds, as I watched the professor use food pellets to bring the random movements of a pigeon under his complete control – speaking all the while of reinforcement contingencies, operant responses, and the like – I could not escape the power of that perspective. Its plausibility will never be lost from me.

Empirical findings can vitalize the discussion of moral and political issues

Debates that involve only abstract theoretical terms can often become dry and seem irrelevant to our lives. However, empirical results can speak with a powerful voice; we can literally visualize the issues in "real-life" terms. I think here of the classic laboratory experiments on obedience by Stanley Milgram (1974). Here an experimenter commanded subjects to deliver what appeared to be harmful electric shocks to another human being. Although seemingly in deep turmoil about their actions, in response to the experimenter's demands, most of them continued to deliver the shocks even after it appeared that the victim was unconscious. The study proved nothing in general, but in the way the research echoed the atrocities of Nazi concentration camps, for example, it continues to stimulate discussion on the nature of responsibility and how to resist blind obedience.

Empirical findings can generate useful information and predictions

Although much experimental research is limited to studying trivial behaviour (for example, how people fill out questionnaires, press buttons, rate ambiguous situations), empirical methods can provide useful information, and generate predictions of broad social utility. For example, we need information on joblessness, poverty, crime, drug use, and the like. And in terms of prediction, political parties wish to predict election returns, insurance companies to gauge the likelihood of car accidents, and prison probation boards to determine probable recidivism. Traditional research can also be used to determine the mental health care needs of a community, or the likely success of students in a special educational programme. Health psychologists have provided much useful information on the social conditions favouring longevity. Of course, when people know what is predicted, they may change their behaviour. In this case the predictions can be falsified. However, for certain purposes predictions can be helpful.

Research Traditions in Transformation

As you can see, the empiricist tradition offers much, but is simultaneously limited. For participants in the constructionist dialogues, these limitations have served as invitations to innovate. Such innovations may be roughly divided into three kinds. There are first innovations that modify traditional forms of enquiry; they resemble the old but with new twists. A second group of innovations are stimulated by the constructionist emphasis on discourse. They carry elements of traditional empiricist work, but with new and significant deviations. And a third group represents major breaks with the existing traditions of research. Indeed, the very idea of research is transformed.

Ethnography and Cultural Understanding

For well over a century, scholars have taken a keen interest in studying groups of people from other parts of the world. Much of this study is now undertaken in the discipline of cultural anthropology. The major form of study, ethnography, typically entails that the researcher lives among the groups he or she wishes to study, takes careful notes, participates in the daily affairs, and upon return to the home country, provides a thoughtful and detailed account of the people in question. This orientation seems reasonable enough, until one considers the practice from "the native's point of view". Think, for example, of what it would be like to have a wealthy foreigner sit in the corner of your room, watching your every move, with an idea of returning to his people to tell them about people like you. Resistance to this form of "studying the other" can be traced to the classic writing of Edward Said, on the scholarly construction of the Orient (Said, 1978). For centuries, European depictions of "Oriental people" – the manners, customs, beliefs, and traditions of cultures from the East – have accumulated, generating in the twentieth century the grounds for entire academic departments. Yet, as Said proposed, the Orient is essentially a "European invention" – a representation of the other growing from the soil of European interests. These interests, Said points out, are not merely ones of curiosity and entertainment. Rather, he sees "Orientalism as a Western style for dominating, restructuring, and having authority over the Orient" (p. 6). In studying "the Orientals" a sense of superiority and justification for political domination was subtly created. As related by an African "native", anthropology is "the diary of the white man on a mission; the white man commissioned by the historical sovereignty of European thinking and its peculiar vision of man".

Such critiques have had powerful effects on the practice of ethnographic study. They have led, for one, to a substantial exploration among anthropologists of the political and value biases that inevitably haunt the attempt to characterize "other people". They have also stimulated anthropologists to develop variants on traditional methods. One of the most important of these variants is *collaborative ethnography*. Luke Lassiter's (2005) research on the songs of the Kiowa Indians from Southwest USA is an excellent example of collaborative ethnography. Lassiter developed friendships among the Kiowa, and travelled with them to their pow-wows. Eventually he developed the ability to sing at these ceremonies. He was so struck by the power of the music that he decided to write about it. In this case, however, Lassiter enlisted the help of his Kiowa friends and others to carry out the project. They not only shared their own views, but helped him in the writing. The work was not his alone, but a joint creation that allowed the Kiowa to share from their own perspective.

New Histories

In the empiricist tradition, the study of history is primarily a search for the truth of the past. Given the available evidence, what is the most accurate account we can give of earlier years? With developments in constructionist ideas, this view could not be maintained. In one of the first significant critiques, the historian, Hayden White, proposed that history was a genre of writing. As such, the historian was guided as much by literary rules as the evidence at hand. History as "one damn thing after another", is of little interest to anyone. It is when the historian uses metaphors, such as "the Age of Reason", "the industrial age", or "the Cold War", that it comes to be significant. Further, the historian is a moralist, White argued, as he or she uses narratives in which there are good or bad endings, according to some perspective. Thus, for example, most Western history books will characterize World War II as a victory of good over evil, and the rise of Stalinism as a menace. In effect, historical accounts are not value neutral. And, as we saw in the preceding chapter, narrative structure will direct the historian's choice of what counts as fact. It is this last concern that stoked the critical fires of numerous minority groups – African Americans, Latinos, Asian Americans, feminists – who felt most of American history had largely been written from the value perspective of upper-middle-class white males. Essentially, it was a history in which they were largely absent.

The result of such deliberations first led to new histories that gave special attention to minorities and the common person. In addition, numerous experiments in "doing history" have resulted. As some scholars propose, if history is a story, then why not make it a good story? Thus, historian Natalie Zemon Davis (1983) began with the case of a French peasant in the sixteenth century who was executed for claiming he was Martin Guerre, a man who was thought to be dead. For years, however, this man had lived with Guerre's wife, who made no distinction. Then Guerre returned. Davis embellishes the tale by reconstructing the lives of the peasants, the religion of the time, and the procedures of the courts. The work adds sparkling vitality to our vision of the times. In another, more controversial case, Edmund Morris (2000) composed a memoir of Ronald Reagan that drew significantly from both public and private documents on Reagan. However, Morris not only wrote the memoir in the first person, but as a fictionalized first person. In effect, he wrote from the point of view of an individual he had invented. We turn now to innovations in research sparked by constructionist concerns with language.

Discourse Study: Exploring Constructed Worlds

As constructionists reason, our patterns of living originate and are sustained in collaborative relationships. Essential to these relationships are our common ways of speaking – in effect, our discourse of the real, the rational, and the good. It should scarcely be surprising, then, that constructionist researchers have opened new ranges of research into language. In some degree, the preceding chapter has furnished a glimpse into outcomes of discourse study. However, because the field is vast, the methods varied, and the aims quite varied, further discussion is needed.

There are two principle orientations in discourse study, the first concerned with the content and the second with process or function. Content studies tend to illuminate people's particular constructions of the world, and the second the way in which discourse functions or what it achieves in relationships. Such study is clearly empirical, in the sense that it uses observations to support its conclusions. However, most of it differs from traditional empirical research in two important ways. First, it does not rely on many of the rigours imposed by traditionalists. You will find little reliance on large samples, measurement, or statistics. Rather, researchers will draw from examples, often richly textured, in order to make their proposals. In part, this free-form approach is adopted because such researchers understand that data never speak for themselves. Rather, the investigator is always making interpretations, which is to say, constructing what the data mean. The traditional rigours of method are not safeguards to interpretation. Further, discourse researchers are not often interested in prediction and control. They understand that patterns of discourse can change over time – sometimes rapidly. It is not so important to "get it right" about the present, because tomorrow may be quite different. Habits of communication on the internet are a good example. The second major difference is closely related to the first. Abandoning prediction and control as research goals, most discourse researchers have alternative goals. Informed by constructionist ideas, they understand that all research is value invested. Thus, they use research to further ends they value. They may, for one, use research as a means of *social critique*. For example, researchers will point out ways in which academic discourse excludes the less educated from understanding. Or, closely related, researchers may illuminate common conventions of language in order to *liberate* us from them. Studies of common but subtle forms of racist and sexist language are exemplary.

For many, the most exciting forms of discourse research are those that challenge the taken-for-granted realities of the times. They point out that what we commonly accept as objective or obviously true is only so because of negotiated agreement among people. Such research removes the authority of those claiming truth, and invites dialogue on alternatives. Thus, for example, significant treatises can be found on the discursive construction of sexuality and gender, race and ethnicity, the value of money, social deviance, mental illness, nature, national identity, and much more (Holstein & Gubrium, 2008). With my own background in psychology, I have found research on the cultural construction of the person especially interesting. In the West we take for granted that our behaviour is vitally influenced by psychological states and conditions. We believe that thinking, the emotions, motivation, memory, and so on are vital to our well-being. Yet, studies of other cultures tell us that all these assumptions are particular to the West. What we take to be "universal human functioning" is quite local.

Unnatural Emotions

In the West we commonly presume that there are a number of natural human emotions, including fear, anger, sadness, disgust, and so on. We also see these as built into our biological systems; we believe we are prepared by evolution to have the feelings we do. But now consider the constructionist thesis: our constructions of emotion in the West are not demanded by the fact that there are emotions there to be observed in the world. The Western vocabulary of emotion is particularly Western. Consider research by the anthropologist Catherine Lutz (1988), who spent time with the Ifaluk people in the South Pacific. By studying the way they use words that we might say are indicators of emotion, the Western categories seemed largely irrelevant. For example, she found the Ifaluk often talked of Fago. There is no direct translation of the term into English, so all Lutz could do was observe the ways or conditions in which it was used. At times the word seemed to stand for something Westerners might call compassion. For example, the Ifaluk would commonly say that they fago those who have no one to take care of them. At other times, it functioned in some of the ways that the word, love, does in Western culture. A woman reported that "I fago my brother and therefore take care of his children". Or in scolding a

(Cont'd)

young boy for his aggressive moves toward his brother, she asks "Don't you fago your brother?" At the same time, the Ifaluk could also talk of their fago in the same way Westerners would of sadness. For example, a woman said, "The last time I had fago was when our mother died two days ago". To complicate matters, the Ifaluk also speak of their fago for those who they admire, on occasions in which Westerners might say they were "homesick", and for someone who is singing a beautiful song. In effect, we find no obvious equivalent in the West for the way in which the Ifaluk identify what we might call an emotional state. As Lutz proposes, "Emotional meaning is a social rather than an individual achievement – an emergent product of social life" (p. 63).

Narrative: Exploring Life Constructions

> Pure unstoried action, pure unstoried existence in the present, is impossible.
> William Lowell Randall, *The Stories We Are*

One of the most active lines of content-oriented enquiry is into the narratives used to construct our lives. Such research often stands in important contrast to traditional research in which investigators test hypotheses about abstract principles. In hypothesis testing, the research investigator's voice dominates; all competitive voices are either suppressed or shown to be wrong. Thus, those under study have no voice in interpreting the results of research in which they have been the objects. In contrast to the dominance of the professional voice, much narrative research features the first-hand accounts of people themselves. Their voices are treated with respect; the researcher conveys their message to the public.

Narrative study is highly varied and cuts across disciplines. Personal accounts have long been used by investigators wishing to avoid the manipulative and alienating tendencies of experimental research. Feminist works, such as Gilligan's *In a Different Voice* (1982), and Belenky et al.'s *Women's Ways of Knowing* (1986), are classics in the effective use of first-hand accounts. Here women's narratives were used to illuminate common ways in which women approach issues in moral decision making and generating knowledge. Other investigators have centred on autobiography, with the hope that people's life stories can illuminate the economic and political forces affecting a society; and still other researchers have used family stories, oral histories, journals, and letters to give us insights into earlier historical times (see, for example, Bertaux, 1981).

Narrative research with a more empathic orientation often attempts to give voice to the unheard and marginalized in society, to generate understanding through sharing first-hand experience. People are encouraged to "tell their story" in their own terms (see, for example, Josselson, 1995; Rosenblatt Karis & Powell, 1995). The attempt here is to increase the public understanding of these lives and an appreciation for the challenges other people confront. Ultimately the hope is to close the distance between social groups, and in many cases, to stimulate social or political action. For example, scholars have documented the experiences of illegal Mexican immigrants in the USA, and the way in which immigrants negotiate their identities as they make their way in the new country. Others have have illuminated the extreme loneliness of Asian refugee women – numbering in the millions worldwide – who are displaced from their home-place, but find themselves with little human connection. Narratives of the American Indian, along with the Maori of New Zealand, have brought attention to the stressful and oppressive conditions of living within these groups. In all these cases the research interests are closely tied to the concerns of the society as opposed to abstract intellectual issues.

Redeeming Narratives

Narrative study may also stimulate reflection on our own lives. From his wide-ranging research, psychologist Dan McAdams (2005) concludes that one of the major narratives around which Americans organize their lives may be called the redemption narrative. The redemption narrative is essentially one in which the individual sees his or her life story as moving upward in a positive trajectory from negative beginnings. (See the discussion of progressive narratives in Chapter 2.) There are many variations on the redemption narrative. There may be movement from early sin to later forgiveness and salvation. Or, one may move from poverty to wealth and social standing, from immaturity to a state of self-actualization, from sickness to wholeness, or from ignorance to knowledge. Such stories are all around us. Most highly visible people – athletes, leading politicians, entertainers, and leading scholars – often tell such stories about themselves. Chances are that you, as reader, also harbour some form of redemption narrative. As McAdams reasons, such narratives are deeply rooted in history. And, as he finds in his study of highly productive adults, they are essential in giving meaning to their good works. Such people gladly sacrifice themselves for others because it makes sense in terms of their life stories.

Additional research suggests that redemption narratives are scarcely limited to the successful. In research on reformed criminals, redemption narratives play a major role (Maruna, 1997). Criminals often account for their lives in terms of early misfortunes. The early years are seldom described in a positive way. The turn to crime is explained in many ways. Among them, crime was viewed as a way of gaining power and control in one's life; for many others, it was a way of getting on successfully with others. It was important to be one of the gang, or to impress others with one's possessions or daring. However, for reformed criminals, there is always a turning point, one in which they "see the error of their ways", and the possibility for building a better life. To be sure, not all can maintain the "straight" life. But typically, when they cannot, it is for a lack of social supports. The policy implications are clear: if we don't wish to see ex-prisoners return to crime, it is essential to find ways to reintegrate them into society.

HORIZONS OF HUMAN ENQUIRY

Narrative research can also serve a critical and creative function. For example, Mary Gergen (1992) was concerned with the gender imbalance in the top echelons of business, government, universities, and the like. Why were women less often in leading roles, even if they had the opportunity? If we live out our lives within narrative, she reasoned, is it possible that the dominant male narratives differ from those of women? Men may see themselves in a story where high level achievement is presumed ("What else is life all about?"), where women infrequently entertain such narratives for themselves ("Why should I want to do that?"). Do women need to expand the range of possible life stories? To explore these possibilities Mary examined the autobiographies of men and women of high accomplishment. The results were unsettling: the successful men did describe their lives in far different terms, but with what seemed like an inhumane narrowness. There was little concern for family, friends, emotions, or their bodies. Consider:

- Richard Feynaman, Nobel prize-winning physicist, reporting on his return to his work in Los Alamos after his wife's death:

"When I got back (yet another tyre went flat on the way), they asked me what happened. 'She's dead. And how's the progam going?' They caught on right away that I didn't want to moon over it". (Gergen, 2001: 63–64)

- Lee Iacocca, CEO of Ford and Chrysler, after recalling his wife's death by heart attack:

"Above all, a person with diabetes has to avoid stress. Unfortunately, with the path I had chosen to follow, this was virtually impossible". (ibid.)

- John Paul Getty, describing the drilling of his first great oil-well:

"The sense of elation and triumph … stems from knowing that one has beaten nature's incalculable odds by finding and capturing a most elusive (and often dangerous and malevolent) prey". (ibid.)

In contrast to the men, the women seemed more diffuse in their goals and more deeply wedded to their relations with others. Consider:

- The opera diva Beverly Sills, talking about her early career:

"I began reevaluating whether or not I truly wanted a career as an opera singer. I decided I didn't … I was 28-years-old, and I wanted to have a baby". (ibid.)

- Tennis star Martina Navratilova, describing her first win at Wimbledon:

"For the first time I was a Wimbledon champion, fulfilling the dream of my father many years before … I could feel Chris patting me on the back, smiling and congratulating me". (ibid.)

- Business executive Nien Cheng, recounting her relations with a spider during her years as a prisoner of the Cultural Revolution:

"My small friend seemed rather weak. It stumbled and stopped every few steps. Could a spider get sick, or was it merely cold … when I had to use the toilet I carefully sat well to one side so that I did not disturb its web". (ibid.)

So much more appealling were the women's stories, that Mary Gergen's concept of accomplishment began to shift. Why should women wish to appropriate the male narratives of success? The world might benefit far more from men expanding their repertoires of self-understanding.

Discourse in Action: The Self as a Conversational Achievement

So far I have described discourse study as largely concerned with the content of what is said or written. However, there is a second and contrasting line of enquiry into process, that is, how language functions, and more specifically, what it accomplishes in terms of relationships. Recall the constructionist emphasis in Chapter 1 on the function of language in doing things together. If someone tells you she is depressed, this is important content. At the same time, the content may also be a request for your care or support. For the constructionist, it is important to *listen twice*, once to the content of what people say, but second, to what this content implies for the actions that follow. To appreciate what is at stake here, consider the sense of identity. The traditional view is that each of us has a fundamental or core sense of self. It is to this fundamental sense of self that "we should be true". To stand firm in one's sense of identity is to have integrity. We shall have more to say about this in Chapter 5. However, consider for a moment the opposite possibility: our sense of our identity is vulnerable and subject to change. Can we ever be certain of our motives, for example, or whether we are truly skilled as opposed to lucky, that our values are deep, our sexual orientation secure, or our love is solid? Consider how rapidly your morning mood can shift if a friend tells you that "you don't look so good today". As many discourse researchers hold, one's self-definition is largely created within conversation. To be sure, one does bring into relationships a sense of self – sometimes quite persistent. However, this firm sense of self owes its existence largely to preceding relationships. And the durability of the past is always in question. The self is always a work in progress.

In what follows we can sample from two lines of research that both approach the discursive construction of the self. First we consider the process of *social accounting*, and then *positioning*. Consider, then, your reaction to the following phrases:

"How could you do that ..."
"You were a jerk ..."
"Don't you remember our agreement ..."
"You didn't listen to what I said ..."

These phrases are representative of the many ways in which we use conversations for purposes of correction. From the scoldings we receive as children to the silences and cold stares we endure as adults, being corrected is simply to live in organized society. These criticisms, attacks, stares, and the like, are all means of sustaining what is often called a *moral order*, a commonly valued way of life. Of course, there is never a single moral order. We all participate in multiple relationships, and each of them will tend to develop its own specific order. What is morally good in one relationship may not be appreciated in another. Social life is complex, and as a result we often violate others' expectations of what a "good person" should do. It is under these conditions that correctives are called into play. The theorist, John Shotter (1985), uses the term *social accountability* to refer to the ways in which correctives function. Essentially correctives ask us to give an account of ourselves, to explain our actions. And if we are successful, we sustain the definition of the good self that has been developed in the relationship.

For example, there are two major ways to account for oneself when confronted with a corrective: *excuses* and *justifications*. Excuses and justifications are based on different logics and function in different ways. Consider some frequent phrases used to make an excuse:

- "I didn't mean to"
- "It wasn't my fault"
- "I wasn't thinking straight"
- "I let my emotions get the best of me"
- "I was drunk"
- "They made me do it".

In each case, the message is: "It wasn't the real me". Each of these phrases attempts to restore the moral order. But notice, the excuse does not challenge the order; it primarily informs the accuser that "You may think I was deviating, but I was not. I am the same person. Everything remains as is".

In contrast, consider some common justifications:

"He deserved everything he got".
"It's the nature of the business ..."
"It was self-defence ..."
"We live in a free country".

The justification recognizes that there are multiple moral orders, and uses one of these to reply that he or she is a good person after all. The person may be blamed for a violation, but shows that the violation is consistent with a moral order, one that the accuser should recognize. The justification informs the accuser, "Yes, I recognize why you blame me, but you should recognize the way in which my behaviour was justified".

A second contribution to the achievement of self in conversations is represented in the concept of *social positioning* (Harré & van Langenhove, 1999). To appreciate the concept, imagine your behaviour toward a revered teacher as opposed to your actions with a child of four. In the former case you may be respectful and listen to the teacher's words; in the latter you may frolic about. The concept of positioning calls attention to the fact that you are positioned to be a certain kind of person by each of these individuals. In the former case, you are positioned as a learner, and in the latter as a playmate. Your identity is dependent upon how you are positioned. Of course, this means that you must first accept the identity claims of the other – that he or she is a teacher worthy of being revered, for example. And, you must be willing to accept the position in which you are placed. Thus, in the case of being accused, you are positioned as someone who must give an account of your actions. As just discussed, by common convention you may give an excuse or a justification. However, you may not accept the right of the individual to take the position of the accuser. For example, we sometimes ask, "Who are you to be blaming me? This is really your fault". Here you are taking the position of the accuser. When viewed through the lens of social positioning, we can see social life in terms of a continuous dynamic of positioning and being positioned to be a certain kind of person. We now turn to a third transformation in research practices stimulated by constructionist ideas. Here we will find the departures most radical.

Imagination in Action: Qualitative Enquiry

Over the past two decades, a quiet methodological revolution has been taking place in the social sciences.

Norman K. Denzin and Yvonne S. Lincoln, *Handbook of Qualitative Research*

As I pointed out earlier, the empiricist tradition in the social sciences is an important one, but it is also limited. It is one approach to research, but from a constructionist standpoint it should not be the only one. For thousands of researchers across the social sciences, this idea has been a breath of fresh air. Here is an invigorating invitation to new departures. Given the shortcomings of the empiricist tradition, what new vistas are now open? What kinds of practices might be imagined? At this point in time, new departures are everywhere in evidence; developments are mushrooming even as I write. Often these developments are placed in the category of *qualitative enquiry*, drawing from an early distinction between systematic, observational, and statistically based research, called *quantitative*, and more personal, subjective, and interpretive research, called *qualitative*. This distinction is based on the realist view that the world is out there to be measured and manipulated, and on this account, qualitative research is defined as inferior. However, in a constructionist frame, all research constructs the world in its terms. The major question is not one of objectivity, but of utility. For what purposes is the research to be used? Qualitative research now moves in many different directions, and the interested reader may wish to consult the references at the chapter's end for a deeper appreciation. For the present, I will touch on three forms of research I find particularly exciting.

Autoethnograpy

Most research separates the researcher from the object of research. Essentially, "we scientists study you". Thus, the research report is in the language – and the tradition of understanding and values – of the research community. Narrative research represents a significant attempt to give more voice to those under study. Many narrative researchers attempt to give voice to the unheard and marginalized in society, to generate understanding through sharing their first-hand experience. The hope is to increase the reader's appreciation and sensitivity. However, the research report and its implications still remain in the hands of the researcher. Much of the narrative is "left on the cutting room floor". A radical break with the traditional split between the researcher and the object of research is represented in the emergence of *autoethnography* (Ellis, 1995). In autoethnographic research, the researcher is simultaneously the object of research. The researcher takes advantage of his or own unique life experiences, and shares these with the reader. Often such reports reveal subtle and intimate details that bear on the issues at stake. For example, in her essay "A Secret Life in a Culture of Thinness", Lisa Tillmann-Healy tells of the fears and the pain of growing up as a bulimic. Here she describes – using three narrative voices – her first attempt to tell a lover of her practices:

"Douglas?" *my strained voice calls out.*
"Umhmm ..."
"There's something I need to tell you".
Probably not a good opening line.
"What's that?" he asks.
"I know I should have told you this before, and I hope you won't be upset that I didn't". Deep breath. Swallow.
It's okay. You're doing fine.
"What is it?" he asks, more insistent this time.
Looooong pause. "Lisa, what is it?"
He's getting nervous. Spit it out.
"Oh, god, Douglas. I don't ... I ... shit!"
You've come too far. Don't fall apart. Just say it, Lisa. Say the words.
"To one degree or another ... I have been ... bulimic ..."
Fuck! I hate the sound of that word.
"... since I was 15".
It's out there. You said it.
Douglas asks several questions about who else knows of the problem, and then queries,
"Well, how bad is it now?"
"It's been much worse".
"That's not what I asked".
"It's not that bad".
Liar.
"Have you done it since you met me?"
If you only knew.
"A couple of times, but I don't want you to be concerned".
Oh, please. Please be concerned.
"You must know what that does to your body".
Believe me, I know. I know everything.
"I'm really glad you told me", he says as I start to cry.
"I love you, Lisa. Tell me how I can help you. Please".
You just did. You can't imagine how much.
He pulls me close, stroking my hair until I go to sleep.
I am 22 years old. (1996: 79–80)

In these lines the writer draws the reader into the experience as she has lived it, revealing bulimia from the inside; she also gives hope to others in this situation.

And, by discussing her experiences in the context of the "culture of thinness", she helps us to see her particular problem as an outgrowth of our culture. At this point we as readers must think again about our own prejudices. Don't many of us subtly value those who are thin, while rejecting those who are fat? And if this is so, don't we contribute to the kinds of problems faced by the author?

Autoenthnography represents a valuable addition to the range of research practices. It enables scholars to share directly their experiences in ways that they may be useful to others. But like all practices, there are limitations. Not all researchers have such unique experiences to share, nor are they skilled enough with words that they can effectively describe their lives or engage readers. Autoethnography also tends to support an individualist tradition in which it is "my experience" that counts. More will be said about this tradition in the next chapter.

Collaborative Enquiry

In empiricist research the investigator remains distant from the subjects of study. The subjects' lives are revealed to the investigator, but the investigator remains aloof and opaque to those "under study". It is most desirable if the researcher has no contact at all with those under study, as his or her presence may bias their behaviour. The use of one-way mirrors, research assistants, and impersonal questionnaires, for example, is helpful for keeping a safe distance. Many constructionists question this tradition because the very idea of unbiased research is misleading. In addition, the model of knowledge has been found to be problematic. It suggests that the ideal means of gaining knowledge of others is to keep them at a distance; to remain aloof and uninvolved. Consider this model of knowledge in terms of what it is to know your family and friends. An exciting alternative to this distancing orientation is to join with subjects to carry out research together. Through these collaborative efforts, the participants and the researcher can become interdependent; everyone's voice counts. Multiple ways of seeing the situation may be revealed. Knowledge is understood as a collaborative achievement.

Earlier I mentioned the development of collaborative ethnography. This is only a beginning. The concern with research as collaboration has stimulated new adventures in enquiry. These take many forms; there are no rules because the course of research will depend on the collective aims and hopes of the participants. In one case, for example, mid-life women joined together with a psychologist to discuss the conventional construction of the menopause and its relevance (or irrelevance) in their lives (Gergen, 1999); in other instances therapists have joined with their clients in writing professional papers about their particular problems and the efficacy (or inefficacy) of therapy (McNamee & Gergen, 1992); and in still other instances, feminist scholars have worked with women on reconstructing the meaning of emotion in their lives (Crawford et al., 1992).

One impressive example of collaborative enquiry is contained in Patti Lather and Chris Smithies' work *Troubling the Angels*. The volume is the result of their collaboration with 25 women with HIV/AIDS. The work emerged over a period of several years in which the women met to discuss their personal lives, common problems, and the potential of making their insights available to others. The hopes were not only to use the interchange itself for mutual support, a way of giving meaning to lives under continuous threat, but also ultimately to provide support and information to other women with HIV/AIDS, along with their friends and families, and to inspire them to advocacy. The work itself offers a fascinating, multi-vocal pastiche. Most prominent are the voices of the women themselves. For example, Linda B tells one of the groups:

I'm more alone now than I've probably ever been in my whole life. Some of it is self inflicted; a lot of it is the fear of being rejected. I'm better off being by myself alone and being sad, rejection is the hardest thing a person has to go through.

Lori immediately responds:

I think it is possible to have relationships. When you're ready, you take a chance on somebody. (Lather & Smithies, 1997, p.103)

Following is a lengthy discussion in which the women share stories and insights on how to tell someone you are infected, starting relationships, safe sex and the like. The participants learn and share experiences on possibilities, dangers, and ways to go on.

In addition to these voices, both the investigators contribute their own feelings, doubts, and hopes to the mix, sometimes revealing personal issues, at others theoretical insights. Also included is relevant scientific information, statistics and research reports on HIV. Finally, in a self-reflexive mode, participants look back on their work and comment on its successes and failures. Researchers in this case don't have the last word. They work together with the research participants to generate a multi-hued world of possibilities.

The spirit of collaboration now extends in many directions. When researchers collaborate on a project, they may set up a discussion board on which they can share their reflections about what they are doing, their doubts as well as their insights. Other researchers then enlist the help of colleagues, who may help them reflect on the values and assumptions they bring to their research. Therapists writing about a case study may invite the person about whom they are writing into collaboration with them. In each case, there are added voices, added values, and a more enriched outcome. Such an appreciation for collaboration is accentuated in participatory action research.

Action Research: Social Change in Motion

The best way to predict the future is to change it.

Alan Kay

Empiricist research, concerned as it is with prediction and control, typically presumes a stable world. Today's careful observations will allow sound predictions of people's future behaviour. From a constructionist standpoint, realities may always be re-negotiated; there is little that we must do; change is everywhere possible. From this standpoint, the researcher is invited to actively engage in social change. The most visible research of this kind is called *participatory action research*. For many, action research sprang to life in the political storms of the 1960s; however it is a movement of many hues – with different emphases and ideological interests across various nations and ethnicities. There is universal agreement among action researchers that it must be collaborative. The ultimate aim of the researcher is to assist those with whom he or she works to improve their condition. At the same time, the researcher typically enters the collaboration with particular political ideals or goals; the collaboration is typically intended to further this agenda. Or in Fals-Borda's terms, "This experiential methodology emphasizes the acquisition of serious and reliable knowledge upon which to construct power, or countervailing power, for the poor, oppressed and exploited groups and social classes" (1991, p. 3).

To illustrate, a group of African descendants in the community of Villarrica in rural Colombia had become increasingly dependent on electrical power for maintaining their way of life (de Roux, 1991). However, during a period of economic decline community members began to find their electricity bills unjustifiably increased, thus favouring the public service utility responsible for supplying their electricity. Individual complaints to the company were typically ignored, and the utility's demands for payment were accompanied by threats of cutting off the electricity. Feelings of frustrated exploitation and hopelessness were rampant in the community. With the assistance of action-oriented organizations from outside, a Villarrica Users Committee was formed. This group initiated a series of community-wide meetings in which people could give voice to their frustrations, and begin to generate a sense of solidarity. Further, these meetings were used to collect stories that detailed the picture of exploitation. A grassroots initiative was then formed to collect copies of individual bills for purposes of documentation. With additional meetings a strategy for action was developed. The community demanded that the public service utility negotiate, and when this demand was backed up by a threat from the community to pay no more bills, meetings began. The ultimate result was not only a vast improvement in the service, but also the creation of a politically energized grassroots democracy.

Where the Action Is

Action research is now one of the most rapidly growing forms of qualitative enquiry. In part this growth can be traced to the idealistic enthusiasm that many young people bring with them into the social sciences. Many become social scientists largely because they want to help in creating a better world. Yet, traditional research practices provide little fulfillment. Such research is geared primarily to publishing. The

(Cont'd)

goal of the research is to contribute to journals and books. Some of this work may eventually be used in helping people, but such outcomes are few and non-obvious. Action research, in contrast, enables the researcher to join with others in directly creating change. Yes, there are journals in which the results of such work can be shared with others but publication is not the driving force behind the work. And also, the need for educated researchers to help in social change efforts is widespread. The researcher does not require a large grant, laboratory equipment, a subject pool, or large data sets. Thus, to name but a few, action researchers have been involved in helping:

- women in prisons to create educational opportunities;
- poor neighbourhoods organize to control drugs and lift themselves up educationally and economically;
- school children to develop decision-making practices;
- women in Nepal to develop grassroots businesses;
- Mayan villagers to develop health care programmes;
- parents and teachers in East Timor to develop better relations;
- Protestants and Catholics in Northern Ireland to bridge their differences;
- diabetes patients and physicians to work more productively together;
- the elderly in the Netherlands to work toward better care;
- teachers in Zimbabwe to develop more dialogic teaching strategies;
- agricultural workers in Iran to develop more collaborative practices.

As you can see, the potentials of action research may be limited only by the imagination (see the further resources section at the end of this chapter).

Performance as Enquiry

Possibly the most radical – and most exciting – openings in research today feature theatrical performance (see, for example, Carr, 1993; Bial, 2003). Although surprising, there are many good reasons for exploring the potentials of performance in social science. For example, anthropologists have long argued that written descriptions of other cultures are inadequate in generating understanding. Written words do little to convey experiences of the war dance, for example, or the ritual roasting of an animal. To truly understand such activities, it is advanced, one must *do them*. As an analogy, it is the difference between reading a book about sky-diving and actually diving. Thus, cultural knowledge invites people to perform the actions they wish to understand. As others propose, performance underscores the plasticity of human behaviour. Traditional research presumes that patterns of behaviour are stable over time. Research is thus largely dedicated to measuring patterns and making predictions about the future. However, as reasoned easier, there is enormous latitude in the way people construct and reconstruct their realities over time, and we are not bound to repeat

Figure 3.1   Performance photos
As Antonia's photo suggests, play is a major means for children to explore multiple worlds. Mary carries out such explorations into professional life in a performance exploring the constructed character of gender

today's actions tomorrow. When we watch something performed, we become aware of the possibilities for change. And in addition, performance can be used to demonstrate alternatives.

To illustrate the potentials of performance, Gary Ross and Christina Sinding (2002) worked with women suffering from metastasized breast cancer to develop a theatre piece. Their hope was to demonstrate the complex issues in communication and care as these women encountered doctors, family members, and friends. For example, such women are sometimes avoided by others because of their illness. Or some people will treat them in terms of their illness alone, without taking into account the rich and complex lives they otherwise lead. Some women also have difficulties expressing their fears to others; people don't want to hear about their suffering. The women not only helped to write the script, but they also worked alongside professional actors in taking parts in the play. Initially the theatre piece was used to educate the hospital staff. The hope was that they might learn more about cancer patients as people, and the treatment would be improved. However, the play was so popular that it moved to a public forum so that family members and the general public might also become educated … and moved.

These adventures – into autoethnography, collaborative enquiry, action research, and performance – are only a sample of the explosion in research practices of recent decades. They vitally expand the repertoire of the human scientist. Further, they are effective in bringing the scientist closer to society. The research not only speaks more directly to issues of social concern, but also does so in a language that can be used by those outside the scholarly profession. There is good reason for optimism in future developments.

Reflection

For me, one of the most exciting outcomes of a constructionist view of research is that it removes the traditional demand for "the correct method" of research. In my graduate school days, multiple courses on methods and statistics were required. There were superior and inferior methods, and the best journals would only accept the former. In effect, if one wished to make a "real contribution" to knowledge, only the superior methods would be acceptable. Much the same view continues to dominate the social sciences. How often I found myself curious about a topic, and inspired to carry out research. Then, by the time all the rigours of method were set in place, all the measures validated, and statistical requirements introduced, the juice was squeezed from the vision. A year was often required to test even the barest hypothesis, another year to gain journal approval, and still another year before the study was published. A snail's pace to trivia, I often felt. From a constructionist perspective, there is "no superior method". The very idea that one can achieve truth through method is challenged. Rather, one is invited to consider multiple ends for research, and to invent ways that will best serve these ends. In this chapter, for example, we have seen research used for purposes of social critique, liberation from unquestioned conventions, challenges to our assumptions about social life, increasing appreciation for alternative ways of life, and direct social change. And, to serve these ends, we have seen imaginations soar. The invitation is there for all newcomers to contribute to the dialogues from which the future will be determined.

Further Resources

On the Problems of Empirical Research

Danziger, K. (1990). *Constructing the subject: historical origins of psychological research*. Cambridge: Cambridge University Press.
Gergen, K.J. (1993). *Toward transformation in social knowledge* (2nd edn). London: Sage.
Slife, B.D. & Williams, R.N. (1995). *What's behind the research? Discovering hidden assumptions in the behavioural sciences*. Thousand Oaks, CA: Sage.

Variations on Traditional Research

Curthoys, A. & Docker, J. (2005). *Is history fiction?* Ann Arbor: University of Michigan Press.
Jenkins, K. (1997). *The postmodern history reader*. London: Routledge.
Lassiter, L.E. (2005). *The Chicago guide to collaborative ethnography*. Chicago: University of Chicago Press.
Smith, L.T. (1999). *Decolonizing methodologies: research and indigenous peoples*. London: Zed Books.

Discourse Study

Schiffrin, S. (Ed.). (2001). *The handbook of discourse analysis*. Oxford: Blackwell.
Wetherell, M., Taylor, S., & Yates, S.J. (2001). *Discourse as data, a guide for analysis*. London: Sage.
Wetherell, M., Taylor, S., & Yates, S.J. (2001). *Discourse theory and practice, a reader*. London: Sage
See also the journals: *Discourse and Society, Discourse and Communication* and *Discourse Studies*.

Narrative Enquiry

Bamberger, M. (2006). *Narrative – state of the art*. Special issue of *Narrative Inquiry*. 16:1.
Clandinin, J. (2006). *Handbook of narrative enquiry: mapping a methodology*. London: Sage.
Elliot, J. (2005). *Using narrative in social research: qualitative and quantitative approaches*. London: Sage.
Josselson, R., & Lieblich, A. (Eds.). (2000). *Making meaning of narratives*. Thousand Oaks, CA: Sage.
Polkinghorne, D.E. (1988). *Narrative knowing and the human sciences*. Albany, NY: State University of New York.
See also: *Narrative psychology internet and resource guide*:
web.lemoyne.edu/%7Ehevern/narpsych/narpsych

Qualitative Enquiry

Camic, P.M., Rhodes, J.E., & Yardley, L. (2003). *Qualitative research in psychology*. Washington, DC: APA Publications.
Denzin, N.K., & Lincoln, Y.S. (2005). *The Sage handbook of qualitative research*. Thousand Oaks, CA: Sage.
Ellis, C., & Bochner, A.P. (Eds.). (1997). *Composing ethnography, alternative forms of qualitative writing*. Thousand Oaks, CA: Sage.
Gergen, M., Chrisler, J.C., & LoCicero, A. (1999). Innovative methods: resources for research, teaching and publishing. *Psychology of Women Quarterly, 23*, 431–456.
Knowles, J.G., & Cole, A.L. (Eds.). (2008). *Handbook of the arts in qualitative research*. London: Sage.
Kvale, S. (1996). *InterViews*. Thousand Oaks, CA: Sage.
Madison, D.S., & Hamera, J. (2006). *The Sage handbook of performance studies*. London: Sage.
Smith, J. (2008). *Qualitative psychology, a practical guide to research methods* (2nd Ed.). London: Sage.
Reason, P., & Bradbury, H. (Eds.). (2007). *Handbook of action research* (2nd Ed.). London: Sage

See also:
Forum: Qualitative Social Research: www.qualitative-research.net
The Qualitative Report: www.nova.edu/ssss/QR/index.html

4

THE RELATIONAL SELF

GENERATIVE THEORY
••••
THE SELF IN QUESTION
Individualism: Separation and its Discontents
The Problem of Isolated Selves
Narcissism and Others as Instruments
Relationships as Artificial
The Tragedy of All Against All
The Exploitation of Nature
The Power Problem
Narrowing the Range of Understanding
••••
SELF AS RELATIONSHIP: FIRST STEPS
Symbolic Interaction: Inter-subjective Selves
Dramaturgy: The Self on Stage
Cultural Psychology: Carrying On
••••
SELF AS RELATIONSHIP: THE EMERGING VISION
Meaning in Relationships
••••
THE RELATIONAL MIND
Mental Discourse as Performance
Performances as Relational
••••
REFLECTION
••••
NOTES
••••
FURTHER RESOURCES

In the beginning is the relationship.

Martin Buber, *I and Thou*

A recent film, *Blindsight*, documents the trek of six blind Tibetan students to the summit of Lhakpa Ri, on the north side of Mt. Everest. Accompanied by Erik Weihenmayer, the first blind man to reach Mt. Everest, the youths successfully confronted the hazards of freezing temperatures, low oxygen levels, avalanches, and deadly crevasses. Such a film dramatically undermines the common stereotype of the poor and disabled blind. The blind mountain climbers not only demonstrated extraordinary resourcefulness, but they succeeded in a task that most sighted people would fail. In effect, the film re-constructs the public's understanding, and in turn, their orientation to the blind. It is just such transformations that a social constructionist vision invites into the world of scholarship. The scholar's task is not to "get it right" about the nature of the world, but to generate understandings that may open new paths to action. The present chapter will give you a taste of how this can be so. The subject of transformation is relevant to each of us, for it is no less than the self. Before we explore attempts to transform our understanding of the self, it is useful to consider more fully the challenge of theorizing.

Generative Theory

Scientists have traditionally viewed theory as a way of summarizing and integrating what is known about the world. Darwin's theory of evolution or Einstein's relativity theory are good examples. However, for the constructionist such a view of theory is limited. Yes, within a tradition of enquiry, such as biology or physics, theories of this kind may be useful. However, they are primarily used to sustain a given tradition of research. They are not intended to create alternative ways of living. But, in the social sciences the way we describe and explain behaviour may enter directly into the conversations of the culture. When scientists describe people as prejudiced, conforming, cognitively impaired, low in intelligence, mentally ill, oppressive, exploitative, powerful, and so on, their accounts may be rapidly absorbed by the surrounding culture. These descriptions enter into the way we understand and treat each other. In this case, we may ask whether a given theory is generative in nature. *Generative theory* describes and explains in a way that challenges the taken-for-granted conventions of understanding, and simultaneously invites us into new worlds of meaning and action.[1] Freud's theories were surely generative, challenging as they did the traditional assumption of consciousness as the centre of action, sexuality as a minor aspect of human functioning, and morality as an essential good. Marxist theory was similarly generative in questioning the "naturalness" of economic class differences, and the wage differences between management and labour. B.F. Skinner's behaviourist theories – holding individual action to be a product of reinforcement contingencies – flew in the face of accepted views of human agency (free will). In each case there were substantial repercussions – including the creation of the psychiatric profession, the Russian revolution, and the overhauling of educational practices. This is not to approve of the consequences of these formulations, nor to argue that they remain generative today. However, it is to recognize that one of the major routes to social change is through audacious theorizing.

THE RELATIONAL SELF

It is important to realize the radical nature of what is being proposed here. From the traditional realist standpoint, the task of the scholar is to furnish accurate accounts of reality, to map or picture the world as it is. In research informed by this tradition there is a strong incentive to use a language of description that is broadly acknowledged as objective or realistic. Thus, if we are confronted with the problem of crime, we carry out research on policies of prevention. By conventional standards it is taken for granted that crime has causes and should be prevented. Thus, to approach an issue *realistically* is to sustain our conventions along with associated ways of life. In effect, such theory is socially conservative; little is changed. The move to generative theory, however, invites us to suspend the traditions, and to experiment with new ways of describing and explaining. What if street crime is viewed as a manifestation of societal ills, for example, or as a means toward enhancing self-esteem, or as a construction created by certain classes of people to punish those outside the class? Each of these alternatives opens the way to new forms of enquiry, and possible ways of going on in the world. In a sense, generative theorizing is a form of *poetic activism*. That is, it asks us to take a risk with words, shake up the conventions, create new ways of understanding, and new images of possibility.

The present chapter represents an expedition into generative theory. In focusing on a single case, my hope is to illuminate the possibilities for creative change. My particular focus is on the self, the way we understand ourselves as separate and autonomous, possessed with powers of reason and naturally given passions. It is individual selves, we hold, who come together to form relationships; indeed, society itself is made up of individual selves. How can we transform such a longstanding tradition? What kind of alternative could we construct? More important, you are probably asking, why should we embark on such a journey in the first place? Let us take up this last question before we proceed.

The Self in Question

It is comfortable to believe in ourselves as conscious decision makers, as individuals who can and should think for themselves. Yet, in the West, we have only been comfortable with such a view for several hundred years. It was only in 1600s that Descartes could confidently proclaim, "I think, therefore I am". It was only in the following century that people began to construct themselves as having "feelings". And, over the centuries that followed, we have steadily increased the number of events and processes that we attribute to the mental world. It is now estimated that in English we have over 2,000 words referring to the inner world of the self. Is it not totally clear to us today that each of us has thoughts, emotions, motives, desires, wants, needs, ideas, will-power, and memory? To be without these ingredients of the mind, we would be something less than human. We feel now that we must find ourselves, identify our needs, and know how we truly feel. Educational systems are devoted to "improving minds". Democracy is based on the idea that each individual "thinks for him/herself".

Yet, even though the belief in ourselves as thinking, feeling agents of our own actions seems thoroughly convincing, many scholars remain skeptical. Consider some of the problems that are created by our common beliefs.

- How can a mental event cause a physical movement of the body? If we make a decision to act (a mental event), how does this mental process stimulate the neurons? What precisely is a "*mental* process" that it can have an impact on our nervous system?
- How can we ever know the world? If we live in our mental world, how can we ever be sure there is anything outside it? We may experience something we call the world, but what if we are mentally creating this experience?
- If we do presume there is a physical world "out there", how does it ever make its way to the world "in here?"
- How can we ever know that other minds exist? Perhaps we are simply making up this idea for ourselves? ......

Yet, my concern here is not with the philosophical shortcomings of the traditional view of the private self. No set of assumptions is without weaknesses; there are no ultimate justifications for any of our beliefs. If we had to locate flawless foundations for our ways of life, we could scarcely go on. The more important question is, what are the implications for cultural life of putting things in the ways we do? Or in the present case, what do we gain and what do we lose by sustaining the tradition of private, individual selves as the wellspring of action? I suspect that most of us would agree that such a conception has made a positive contribution to Western culture. As indicated earlier, the assumption of individual thought is essential to the institution of democracy. Closely coupled with our commitment to democracy, the value we place on public education derives from the belief that it will cultivate independent minds. As often argued, the stronger the minds of individuals, the more effective the democratic process. Further, without a belief in individual agency, our institutions of moral responsibility would begin to crumble. It makes no sense to hold each other responsible for our actions – both in daily life and courts of law – if we are not capable of individual choice. Clearly, we owe an enormous debt to this, the *individualist tradition*. We would scarcely wish to abandon it. However, we must also consider the dark side.

Individualism: Separation and its Discontents

None of us lives without a reference to an imaginary singularity which we call our self.

Paul Smith, *Discerning the Subject*

In recent years discontent with individualism – and its companion discourse of individual minds – has accelerated at a rapid rate. As inhabitants of the Western tradition we have tended not only to presume its truth, but its universal application. Yet, as the globalization process is increasingly extended, and the challenge of difference mounts in magnitude, what are the implications of our Western commitments? Who gains and who is crushed? Can individualism see us successfully through the twenty-first century? Should we seek to cultivate alternatives? There are many who believe that individualism is a cultural ideology that is now dangerous to the world. Although its history has been a promising one, this *ideology of the self-contained individual* must now be replaced. Consider the following lines of critique.

THE RELATIONAL SELF

The Problem of Isolated Selves

If what is most central to me is within – mine and mine alone – then how am I to regard you? At the outset, you are fundamentally "other" – an alien who exists separately from me. I am essentially alone, I come into the world as an isolated being and leave alone. Further, you can never fully know or understand my private world, for it is never fully available to you, never fully revealed. By the same token, if what is most significant about you – what makes you tick – always lies "behind the mask", then I can never be certain of you, can never know what you are hiding from me, what you truly want. Even in our most intimate moments I cannot know what you are truly feeling. In effect, our mutual isolation is locked arm in arm with distrust. Because we cannot be certain, no words or actions are fully trustworthy, then suspicion always lies just over the shoulder. If this is our dominant orientation to life, what is the fate of close and committed relations, and how can we build cooperative relations on a global scale?

Narcissism and Others as Instruments

> I celebrate myself.
>
> Walt Whitman, "Leaves of Grass"

The prevailing sense of isolation, alienation and distrust also feeds a second problem deriving from individualist ideology. If the self is the centre of one's existence, and one can never fully know or trust another, then our primary mission must be to "look out for number one!" We thus spend hours at self-improvement, building self-esteem and ensuring that we are somehow better than those around us. This is only natural; to expend effort on behalf of others is unnatural. Regarding others, one must continuously ask the question "how does he or she help me; what does it cost?" More broadly, this orientation is labelled *instrumentalist* (or alternatively, *utilitarian*). On this view others have no intrinsic worth; rather, our actions are only rational if they are instrumental to achieving self-gratification of some kind. To be sure we may help others, but only because altruism will bring one rewards – praise, gratitude, a better community, etc. Christopher Lasch's *The culture of narcissism* (1979) is one of the most condemning statements of the "me-first" attitude favoured by the individualist impulse. For Lasch, when we are instrumentalist in our orientation, then we reduce to trivia emotional relationships and sexual intimacy. If one engages in love and sexual intimacy only to achieve self-gratification, then the traditional value of these actions is undermined. Similarly, scholarly research conducted only to "help my career", and political activism designed "to help me win", are also emptied of their deeper worth.

Relationships as Artificial

Consider some common phrases: "We need to work on our relationship", "This relationship is falling apart", "We must develop better teamwork", "He really helped

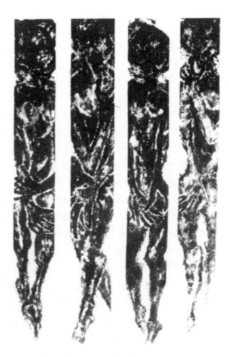

Figure 4.1   The artist, Regine Walter, suggests here that to understand the world in terms of separate individuals is to invite a way of life in which alienation prevails

build the organization". All of these phrases are lodged in the premise of individualism: if we believe that selves are primary – that society is made up of individual actors – then relationships must be "built", "made", or "repaired". In effect, the self is the primary reality; relationships are artificial, temporary, and desirable primarily when one cannot function adequately alone. In the celebrated volume *Habits of the heart*, Robert Bellah and his colleagues (1985) propose that in its emphasis on self expression, freedom, self-development, and self-fulfillment, the individualism of today undermines the kinds of social institutions that are central to a viable society. For example, "If love and marriage are seen primarily in terms of psychological gratification, they may fail to fulfill their older social function of providing people with stable, committed relationships that tie them into the larger society" (Bellah et al. 1985, p. 85). On the individualist account, if one finds that marriage frustrates one's desires for freedom or self-expression there is little reason to remain in the marriage. Self is the essential unit, and if marriage is an uncongenial companion then it must go. Similarly, Bellah and his colleagues are concerned with the potentials of communities to govern themselves, and indeed people's willingness to engage in public life, voluntary services or community politics. Because these activities typically require time and energy, they may seem inimical to self-development and personal gain. The individualist, then, is likely to "look on bonds as restraints, values and customs as impositions" (Wallach & Wallach, 1983, p. 1).

THE RELATIONAL SELF

The Tragedy of All Against All

In his famous work *The Leviathan*, the seventeenth-century philosopher Thomas Hobbes developed a compelling case for civil law and a strong central government. As he saw it, humans in their natural state prefer themselves above all others. Thus, the underlying condition of human existence is a "war of every man, against every man" (1651: 13.8). In this state of things, human life is "solitary, poor, nasty, brutish, and short" (1651: 13.9). As a result of this condition, both civil law and a strong central government are essential for our well-being. Hobbes's vision of society is a cornerstone in present-day individualism – whether in daily life, or in our institutions of government, education, and business. The pervasive view is that our fundamental condition is one of isolation and distrust. When "push comes to shove", what is there to do but "look out for number one?" No one can be fully trusted; everyone is primarily motivated by self-gain.

In slightly different terms, individualism invites us into a posture of competition. We enter a college classroom, and we are typically thrust into competition – only a handful will emerge with top marks. We enter the workplace, and again we traditionally find ourselves in competition: only a few will rise to the top. Both education and the workplace represent individualism in action. As we understand the economic world, it is also made up of individual agents each attempting to maximize his/her own gain and minimize losses. On a planet of limited resources this means that we are each pitted against the other in a dog-eat-dog world. Must this sense of continuous embattlement remain; must we continue to build institutions that embody this view; and if this view is extended into global relationships, what kind of future can we anticipate?

The Exploitation of Nature

The celebration of the self also enters into our orientation to nature. If the self is first, then nature is evaluated in terms of its benefits (or threats) "to me". It is this mentality – extended to organizations such as business and government – that many view as catastrophic. Natural resources (coal, iron, oil) are pillaged, forests are turned to stubble, water resources are fouled and depleted, and vast ranges of animal species are eradicated – all for the purpose of increasing individual gain. As many argue, unless we shift from a posture of personal gain (more growth, gain, profit, well-being) to one of sustainability, the planet will be laid waste (for further discussion see Meadows et al., 1992).

The Power Problem

> "Divided we fall …"
>
> Patrick Henry

In large measure we have followed the Hobbesian view of governance. Because we see ourselves as isolated, untrustworthy, self-serving and competitive, we establish institutions to keep us in check – organizations of surveillance, evaluation, punishment, incarceration, and eradication. Once these organizations are set in motion, however, they often come to have a life of their own – unmonitored and unchecked by those who have brought them into being. The KGB and the CIA are good illustrations from the past; even government officials were placed in fear by their uncontrollable powers. It is not simply the suspicion of the untrustworthy individual that is at stake here. In addition, it is through an individualizing process that the overarching powers increase their control. Foucault proposed that in earlier periods of Western history there was little demand that written books be attached to the names of single authors. Writing was not viewed as the expression of an individual mind. The concept of the author as origin came into prominence, proposed Foucault, when the French royalty became fearful of political tracts critical of their governance. By making it unlawful to publish written materials without the name of an author attached, control was secured. Likewise, many are concerned today with the quantification of the individual, and the ways in which massive amounts of information about a person are now assembled and available on the internet. As Rosy Stone (1996) argues, we have become subjects on whom a numerical value is placed by others and who can be identified and called to answer at any time.[2] Resistance to individualization is essential in order to sustain a free society.

Narrowing the Range of Understanding

Because we believe in self-contained individuals, who think, feel, weigh evidence and values, and act accordingly, we also inherit a handy way of understanding bad action – weirdness, crime, harassment, bigotry, and so on. In all cases we are led to suspect a fault in the internal functioning of the individual. Weirdness is traced to "mental illness", we see crime as the outcome of a decrepit "sense of right and wrong", harassment and bigotry are traced to "deep-seated prejudice", and so on. Individuals cause problems and individuals must be repaired – through therapy, education, imprisonment, and so on.

But consider again. Does anyone's action entirely originate within the self, independent of any history or circumstance? If I am prejudiced, did this prejudice spring naturally from within? It is difficult to imagine such a possibility. Yet, if we are deeply immersed in the world, in relationships, jobs, physical circumstances and the like, why do we select the individual mind as the source of problematic behaviour? If my job is boring and my boss a tyrant, why should I be treated for my feelings of depression? Why not change the workplace? In broader terms the individualist presumption operates like a blinder. It is a crude and simplistic way of reacting to problems. We fail to explore the broader circumstances in which actions are enmeshed, and focus all too intensely on the single body before our eyes. Not only is the individualist option highly limited, but if the broader circumstances of individual lives are not addressed it may also be disastrous.

These are only a few of the critiques of the Western tradition of individual selves. Despite its value, the presumption of individual selves is deeply flawed. When the self is the essential atom of society, we find invitations to isolation, distrust, narcissism, and competition; we find relationships reduced to manipulation and artifice; and we find a stunting simplification of the problems we confront. In all these ways we might wish

87

for more promising alternatives, new conceptions of the self that might render social life less chilling – and possibly create a more promising global future. No, it is not essential that we abandon tradition; social constructionist ideas do not invite the eradication of any tradition. However, we are invited to develop generative alternatives to carry us into the future. It is to this possibility that we now turn.

Self as Relationship: First Steps

> The ability to tolerate and the will to encourage fluid and multiple forms of subjectivity is an imperative and fully ethical position.
>
> Jane Flax, *Multiples*

Let me be clear here about what is being proposed: if we inherit a strong reality of the individual self – a self that senses, thinks, feels, and directs action – and we find this construction of the person flawed, can we set out to reconstruct reality in a different way? And toward what kind of alternative should we strive? In what way can we conceptualize persons such that the individualist ills are not duplicated, and the possibilities for more promising forms of societal life are opened? Although we should not foreclose other avenues of departure, one promising possibility emerges uniquely from social constructionist dialogues.

As outlined in the preceding chapters, social constructionism traces commitments to the real and the good to social process. What we take to be knowledge of the world grows from relationship, and is embedded not within individual minds but within interpretive or communal traditions. In effect, there is a way in which constructionalist dialogues celebrate relationship as opposed to the individual, connection over isolation, and communion over antagonism. Yet, the question remains, can we compellingly reconstruct what it is to be a person in a way that moves us away from the individualist premise and toward the relational? This is not an easy task, in part because the language we inherit from the past is so deeply embedded in individualism. As mentioned earlier we have over 2000 terms in the English language that refer to ("make real") individual mental states; we have very few that refer to relationships. Even the concept of relationship itself, as we inherit it, presumes that relationships are built up from the more basic units of single individuals. It's as if we have become enormously sophisticated in characterizing individual pawns, rooks, and bishops, but have little way of talking about the game of chess. How, then, can we embark on a generative form of theorizing without a ready vocabulary to hand?

Because we cannot start from scratch, generating meaning outside any tradition, we may benefit from a closer examination of the past. Specifically, if we scan our traditions can we find pockets of intelligibility that offer resources for the future? How can we use these resources; in what ways are they limited? Let us consider, then, three significant roads toward relational being: symbolic interaction, dramaturgy, and cultural psychology. Let us also consider the ways in which we might wish to press beyond these traditions.

Selves can only exist in relationship to other selves.

George Herbert Mead, *Mind, Self and Society*

Since the 1930s the discipline of social psychology has largely been committed to an individualist view of the person. Labouratory experiments are used to manipulate *stimulus conditions* in the environment, to which the individual – based on processes of cognition, motivation, emotion, and the like – *responds* with more or less aggression, altruism, prejudice, attraction and so on. Relationships, on this account, are the byproduct of independent individuals coming together. Because relationships are thus derivative of individual minds, they are of little interest to most social psychologists. Not only is individual functioning the centre of research attention, but most theories in social psychology also demonstrate an underlying prejudice against the intrusion of others into one's life. That is, other persons are typically treated as disruptive to the optimal functioning of the individual. In this tradition, it is "other people" who cause one to conform, demand obedience, elicit aggression, or bring about a deterioration in thought (for example, "group think").

The profession could have been different – both in terms of research emphasis and in the value placed on others in our lives. A significant alternative was generated in 1934, with the publication of George Herbert Mead's classic work *Mind, self and society*. As Mead proposed, there is no thinking, or indeed any sense of being a self, that is independent of social process. For Mead, we are born with rudimentary capacities to adjust to each other, largely in response to gestures – with the hands, vocal sounds, facial expressions, gaze, and so on. It is through others' responses to our gestures that we slowly begin to develop the capacities for mental symbolization; or in effect, our gestures and the reactions they elicit from others come to be represented mentally. Language becomes possible when people share a common set of mental symbols, for example, when words call forth the same symbols to both parties in a conversation.

Our ability to share symbols also benefits from our innate capacities for *role-taking*. That is, as we watch others respond to our gestures, we take their role; we begin to experience their responses within us, and we are able to gain a sense of what the other's gesture symbolizes for him or her. For example, if, as a child, I scream in anger and my father raises his hand in a threatening way, I become fearful and stop my screaming. In doing so, however, I also gain a sense that my father finds my screaming unacceptable. By taking his role in the situation, I understand that in his symbolic world, he can't tolerate my screams.

As Mead also proposes, it is through role-taking that I become conscious of myself. By taking the role of the other, as he or she responds to my actions, I come to understand who and what I am. Over time I come to develop a sense of a *generalized other*, that is, a composite of others' reactions to me across situations. It is out of the sense of the generalized other that I develop a coherent sense of self, or "what I truly am".

Although largely disregarded in social psychology, Mead's work did give rise to a small but vital movement called *symbolic interactionism*. Symbolic interactionists have taken a special interest in the ways both social order and deviance come about. Of major importance is the concept of *social role*. From the symbolic interactionist perspective, social life is played out in the roles we acquire, invent, or are forced into.[3] In this sense, if you look ahead in life you can see stretched out before you a structure of roles – teacher, manager, therapist, and the like, or wife, father, lover. Even the deviant from mainstream society – the drug addict, the thief or the "mentally ill" – can be viewed as playing out scripts that were largely determined before he or she ever arrived on the scene.

It is also clear that symbolic interactionism makes a substantial contribution to an appreciation of human interdependency. Because each of us draws our sense of self from others, we are thus thoroughly interrelated. For Mead, "No hard-and-fast line can be drawn between our own selves and the selves of others, since our own selves exist and enter as such into our experience only in so far as the selves of others exist and enter as such in our experience also" (1934, p. 164). Similarly in role theory, we need others' recognition in order to play a role. If you play the role of a doctor when others don't agree that you are a doctor, you my end up in jail. We are all in it together.

Yet, in spite of its intellectual significance, symbolic interactionism doesn't take us far enough. The problems are several. First, in spite of the relational emphasis, symbolic interactionism retains a strong element of individualism. For Mead, one is born into the world as a private subject, and as a private subject must come to "experience" others, and then, mentally "take the role of the other," in order to develop a concept of self. Communication is ultimately from one individual subjectivity to another. Further, symbolic interactionism leaves us without a way to explain how it is a person is able to grasp others' states of minds from their gestures. If I am a child, and my father raises his hand, how do I know what this gesture means to him? This is again the problem of "knowing other minds". Finally, there is a strong flavour of social determinism in symbolic interactionism. For Mead there is a "temporal and logical pre-existence of the social process to the self-conscious individual that arises in it" (ibid., p. 186). That is, how we think about the world and self is ultimately determined by others; without their having views of us, we could have no conception of ourselves. The deterministic view also haunts the analysis of social roles: are we simply determined to play out the roles already laid out for us? Do we ultimately wish to have a theory in which we are simply the products of others' actions?

Dramaturgy: The Self on Stage

The idea that people are like dramatic actors, playing out theatre roles, has been with us at least since Shakespeare's time, and his lines, "All the world's a stage. And all the men and women merely players". This view was born again in the twentieth century works of Erving Goffman. As Goffman explored in perhaps his major work, *The presentation of self in everyday life* (1959), we are constantly giving off signals that define who we are to others. Like actors on a stage, we choose our clothing, hairstyle, jewellry or watch, and so on, for the specific purpose of creating a public identity. In our actions – words, facial expressions, gestures, and so on – we invite others to treat us as this kind of person. In Goffman's words, "when an individual plays a part he implicitly requests his observers to take seriously the impression that is fostered before them" (1959, p. 17). One of Goffman's carefully chosen quotes deliciously illustrates the point: the novelist William Sansom describes Preedy, an Englishman, making his first appearance on the beach of his summer hotel in Spain.

> But in any case he took care to avoid catching anyone's eye. First of all, he had to make it clear to those potential companions of his holiday that they were of no concern to him whatsoever. ... If by chance a ball was thrown his way, he looked surprised; then let a smile of amusement lighten his face (Kindly Preedy) ... looked around dazed to see that there were people on the beach, tossed it back with a smile ... But it was time to institute a little parade of the Ideal Preedy. By devious handlings he gave any who wanted to look a chance to see the title of his book – a Spanish translation of Homer, classic thus, but not daring, cosmopolitan too – and then gathered together his beach-wrap and bag into a neat sand-resistant pile (Methodical and Sensible Preedy), rose slowly to stretch at ease his huge frame (Big Cat Preedy), and tossed aside his sandals (Carefree Preedy, after all.) (Sansom, 1956)

At the same time we are creating a public self, proposed Goffman, we are also shielding others from what he called a *back region*, a region of action hidden from the observer. If others could see life in the back region, they might be unwilling to accept the identity of the person. For example, when university students are with their parents, their back region might be the life they lead with their friends on a Saturday night; if their parents could see them in this region, they wouldn't believe the tidied up identity their son or daughter may present to them. In the same way, however, for the parents, their life in their bedroom might be a back region; they don't wish to have the selves they present in that region exposed to their offspring. In effect, when parents and offspring are together they create a set of local identities that they ask each each other to take seriously – yet in some sense, these are a sham for the moment. Goffman's approach is called *dramaturgical*, in that it paints a picture of social life as a stage, where we all perform for each other, knowing at the same time that what we seem is never quite who we are.

As you can see, the dramaturgical view defines the person as fundamentally social. Our every action is *for* others. It also defines the person as an agent of his or her own actions, rather than as a byproduct of others. At the same time, this view has unsettling consequences. After all, if we take this view seriously, what would it do to our relationships? Goffman's analysis suggests that we are much like con artists, trying to con others into believing we are who we present ourselves to be. Our presentations are like masks, but behind the mask is just another mask. Sincerity itself is just another con, which might even succeed in duping the actor. To accept such a view is to invite a deep skepticism about others and the self. It is to generate distrust and doubt in all support, gratitude, or affection. Nor, in the end, can we trust or accept ourselves. Thus, while fascinating in its implications, and deeply social in its perspective, this is scarcely an acceptable alternative to individualism.

Cultural Psychology: Carrying On

> Speaking/thinking ... is social-cultural activity.
>
> Lois Holzman, *Schools for Growth*

As we saw, the field of social psychology could have developed in directions that emphasized relationship over the individual, but it did not. There is a similar story to be told about developmental psychology. Researchers might well have come to see human beings as fundamentally social in being. However, in the main they have followed the direction of the social psychologists, defining human development in terms of the self-contained individual. In the main, developmentalists have based their work on either one or two major metaphors of the person: the machine or the flower, or what are often called the *mechanistic* and the *organismic* conceptions of development.[4] In the mechanistic case, the infant is largely viewed as an input–output machine, that is, as an organism whose development – or behavioural output – is largely shaped by environmental conditions (the input). Here investigators trace, for example, the influence of early stimulation on the infant's intelligence, or the impact of different child rearing patterns on the child's attachment, or feelings of self-esteem. In effect, child behaviour is the output resulting from machine (environmental) inputs. The mechanistic orientation to development is often called *behaviourist*. In contrast, the organismic theorist stresses the genetic basis of development. Like a developing daffodil, the direction and stages of development are predetermined – inherent in the nature of the organism. Here the work of Piaget is illustrative, emphasizing as it did the way in which the child's capacities for thought develop naturally – from rudimentary sensory reactions in infancy to abstract conceptual skills in later childhood. In both the mechanistic and organismic case the child is fundamentally separate from his/her surrounds.

How could we think outside these two metaphors? One innovative answer is supplied by the early work of the Russian psychologist, Lev Vygotsky. For Vygotsky, separating the individual – either as a machine or a flower – from the surrounds can only be accomplished analytically – as an exercise in theory – for in truth, they are inseparable. Of particular interest for Vygotsky were the "higher mental functions", such as thinking, planning, attending, and remembering. Psychologists typically view these functions as biologically based, and thus as universal. Research is devoted to the "nature of individual cognition" in general, and almost never to cognition within, let us say, differing ethnic or religious traditions. Yet, for Vygotsky, these higher processes are lodged within relationships: "Social relations or relations among people genetically underlie all higher (mental) functions and their relationships" (1981, p. 163). In effect, mental functioning reflects social process; there is no strictly independent thought. Thinking is always embedded in and reflects social life. As Vygotsky proposed, there is nothing in the mind that is not first in society.

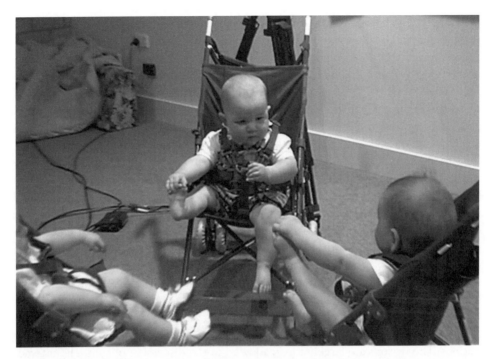

Figure 4.2   Developmental psychologist, Ben Bradley, believes that the human capacity for
social collaboration is present in the very early stages of life. Here are three infants, all under
a year old, participating in one of Bradley's studies. Note the way in which they orient their bodies to
each other. This capacity for collaboration may furnish the basis for cultural similarities in thoughts
and feelings.

Vygotsky's theories have sparked the development of a contemporary movement
called *cultural psychology*. One of its chief proponents, Jerome Bruner, has proposed
the stimulating idea that the everyday accounts of why people act as they do, what
we often call *folk psychology*, reflect the essential elements of thought. For example,
we explain people's actions in terms of desires, beliefs, goals, and wants. We say, "he
wanted to win", or "she believed that it was true". As Bruner proposes, this way
of talking – a folk talk – reflects our forms of thinking. Without our sharing a folk
psychology we would scarcely know how to carry out relationships. Society as we
know it would come to an end. For Bruner, folk beliefs are carried within the mind
as narratives; that is, we understand others by thinking in narratives. We think, for
example, "Alex became angry because he wanted the prize, and Suzie won; that's
why he isn't speaking to Suzie". Further, proposes Bruner, these mental narratives
organize the way we experience the world, and regulate our feelings. Because of our
narrative knowledge we understand which feelings are appropriate on a given occasion
and which are not. "Indeed the very shape of our lives – the rough and perpetually
changing draft of our autobiography that we carry in our minds – is understandable
to ourselves and to others only by virtue of (our) cultural systems of interpretation"
(Bruner, 1990: 34).

THE RELATIONAL SELF

Cultural psychology is an important development not only for intellectual reasons but practically as well. The cultural view has particularly important implications for educational practice (see, for example, Moll, 1990). Traditional education has centred on improving the mind (reason, knowledge, understanding) of the individual student. The student is exposed to educational materials and expected to learn. From the cultural standpoint, however, the focus of the educational process moves from the mind of the individual student to relationships between teacher and student, and among students themselves. For Vygotsky, in particular, the site of learning is within relationships. In carrying out activities with others, one metaphorically steps outside the self and takes on some aspect of the other. One interesting application of these ideas is to the education of learning-disabled students. The traditional approach to such students is one of care-taking. There is close supervision and surveillance. As it is reasoned, however, this approach limits their learning. Students must interact with each other and the world around them in ways that are specific to their needs and stage of development. Thus, an emphasis is placed on peer-collectivities, that is, students working and playing together, a process that hastens their educational growth (Rodina, in press).

Yet, in spite of the important contributions of cultural psychology, we must once again ask whether this is a satisfactory resting place. You may already suspect the limitations. The reasons are largely foreshadowed in the discussion of symbolic interactionism. Like Mead, the cultural psychologist confronts the enigma of explaining how the cultural understandings are incorporated into the individual mind. If the mental world is a blank slate, how could the voices or actions of others be understood? As infants – with no comprehension of language or action – how could we learn to absorb the words or actions of our parents? And if we are born with our higher mental processes already intact, then cultural psychology cannot be telling us the whole story. Further, there remains the problem of social determinism. If all thought is the result of taking in the cultural surrounds, is the individual anything more than society's robot? Are we just carrying on the traditions of the past in our thinking? Is there no means of transforming our traditions? And, if culture does give birth to individual minds, then what is the origin of culture? Let us press further.

Self as Relationship: the Emerging Vision

> I look for the way
> things will turn ...
> not so much looking for the shape
> as being available
> to any shape that may be
> summoning itself
> through me
> from the self not mine but ours.

> A.R. Ammons, "Poetics"

The preceding discussions – on symbolic interaction, dramaturgy, and cultural psychology – are similar in one major respect: they presume that the world of the mind emerges from participation in the social world. Notice, then, that in each case there is a social world that preexists the mind. In effect, the mind becomes socialized. And, while this is an inviting way to see the self as fundamentally social, it still leaves us with quandaries. It is not simply that it is difficult to see how the social world "gets into" or leaves a mark on the mind, but that we are still left with minds inside heads – separated and unknowable. If we are to move successfully beyond individualism, it seems that a more radical departure is needed. We must undermine more fully the traditional separation between self and world, self and other, self and society. We must locate a way of understanding ourselves as participants in a process from which the very idea of self and world become meaningful. How can this be sensible? Let us first consider more carefully the process of making meaning, and then extend the implications to see how it is that virtually all human action is born in relationship.

Meaning in Relationships

He is not, after all, the first speaker, the one who disturbs the first silence of the universe.

Mikhail Bakhtin, *Speech Genres and Other Late Essays*

Traditionally we hold that meaning resides in the individual mind. Thus we hold that when I talk or write, I am putting my private meaning into words. Or, as we say, "I am trying to make my meaning clear". And if you don't understand me, you may ask, "What exactly do you mean?" You expect me now to give you a better picture of what's going on inside my head. On this account, there is *first* individual meaning, and *then* there is a public expression. On this view, words, gestures, and facial expressions are only the vehicles through which we try to make out thoughts, feelings, and so on, clear to others. It is in the mental world that meaning originates. Language is simply a carrier or a conduit for transferring the meaning to others. But let's put this view to the test.

Understanding "Other Minds"

Place yourself for a moment in the chair of the psychiatrist. You listen to your client, Fred, who says:

"Ever since the death of my father I haven't felt right. I haven't been able to do anything. I just can't seem to get started. I don't feel motivated. Work doesn't interest me. I don't know what's the matter with me".

Fred's words are clear enough. But what are these expressions telling you about his mental life? Essentially you confront the difficult challenge of using words to penetrate an underlying meaning, an exterior as a guide to a hidden interior. Now

THE RELATIONAL SELF

the fun begins. Obviously you have no direct knowledge of the individual's mind. You can never peer behind the veil of his eyes. So, how are you to draw conclusions about his inner world, what truly drives him, what he actually feels, or is trying to say? How can you proceed? How do you solve the problem of understanding? If you are hesitant in answering how it is you can discern what's on Fred's mind, you are in good company. In fact, the problem of interpreting other minds has challenged some of the West's most learned scholars for several centuries. It is no less profound than the challenge of trying to understand God's intentions from the words of the Bible, understanding the Prophet from the verses of the Koran, or trying to understand the thoughts of a poet when you read a complex poem. Much may hang on our reaching the "correct interpretation". (Indeed, many have died because of others' interpretations of their words.) For some 300 years, the discipline of *hermeneutic* studies has been devoted to working out a plausible rationale for justifying interpretations. Importantly, there is no commonly accepted solution.

Yet, you may respond, we do seem to understand each other most of the time, so obviously we have good resources to do this. Our cultural traditions are one major resource. For example, in the present case you have the tradition of psychiatry. As a participant in this tradition, you might guess that Fred's words were an expression of low self-esteem, depression, repressed anger, or perhaps a dysfunctional cognitive system. To be sure, these assumptions are congenial to the psychiatric community. But, how did this community come to know about these things? Do we have concepts of "self-esteem", "depression", "repression", or "cognitive systems" because the experts of previous generations observed them directly? How did they accomplish such a feat? And how could we ever judge between competing traditions? A priest might conclude that Fred was suffering from the lack of spiritual nourishment; and a neuroscientist might say Fred is expressing a state of the brain.

Again, you may resist, arguing that you could ask your client questions bearing on your interpretations. His answers would suggest whether your interpretation was valid. So you suggest to the client that he may be depressed ... and he nods assent. Ah, now you feel you are on the right track. But what precisely has taken place here? Has the client considered your suggestion by turning back into his mind and trying to match the term "depression" against his inner state to see if you might be correct? "Ah, yes, now I spot a depression running about in here ... how could I have missed that ... you are quite correct". Scarcely!

You resist again, because after all, you don't have to trust his words alone. You can observe his conduct – how much he eats or sleeps, how many days he misses work, and how he spends his leisure hours. His behaviour will give you some clues as to whether he is depressed, or something else. And if you cannot observe these actions directly, you can rely on carefully developed psychological tests of depression. On these tests the client can rate how much of the time or how often he "feels tired", "has trouble sleeping", or "has little energy". But are you on solid ground here? Are people's actions truly windows to the mind? After all, bodily actions are no different in principle than a person's words in terms of drawing conclusions about what's on their mind? In both cases we are using external observables to draw conclusions about an unseen interior. If I smile, how can you know that it is an outward expression of happiness, as opposed to satisfaction, ecstasy, surprise, or bemusement? Could it be an expression of anger, love, or giddiness? On what grounds could any of these interpretations be dismissed? Because I tell you so? How would I know? And if I report on a battery of tests that I often feel tired, or have trouble sleeping and eating, how could you know these were obvious symptoms of an underlying depression? After all, where did we come up with the idea that depression exists in the human mind, by observing it? In effect, our actions – whether observed or reported on a psychological test – do not speak any more fluently or transparently about mental states than our words.

It now becomes evident that we have no means of knowing what's on someone's mind, or indeed, whether they have a mind at all. No matter how many ways in which an individual tells you he is depressed, and no matter how he behaves, you have nothing to go on outside a tradition of interpretation. You may heap one piece of evidence upon another to draw a conclusion, but in the end you never move beyond the web of convention.

Let's consider then, the assumption that meaning lies somewhere inside the head. Is this truly sensible? The questions raised at the beginning of the chapter surely give us pause for thought. There we encountered a variety of thorny problems with the traditional view of a mind inside the head. We add to these problems when we presume that meaning lies inside the mind. If understanding requires that we are in touch with each other's private meanings, we will never understand each other. We will return to the question of understanding shortly. In the meantime, let us consider an alternative account of meaning.

Meaning as Co-action
Return for a moment to the first chapter of this book. There I put forward the basic constructionist premise that the world becomes meaningful in relationships. From this perspective, we might thus look to relationships as the source of meaning. Let us take a closer look at this process. Let's say we are friends, and the morning after a party, I say to you, "Hey, wasn't that a great party?" Consider some possible responses on your part. For one, perhaps you couldn't hear me over the sounds of the music you were listening to. You make no response. Or, you might smile and say, "Yeah…it was terrific". Or, you might say, "Well, honestly, I think you are one of the few people who would say that". Now consider what these responses have done to my utterance. In failing to respond, you have reduced my utterance to a non-event. I might as well have been silent; for practical purposes I have said nothing. In your saying the party was terrific you have affirmed my statement. In your final response, you have turned my statement into a problem. In effect, my statement in itself was not meaningful. It came into meaning, or not, depending on how you treated it. I needed you in order to become a meaningful person. In affirming my statement, you gave it life; in questioning it, you reduced it to a mistake. At the same time, your responses would be nonsense without my statement. You cannot agree or disagree until I have made a statement. It would be nonsense for you to approach me and

THE RELATIONAL SELF

say, "I think you are one of the few people who would say that". In effect, your responses have no meaning without me. You needed me, as well, to become meaningful. We find then, that the production of meaning requires coordinated action, or in short, *co-action*. Like dancing the salsa or swing, neither of us can do it alone.

The process of co-action is not simply an exchange of words alone. As we coordinate movement together we are also co-creating meaning. Thus:

> If I thrust out my hand and ... you grasp it in yours,
> I have offered a greeting.
>
>   ... you push it aside to embrace me,
> I have underestimated our friendship.
>
>   ... you kneel and kiss it,
> I have demonstrated my authority.
>
>   ... you turn your back,
> I have been insulting.
>
>   ... you give me a manicure,
> I am your customer.

The process of co-action can also be extended indefinitely. If you bring me flowers, and I am pleased, I have affirmed that the flowers are a heart-felt gift. However, if I later find that you need a recommendation from me, I may now treat the flowers as manipulation. In this sense, meaning is always in motion. Nothing that is said or done is ultimately clear. Each attempt to clarify meaning is to offer a new possibility. Meaning is forever subject to the next turn in the conversation.

Now consider the broader implications. It is in this process of co-action that we may locate virtually anything that is meaningful to us. Words and actions come into meaning as they function in our relationship. It is in this process of coordination that we come to value certain words and actions, and find others scornful. The ways in which we walk, talk, laugh, cry, worship, engage in warfare, and virtually everything else we do, become sensible – or not – by virtue of collaborative action.

The Relational Mind

As I am proposing meaning lies not within the private mind, but in the process of relating. If this seems reasonable, a new and exciting possibility emerges: everything we have considered "in the mind" of the individual is born in relationships. As we saw, mental talk is central to our daily lives: "I feel ...", "I think ...", "I need ...", and so on. However, let us not view these utterances as reflecting or reporting on an inner world. Rather, let us view them as actions within relationship, actions that gain their meaning through social collaboration. How is this sensible? Let's consider two theoretical steps in this direction and then turn to some specific cases.

Mental Discourse as Performance

This first move follows quite naturally from preceding arguments. As we have seen, there is no way of understanding such utterances as, "I love you", or "I am angry" as

Figure 4.3

reports on an inner state of mind or the neurons. However, the utterance, "I love you" can be a powerful statement within a relationship, possibly drawing the other into greater intimacy or commitment, or in some cases, sending the other person running. In effect, the utterance functions as an important part of the relationship; it invites the other to create the relationship as one kind of thing and not another. In this sense near synonyms to "I love you" – phrases such as "I care", "Love ya …", or "I am mad about you" – are not other ways of saying the same thing, nor are they each tagged to a different mental state. Rather, each functions socially in a slightly different way, to modify or adjust the relationship in subtle ways. "I care …", for example, has a way of transforming a passionate relationship into possibly a friend-ship. "I'm mad about you", is more stylized, echoing relationships in film or on the stage, and thus removes some of the sense of sincerity often carried by "I love you". The phrase "Love ya" is a more casual expression that can be used in friendships and more significant relations.

As you can also see, we are not dealing here with "mere words". Expressions of love, anger, hope, desire, and so on, are typically embedded within full-blown per-formances – including gestures, gaze, and posture. For example, if spoken in a faint voice, eyes on the floor, and with a smile, the words "I am angry" would not seem to count as anger. One wouldn't know what meaning to assign to action. In order to per-form anger properly within Western culture, voice intensity and volume are typically enlisted; a stern face and a rigid posture may be required. It is useful, then, to replace the image of private "feelings" with public action; it's not that we *have* emotions, a thought, or a memory so much as we *do* them (see also Schaeffer, 1976). And, it

99

should be clear, words may not be required at all. Sweet smiles, gifts, and monetary support may replace words of endearment, in the same way that a snarl or glare may carry the same weight as a criticism.

It is important to point out that in saying we perform the mind, we should not conclude that our expressions are either superficial or calculating. Think of your own actions in the midst of a heated sports event – running, jumping, excited, fully engaged. You would scarcely say that your actions are contrived, artificial, or merely done to achieve an effect. Yet, the game itself is a cultural invention. In this sense we may say that much of daily life is a *serious game*. And so it is when we are "speaking our minds". In doing anger, love, memory, and the like we may be fully engaged, "doing what comes naturally", even if these doings are born within a history of relationship.

Performances as Relational

Performances in the theatre are fully social. They have been prepared for the purposes of social presentation. Much the same can be said of performances of mental discourse and related actions. First, our expressions have acquired their potential to be meaningful through a history of relationship. In many cases they have been prepared by centuries of co-action. A century ago it was possible for a husband to "fly into a jealous rage", at his wife's infidelity and "just naturally" slay both her and her lover. Over time, this view of jealousy has been tamed; slaying as a natural act has been replaced by couples therapy or divorce. Mental performances are also addressed to an audience. When we speak about psychological states ("I want …", "he feels …", "she thinks …",) we are always addressing someone – either explicitly or implicitly – within some kind of relationship. To say that the performances are addressed is also to say that they are fashioned with respect to the recipient. One's expressions of anger, for example, are not likely to be the same when addressed to one's children as opposed to one's peers or one's parents. The other enters the expression, then, in its very formulation.

One's performances are thus possessions not of the mind but relationship; they are inhabited not only by a history of relationships but as well by the relationships into which they are directed. By making these two theoretical moves, first treating psychological discourse as performance and then embedding performances within relationships, we are now positioned to see the entire vocabulary of the mind as constituted by and within relationship. There is no fully private self, as in the traditional accounts. Rather, there is embodied action, and such action has meaning only within and because of relationship.

Let us see how these ideas apply to daily life. In particular, I will focus on rational thought, memory, and emotion.

Reason as Relationship

Let us return to Descartes for a moment for it was during the sixteenth century that the concept rational of thought became so central to the Western view of the self. Descartes found that he could doubt the existence of all things, but not the act of doubt itself. And because doubt is an act of human reason, reason stood as the chief attribute of the human being. But let us ask, how did Descartes know that he was reasoning? Did he somehow look into his brain and find, lo and behold, there was a thought in this corner and an emotion in another? This scarcely seems plausible. Rather, in order to write about rational thought, Descartes must have already had the words in his vocabulary. And if this is so, then it is to his relations with others that he owes the capacity to write about reason. In effect, the concept of human reason is not a reading of human nature, but a communal construction.

At the same time, like Descartes, we do talk as if we possess the capacity for rational thought. We say, for example, "Let me think about it", "my reasoning is…", "you miscalculated", or, "you are being irrational". From the present standpoint these are social performances. They sustain our traditional patterns of relationship. For example, if I am evaluating a student essay and I write in the margin, "good thinking", I am not evaluating a process inside the student's head. Rather, I am commenting on the way he or she used words. As some scholars put it, reason is not distinguishable from effective rhetoric (Myerson, 1994). In the academic setting, good reasoning is basically the ability to argue according to academic rules (Billig, 1996). If lost in a forest, good thinking may be the ability to use the compass; if confronting a bully in the playground, the child who can find a way of avoiding a fight is a "good thinker". Reason is socially credited action.

You may be suspicious at this point; is this analysis denying our subjectivity, all that we do privately and alone? Surely we are doing something privately in our prolonged gaze into the distance as we prepare to write a term paper, or ponder the meaning of another's harsh words. Why aren't these specifically *inner mental* processes? They are not performed publicly. Consider more closely: when we are preparing a term paper, for example, in what kind of process are we engaged? Are we not readying ourselves to put meaningful arguments on paper, that is, preparing to engage in a social action? Similarly, being rejected by a friend is only meaningful within particular traditions of relationship. Thus, we may be doing something privately – which we might want to call reasoning, pondering, or feeling – but from the present standpoint these are essentially public actions carried out in private. To illustrate, consider the actress preparing her lines for a play. These lines are essentially nonsense that are independent of their placement within the play; that is, they require a relationship to be intelligible. Yet, the actress can rehearse the lines in private, speaking loudly in her empty room, or she can sit quietly and let the words form without voicing them. In the latter case we might say she was "imagining", or "thinking them through". But essentially she is carrying out a public action, only without an audience and a full performance.[5] You can gain an appreciation of this last point by considering your own thinking process when you are writing a report or preparing a presentation. As you sit quietly, you can virtually "hear" the voices of others, the approval and disapproval of colleagues, teachers, friends, and so on. And with each voice the words take shape. "I should not say that…", "This is really important to include," "Chris will love this one…" and so on. As many now hold, thinking is not an expression of an autonomous mind, but is a public dialogue carried out privately (Hermanns & Kempen, 1993).

Let us expand on this vision of the relational self by considering the practices of memory and emotion.

Collective Remembering

"Do you remember the time that ...?"
"What is the square of the hypotenuse?"
"Can you describe the events that took place on the night of 5 March?"

Questions of memory are always with us, and how we respond may sometimes change the course of our lives. Many psychologists presume that the word "memory" stands for a specific kind of process inside the head of the individual, a process that is neurologically based and universal in its functioning. Is there a relational alternative to this individualist view? First, it makes little sense to view the phrase "I remember" as a report on a particular psychological or neurological condition. What kind of condition would we be reporting on, how would we be able to "look inside" and recognize when we had a memory as opposed to a "thought" or a "desire"? Rather, as John Shotter has put it, "Our ways of talking about our experiences work not primarily to represent the nature of those experiences in themselves, but to represent them in such a way as to constitute and sustain one or another kind of social order" (1990, pp. 122–123).

In this sense it may be said that memory is not an individual act but a collective one. Consider the following conversation fragment recorded in a group of British students recalling a movie (*E.T.*) they had seen together:

Diane:	it was so sad
Lesley:	that little boy was a very good actor
Diane:	he was brilliant he really was
Tina:	especially at the end when he ...
Karen:	he was quivering, wasn't he
John:	how many didn't cry at it
Lesley:	[*emphatically*] I didn't and I'm proud of it too
Diane:	tell you what got me the bit when he didn't get on the space ship right at the beginning ... the actual story line was really boring wasn't it
Karen:	yeh
Lesley:	yeh dead boring
Tina:	it was the effects that did it
Paul:	it has some incredible little funny bits in it when he got drunk and things like that
Lesley:	yeh

(Middleton & Edwards, 1990, pp. 31–32)

There are countless ways a film can be described. One can talk about the use of colour, the length of various scenes, character development, the moral lesson, and so on. But what we find here is that the students begin to converge in their description. As they talk they generate an account of "what happened". As they come to agree on the sadness, the good acting, and the boring plot so too do they create what it is to remember. They will draw from these agreements in answering someone who later asks, "Did you see *E.T.*? What was it like?" Similarly, if a child at school is asked "what does 3 times 3 equal?" and she answers with "9", she is not giving a report on an inner condition of her mind. Rather she is acting within a social tradition of what it is to "remember your multiplication tables". And when the family gathers at a reunion, the stories of the past are not "movies in their minds", but forms of conversation that have typically been incubated in a long history of conversation. In their study of how people recall political events, such as wars or revolutions, my Spanish colleagues conclude, "Every memory, as personal as it may be – even of events that are private and strictly personal and have not been shared with anyone – exists through its relation with what has been shared with others: language, idiom, events, and everything that shapes the society of which individuals are a part" (Iniguez et al., 1997, p. 250).

Distributed Cognition

Another way of talking about memory and other mental processes as relational is to say that they are socially distributed. What does this mean? Consider the child who is being taught the alphabet. The mother asks, "Laura, what comes after F?" The child is silent for a moment, and the mother says, "good ... goose ... gravy ..." Laura brightens and immediately responds "G!" In this case the production of "the correct memory" is essentially distributed between the mother and the child; the child reports but the mother's prompt is essential to the performance. As scholars propose, memory is very often distributed in this communal way. For example, what is recalled about a historical figure or event in a given nation may be distributed not only across a range of conversations, but also across textbooks, newspapers, television productions, and films (see, for example, Schudson, 1992). In this sense, the history of a nation is a social construction, and as every savvy politician knows, always subject to reconstruction.

In the same way we might say that rationality is socially distributed. As Mary Douglas (1986) proposes, because rational decisions emerge from a multiplicity of conversations within organizations, we can justifiably say that "organizations think". Stupid decisions are not the result of any single mind; they are a byproduct of the entire group – including the way they speak together, and who is included or excluded from the conversation. In this context, important research has explored the crew of large aircraft who must work together in close coordination to generate "intelligent decisions" concerning flight paths, weather conditions, landings, and so on (see for example, Engestrom & Middleton, 1996). Obviously these coordinations have life and death consequence. As the research suggests, a significant number of air catastrophes can be traced to cases in which the advice of a junior-ranking crew member was unheeded by a senior. It is the defect in collective reasoning that has brought death.

Emotional scenarios

We tend to think of emotions as "natural givens", simply part of human nature. Mothers generally assume their infants are born into the world with fully functioning

THE RELATIONAL SELF

emotions (Gergen et al., 1990). The child's cry is taken as a sign of anger, her smile as an expression of happiness. Scientists support this view in their treatises on the genetic basis of emotions. Psychologists try to locate the physiological basis of emotion, and argue for the universality of what are called "the basic emotions (see Lillard, 1998). Yet, this traditional view not only places the emotions inside the individual head (and body), but also suggests that there is little we can do about emotions such as anger, jealousy, or hatred. We are genetically drawn toward doing what comes naturally. Yet it is dangerous to presume that what we in the West assume to be "natural" is universal. What the Ifaluk call *fago* or the Japanese call *mayae*, for example, are simply deleted from what we in the West presume to be "basic emotions". In this sense, we are in danger of a cultural imperialism that reduces the understandings of other cultures to "mere folk belief".

If we view emotional expressions as culturally constructed and performed, we not only avoid the problems of stasis and imperialism, we also open new vistas of possibility. Consider first that in spite of the view of emotions as biologically demanded, there are complex social rules about when and where an emotional expression can occur. You cannot walk down the street and shout, "I love you" to a passerby, any more than you can interrupt a funeral to express your joy. If you disobey the rules, you are likely to suffer. And, as well, there are conventions about the way such emotions are performed. If you smile while performing anger, it simply isn't anger. Now consider: if you perform an emotion, there are also implicit rules for how others can respond. If I tell you that I am afraid of something, you cannot begin to do cartwheels; if I tell you of my sadness, you cannot jump for joy. In doing so you would exit the culture.

Now compare these failures to follow the rules with a positive case: you tell me that you are fearful about an upcoming exam, and I "do the right thing" culturally by asking you why this exam is so frightening. It is now your turn to speak, and again, you are bound by cultural convention. If you flap your arms like a bird, you are out of culture; if you tell me about the fact that you haven't had time to study, you are making sense within the conventions. Now it is my turn once again, and once again there are only certain things I may say that will make sense. For example, I can reassure you but not stamp on your foot. We now see that the emotional performance is part of a more extended pattern of interchange. It is helpful here to use the concept of a *scenario*, that is, a scripted set of interdependent actions such as we might find in a play (see also Gagnon & Simon, 1973). Each action in the scenario sets the stage for that which follows; what follows lends sense to that which has preceded. In effect, the performance of each actor is required to give the play its coherent unity; each performance depends on the others for its intelligibility. In these terms, we can view emotional performances as parts of a play in which other actors are required. This is to propose that the angry shout or the sluggish expression of depression only make sense by virtue of their position in emotional scenarios. Further, like good drama, many emotional scenarios also have *beginnings* and *endings*. If it is late at night and your electric power is suddenly lost, that is the beginning of a scenario in which expressions of fear (as opposed, let's say, to jealously or ecstasy) would be appropriate. In contrast, if someone is telling you of her sorrow, you may continue to give her nurturance and support until she smiles. At that point the scenario is terminated, and you may be free to make a silly joke or speak of your vacation.

The Plasticity of Pain

Isn't pain primarily a biological matter? After all, biological research clearly shows the existence of pain receptors in the nervous system, and when these receptors are fired people reliably report the experience of pain. It also follows that because the biological makeup of the human species is more or less the same across cultures, the experience of pain is universal. An electric shock or a burning stove will be painful the world over. Yet, social constructionist views raise important questions about the limits of this view. For one, history presents too many counter examples. Historian Esther Cohen reports that before the 1600s, very few people wrote about experiencing pain; in medieval times authors seldom wrote of their physical sensations, and autobiographies were far more likely to dwell on mental as opposed to physical anguish. During the thirteenth to the fifteenth centuries, it was believed that pain was not primarily lodged in the body, but in the soul. In this way, the experience of pain took on a spiritual dimension. Because Christ suffered for humankind, many sought out pain as a way of both sharing Christ's pain and achieving redemption. Self-flagellation, fasting, and even martyrdom were embraced by the devout. Similarly, in his summary volume, *The Culture of Pain*, David Morris describes wide variations in the experience of pain. During battle, for example, wounded soldiers in early times might become euphoric because their wounds meant they would be removed from the threat of battlefield death. Micronesian women in labour give so little evidence of pain that Western doctors can identify their contractions only by placing a hand on their abdomen.

   For the constructionist the question thus becomes: in what degree can an experience commonly called pain be reconstructed so that its suffering is lessened or removed? Professional boxers, football players, and wrestlers seldom talk about the experience of pain. And yet, if most of us were to experience the blows they endure, we would most likely be in agony. Further, there are significant numbers who take erotic pleasure in being beaten. More formally, Arthur Frank's classic volume, *The Wounded Storyteller* connects pain to the narratives we use to explain it. He illuminates three significant ways in which serious illness can be encountered. The first is to understand the illness simply as a deviation from the normal condition of good health, and the task is that of *restitution*. One wishes only to clear it up and get on with life. More extreme is the *chaos* narrative, in which the illness throws one into a state of futility or helplessness. There is no obvious means of coping or resolving. Finally, and less common, is the *quest* story. Here one understands his or her illness in terms of a journey in which significant meaning is realised. Important for present purposes are the differences in

(Cont'd)

105

the suffering attending these contrasting interpretations. With the restitution narrative, one endures the suffering but is buffered by the promise of recovery. Within the chaos narrative there is anger and frustration at the meaningless and unending anguish. For those who engage in a quest, however, there is the sense of achieving a deeper meaning about life and human relationships. In this case, according to Frank, suffering is alleviated.

From this perspective, emotions are not the private possessions of the individual mind, but are the property of ongoing relationships. "Your joy" is not yours but "ours", "my anger" is "our anger", and so on. The implications of this shift in understanding are substantial. Consider the case of depression, a "mental disorder" that is now said to strike one in ten people. From the present standpoint depression is not an individual disorder; an individual "does depression" as a culturally intelligible action within a context of relationship. Therapeutic attention thus moves outward from the individual mind ("what is wrong with him?") to the relational scenarios in which the person is engaged. In what kinds of relationship is the depression invited, with whom, and under what conditions? In contemporary Western culture, it is appropriate to become depressed if one has failed. But, we may ask, is this the only possible response? Failure doesn't require depression as a biological response. Is it possible, we might ask, to remove oneself from the situation with meditation, or even to find ways of appreciating failure? Similarly, spouse abuse is not a "natural eruption" of anger, but is more likely to be embedded within subtle forms of interchange – with family members and others outside or in the past. It has a time and a place when it "feels natural", but we may now ask whether we can change the scenario. If my spouse is angry with me, I am not required by biology to become defensive or return the anger. Can we not "change the rules"?

On the more positive side, the relational orientation suggests that all our pleasures – the joy of tastes, smells, colours, eroticism and the like – are not the result of individual biology. Rather, we owe all pleasures to our existence in relationships. I never liked opera till there was Shirley; I never enjoyed scotch whisky till there was Mike; baseball was a bore till there was Stan ... I could go on. Perhaps you could as well.

Reflection

Perhaps it is obvious that I am very excited about the idea of the relational self. In part my excitement stems from promise of a future in which greater value is placed on the well-being of *relationships* than on the well-being of single *individuals*. From the constructionist standpoint, it is through relationships that we construct worlds of good and evil, joy and sorrow, happiness and despair. If this is so, then it is through relationships that personal well-being is achieved. If we wish to see a better world, it is in relationships that we should invest our energies. If we care for relationships, there is little room for alienation, narcissism, power struggles, and the kind of antagonisms that lead to bloodshed. Yet, I also realize that so far in this book, I have only considered relationships among people. This is a shortcoming. In the long run, the concept of relationship must be expanded to include the environments of which we are a part. In the same way that we have come to view people as isolated entities, we have also come to make separations between humans and the environment. The effects have been virtually catastrophic. Similar to the case of human interaction, we have become alienated from the environment, treating it as instrumental to our own well-being, and as a domain over which we must have power. Relational conceptions are much in need. We must come to see ourselves as intimate partners with nature, with whom we must learn to dance successfully. In the long run we may replace the longstanding concern with individual units (persons, communities, religions, nations, and the like) in favour of a full investment in nurturing relationships. I like the Lakota Indians prayer that begins by honouring, "All my relations ...".

Notes

1 For a more fully developed account of generative theory see my book, Gergen K.J. (1993) *Toward transformation in social knowledge* (2nd edn.). London: Sage.
2 Interestingly, as a commentator on internet technology, Stone champions the development of multiple identities on the internet as a means of resisting individualization.
3 Interesting examples of research and theory in this domain include Hochschild, A. (1983). *The managed heart: commercialization of human feeling*. Berkeley, CA: University of California Press; Turner, R.H. (1978). The role and the person. *American Journal of Sociology*, 84, 1–23; Matza, D. (1969). *Becoming deviant*. Englewood Cliffs, NJ: Prentice-Hall.
4 The classic discussion of this distinction is that of Overton, W.R. & Reese, H.W. (1973). Models of development: methodological implications. In J.R. Nesselroade & H.W. Reese (Eds.). *Life-span development psychology: methodological issues*. New York: Academic Press.
5 For further discussion of this point see Harré, R. (1979). *Social being*. Oxford: Blackwell.

Further Resources

Deliberations on Individualism

Bellah, R.N., Madsen, R., Sullivan, W.M., Swidler, A., & Tipton, S.M. (1985). *Habits of the heart*. Berkeley, CA: University of California Press.
Sampson, E.E. (2008). *Celebrating the other: a dialogic account of human nature*. London: Harvester-Wheatsheaf.

Symbolic Interactionism

Blumer, H. (1986). *Symbolic interactionism, perspective and method*. Berkeley: University of California Press.

Denzin, N. (1992). *Symbolic interaction and cultural studies: the politics of interpretation*. Oxford: Blackwell.

Hewitt, J.P. (1994). *Self and society*. Boston, MA: Allyn & Bacon.

Life as Theatre

Caughey, J.L. (2006). *Negotiating cultures and identities: life history issues, methods, and readings*. University of Nebraska Press.

Hochschild, A. (1983). *The managed heart*. Berkeley: University of California Press.

Cultural Psychology

Bruner, J. (1990). *Acts of meaning*. Cambridge, MA: Harvard University Press.

Cole, M. (1996). *Cultural psychology*. Cambridge, MA: Harvard University Press.

Heine, S.J. (2007). *Cultural psychology*. New York: Norton.

Karpov, J. (2005). *The neo-Vygotskian approach to child development*. Cambridge: Cambridge University Press.

Relational Self

Burkitt, I. (2008). *Social selves* (2nd ed.). London: Sage.

Edwards, D. (1997). *Discourse and cognition*. London: Sage.

Gergen, K.J. (2008). *Relational being: beyond the individual and community*. New York: Oxford University Press.

Hermans, H.J.M. & Kempen, H.J.G. (1993). *The dialogical self*. New York: Academic Press.

Middleton, D. & Brown, S.D. (2005). *The social psychology of experience, studies in remembering and forgetting*. London: Sage.

Pennebaker, J.W., Paez, D., & Rime, B. (Eds.) (1997). *Collective memos of political events*. Mahwah, NJ: Erlbaum.

Wertsch, J.V. (1991). *Voices of the mind*. Cambridge, MA: Harvard University Press.

5

DIALOGUE: CONFLICT AND TRANSFORMATION

Dialogue rejects the tyranny of a single system or dogma; it welcomes new ideas and guarantees them equality ... it refuses to censor "dangerous" ideas; it cherishes and protects its capacity to learn and to grow; it guards as something precious its own access to joy and laughter.

Robert Grudin, *On Dialogue*

We now confront one of the most profound problems in the contemporary world: living with differences. Or, one might say, "dying because of differences". In the opening chapter we recognized the enormous significance of communal creations of the real and the good. When we successfully coordinate our actions we come into a world of reliable meaning, a sense of personal identity, an understanding of right and wrong, and a purpose for living. Through successful coordination we build the most significant relations of our lives, relations that are trusted, significant, and nourishing. Yet, herein lies a fundamental irony. In many respects, the very source of worth, joy, and comfort – these esteemed traditions of relationship – are also the source of enormous agony. Much of the world's bloodshed may be traced to their existence. Why is this so?

From a constructionist standpoint the reasons are many. First, in constructing a desirable world together, we simultaneously create an alternative world of the less than desirable. For everything in which we place value, there is also a negative exterior, the not-valued. The world of the not-valued is primarily inhabited by others, those who are not part of us. Whether we are speaking of couples, cliques, clubs, teams, organizations, religions, or nations, there are strong tendencies to create the reality of "we are better". With the glorification of *us*, there is an accompanying defamation of *them*. The invited result is mutual antipathy, physical avoidance, and the mutual creation of "the evil other". And, there is a certain joy to be derived from telling jokes about the other, in hate talk, and physical violence. All such activities may be affirmed and honoured by one's mates.

At this point we enter a familiar territory of inter-group hostility. As abundant research, and the deaths of millions attest, bonded groups of true believers can be a danger to all those outside the boundary.[1] In these communities we give birth to "hate talk", segregation, incarceration, and ultimately the elimination of the evil other. I am not speaking here only of the commonly recognized villainies – pogroms, invasions, genocides, terrorisms and the like. Rather, I include here the walls that are everyday erected around friendships, athletic teams, fraternities, communities, ethnicities, economic classes, political movements, religions, and nations. All may be cherished, but all harbour seeds of separation and hostility.

We stand now at a critical juncture. The real, the rational, and the good are always in the making. And we are pleased when our efforts bring about the harmony, trust, satisfaction, and joy of bonded relationship. Yet, this same achievement of bonding also carries with it seeds of separation, self-eradication, antagonism, and mutual annihilation. In my view, forces are at work today that dramatically increase the likelihood of global barricades and resulting bloodshed. Communication technologies increasingly permit otherwise scattered voices to locate each other, to unite, and to activate an agenda. For example, through radio and television a religious fundamentalist can find ideological and emotional support around the clock. Through the internet a white supremacist can find dating and mating services to ensure a lifetime's devotion to the cause. With cell phones and the internet, terrorists may plan and execute global destruction. Banding and bonding are no longer limited geographically, and no circling of wagons can prevent alien intrusion (see, for example, Hunter, 1991).

I can scarcely offer a compelling slate of solutions to the emerging challenge. However, a constructionist orientation does underscore the importance of one major resource: dialogue. If collaborative relationships are the source of inspiration and action within a group, it is essential that such relationships be used to reduce conflict across groups. Yet, how is such dialogue to proceed? The remainder of the chapter is devoted to this question. To begin with I will take up two issues that are essential to creating effective dialogue. The first concerns the problem of understanding. We often say that effective dialogue leads to mutual understanding. But what is it to understand another person? Success in dialogue importantly depends on how we answer this question. The second issue concerns the participants in dialogue. We typically hold simplified views of each other; one is either *for* or *against* a given proposal. Our possibilities for dialogue are thus reduced. An alternative vision must be explored, one that may be called, multi-being. After discussing these issues, I will turn to a number of traditional practices of resolving problems through dialogue. As we shall find, from a constructionist perspective they are insufficient. These discussions set the stage for exploring what we may call *transformative dialogue*, that is, dialogue specifically aimed at bringing about new and more promising relationships among participants.

Understanding as a Relational Achievement

"You just don't understand me ..."
"You can't know what I feel ..."
"I don't understand what you mean ..."
"You just don't seem to hear what I'm saying ..."

These common refrains underscore the problem of understanding in everyday life. If we are to live successfully together, it is essential that we understand each other. But so often we do not. How is it then, that we come to understand each other, and why is misunderstanding so common? Are there ways to increase our ability to understand each other? All are important questions, but through the lens of social construction we realize that our traditional way of approaching the problem of understanding is misguided.

Traditionally we say that we understand someone when we "know what's on his mind", "what's in her heart", "what she is thinking", and the like. However, as determined in the preceding chapter, if understanding means penetrating the mind of the other, we will never understand. We will be ships sailing past each other in the night, each living in our own private world. Let us approach the problem, then, from another perspective. First, consider Wittgenstein's (1953: 154) warning, "Try not to think of understanding as a 'mental process' at all. For *that* is the expression which confuses you. But ask yourself: in what sort of case, in what kind of circumstances, do we say, 'Now I know how to go on'". As Wittgenstein suggests, we should stop viewing meaning as accessing another's private meaning.

Now recall from the preceding chapter that meaning is achieved in coordinated action. Thus we may say that we understand each other when we *effectively coordinate our actions* – drawing from traditions in ways that are mutually satisfactory. To illustrate, consider the question of how we can understand what another person is feeling. If emotions were private events – somewhere behind the eyeballs – we could never understand each other's feelings. That you take my tears to represent an expression of sadness is not a result of your looking into my private world and finding that I am sad. Rather you reach this conclusion by virtue of participating in a culture that defines "tears" as sadness (among other things). And, in Western culture it is appropriate to respond to tears with sympathy (among other things). If you come to me in tears and I am sympathetic, there is evidence that I understand. However, if I respond to your tears with laughter and say, "what kind of joke is this?", you may well conclude that I don't understand you at all. My failure to understand in this case is not because I fail to grasp the inner workings of your mind; it is rather a breach in the common pattern of coordination. Or imagine a friend coming to you and revealing her anger over the way she has been treated by her boss. In every way she deserved a promotion, and instead of promoting her they chose her assistant for the position. You reply, "oh well ... but, look, I really want to talk with you about this super vacation I am planning". With this response, your friendship will very likely suffer. You show no understanding; your world is all about you. In contrast, if you reply with concern about the situation, and suggest possible routes to restoring justice, you are likely to remain friends. You have demonstrated sensitive understanding. What you have done is to coordinate your actions in a way that by conventional standards counts as understanding. Mutual understanding, then, is akin to dancing smoothly together, sailing a Frisbee to one another, or effectively paddling a canoe together.

How does this account apply to our failure to understand complex books or poetry? The mistake we typically make in such cases is to believe that the author has a meaning locked inside his or her head, and that we are failing to comprehend. In a relational frame, we can abandon this idea. The author was engaged in a social performance, not a revelation of the mind. And, similar to the author, you as reader are also engaged in a social performance. The problem in failing to understand is that you are not fully socialized in the conventions of coordination that would count as understanding. In a philosophy class, to understand a Hegel or Heidegger is thus to write or speak about their works in ways that are currently acceptable. For some schools of philosophy (continental), such writing requires years to master; for other schools of philosophy (logical empiricist), the same texts are sources of great laughter.

Multi-being: What Shall We Become Together?

To prepare the way for a discussion of dialogue, I have first proposed that understanding is not an individual but a relational achievement. To further the preparation it is useful to consider that all of us are engaged in multiple relations. We have a range of friendships, often with people who are quite different from each other. And we have ongoing relationships with family members, neighbours, teachers, along with members of religious, athletic, political groups, and more. In addition to these ongoing relationships, we also carry with us traces of past relationships – a childhood friend, a first grade teacher, a class bully, an early "crush", and so on. In each of these relationships we have developed a unique pattern of understanding. In constructionist terms, we have created many different realities together, along with values, rationalities, and practices of relating. Although these realities may overlap in important ways, they are all quite unique. As a result, we carry the capacity to live in multiple worlds. What is real, rational, and good when we are talking with parents or a clergy member may be quite different than when we are relating with pals at a party or a football game. The world we create with a younger brother or sister may be very different from the world we share with a teacher or a grandfather. One might say, then, that we are *multi-beings*, capable of being many persons. The below figures illustrate this condition of multi-being, with each oval representing a given relationship. Echoing the theme of the preceding chapter, we may view the person as the intersection of multiple relationships:

Figure 5.1   Single wing

Let us extend this image of the person. When we share a given world with someone, we also recognize what is "not this world". If we share a world in which God exists, we also know what it is to be an atheist. If we share the value of democracy, we also know that it is not totalitarianism. In effect, for every way of being that we embrace, we also know how to act in a way that would oppose it. This is not to say that we would necessarily take the opposing position, but we know roughly how it could be done. In this sense, we are multi-beings who have the capacity to take many positions, along with their opposites. Now consider how we usually go on together. Or, as in the following figure, what happens to us when we come together as multi-beings?

Figure 5.2   Double wing

One of the most important effects of coming together is typically to *negotiate a common reality*. I cannot be everything I know how to be, all at once, nor can you. And, if we continue to shift from one moment to the next – speaking formally, childishly, demandingly, sweetly, passionately, and so on – we will fail to coordinate with each other. Or, following the preceding discussion, we will fail to understand each other. In effect, we locate an agreeable reality, along with what we will value together, how we will talk about it, and so on. Often this common reality is superficial; with little effort we can usually agree on the weather, the price of gasoline, or the winnings of some sports team. If the relationship is to be more enduring, for example, if we are in the same class room, on the same team, or work in the same organization, the negotiation becomes more complex. We must learn what we can and cannot say, what gives life to our relationship as opposed to those spaces of danger. I was once a naval officer, and at the officers' dinner on shipboard, we were forbidden to speak of politics or sex. Differences of opinion in these areas might have spoiled our working relationships. This was simply a formalizing of what we had learnt to do in daily relationships.

Now consider the results of negotiating a common reality: we bring to the relationship enormous capacities for being. But as we coordinate our actions, we reduce the potentials to a narrow range. We come to live within *bounded identities*, and we are trusted to remain true to them. We become known as someone who holds a particular political position, has certain religious beliefs, is committed to certain ends, and holds certain values. If we fail to live up to these bounded identities, we may be condemned. If we take multiple stands – seeing the world from "both sides" – we may be criticized as superficial, wishy-washy, or untrustworthy. Thus, we find, when we are with our peers we may be fully committed to a given reality, set of values, and way of life. However, this commitment also shields us from the fact that our potentials are far greater, and this may include the capacity for negating all these commitments. With these ideas in focus, let us now turn to the challenges of dialogue.

Dialogue and Difference

As we construct local realities and invest them with value, so do we also plant seeds of conflict. We come to see those who don't share in our way of life as lacking in some way – taste, sophistication, know-how, conscience, ability, intelligence, and the like. When we become committed to these realities and values, the potentials for conflict are intensified. Now those who do not share our way of life become threats, possibly dangerous, and possibly requiring control, prison, or even elimination. For all of us, then, certain groups of people will seem just plain wrong-headed or evil – perhaps for you these could be neo-Nazis, the KKK, the Mafia, or terrorist groups. This sense of alienation is virtually an inevitable outcome of social life. And is it not ironic? The very relations from which the meaning of life is derived, from which all that is good and worth doing is nurtured, are also the sources of discord and alienation.

Prejudice is not, then, a mark of a flawed character – inner rigidity, decomposed cognition, emotional bias. Rather, so long as we continue the normal process of creating consensus around what is real and good, classes of the undesirable are under construction. Wherever there are tendencies toward unity, cohesion, brotherhood, commitment, solidarity, or community, so is alienation under production. Virtually none of us escapes from being undesirable to at least one (and probably many) other groups. The major challenge that confronts us, then, is not that of generating warm and cosy communities, conflict-free societies, or a harmonious world order. Rather, given strong tendencies toward conflict, how do we proceed? How can we prevent ever-emerging conflict from yielding oppression, terrorism, warfare, or genocide – in effect, the end of meaning altogether? As I mentioned earlier, the major challenge for the twenty-first century is how we shall manage to *live together* on the globe.

What resources are available to us in confronting this challenge? At least one important possibility is suggested by constructionist theory itself: if it is through dialogue that the grounds for conflict emerge, then dialogue may be our best option for treating conflicting realities. To communicate across barriers of antagonism is to seek new means of coordination. In the remainder of this chapter, I shall first consider some traditional practices of dialogue used in conditions of conflict. Although they can be effective, they are limited by their realist assumptions. Then I shall turn to what may be called *transformative dialogue*, an approach that emerges more directly from the relational perspective developed above.

From Argumentation to Mediation: Hopes and Hesitations

Here's to you, and here's to me
And if we two should disagree,
To hell with you!

Traditional toast

If we disagree on the state of things and wish to avoid mortal combat, an obvious option is "to discuss it". As we all know, however, such discussions are often far from ideal: they are replete with misunderstandings, subterfuge, and subtle power tactics, and often lead to strained or broken relations. One of the major reasons that many dialogues break down is that the participants are immersed in both realist and individualist traditions. That is, on the realist side, they presume a world of identifiable gains and losses. There is real money at stake, real territory, oil, environmental welfare, religious tradition, and so on. On the individualist side they tend to view persons as independent actors, ideally using rigorous reasoning in achieving identifiable goals. One solution to these problems is formalization. Joining these perspectives it should ideally be possible to locate a single best logic (rational procedure) for resolving differences between competing parties. Those advocating *argumentation* as a means of solving conflict furnish a clear example. Here, "the discussants must advance statements in which the standpoint under discussion is attacked and defended ... In an argumentative discussion the participants try to convince one another of the acceptability or unacceptability of the expressed opinion under discussion by means of argumentative statements. These are designed to justify or refute an expressed opinion to the listener's satisfaction" (van Eemeren & Grootendorst, 1983, p. 2). Specific rules of argumentation are thus designed for broadest (and potentially universal) application. A good example of the argumentation orientation is the judicial process. Both the prosecution and the defence use reason and evidence to defeat the other. Seldom do both sides conclude that "justice has been done".

Sharing much with the argumentation approach, many practitioners rely on a *bargaining orientation*. Here each party in the conflict determines the costs and benefits of various outcomes, and attempts to negotiate trades to achieve the highest possible pay-off for the self (maximization). As one bargaining impresario puts it, because of the common "clashing of preferences" among parties, "Bargaining is a search for advantage through accommodation" (Lebow, 1996, p. 1). In the bargaining domain, there is a heavy emphasis on reason; an optimal bargaining strategy would maximize gains while minimizing loss. A good bargaining strategy is to exploit the other's weaknesses; when a weakness can be located one can use threat. The attempt is to achieve the greatest advantage while conceding as little as possible. Bargaining procedures are typically used when there are intense conflicts in business and political arenas.

As you can imagine, the bargaining process can become cut-throat; each adversary seeks his or her own gain without regard to the other. Attempting to soften the relationship, other conflict experts have developed what may be called a *negotiation orientation*. Here the emphasis shifts from maximizing one's own gain to maximizing joint reward: "the best we can both achieve under the circumstances". In a bestseller such as *Getting to yes* (1992), Roger Fisher, William Ury and Bruce Patton outlined strategies by which each party to the negotiation may generate options for mutual gain. Each party is encouraged to identify their basic interests, what they want from the negotiation and how important it is for them. With their hopes on the table, participants are encouraged to search for those particular interests that are shared in common. Are there goals they are both seeking (for example, safety, peace)? Then solutions can be sought that all parties would find acceptable. Negotiation practices are most often found in business and government contexts where there is reasonable trust between the parties. However, the sense of fundamental separation remains.

Although similar to negotiation, we may justifiably separate out the *mediation orientation* for its stronger emphasis on reducing antagonism between the participants (see, for example, Bush & Folger, 1994; Susskind & Cruikshank, 1987). In mediation a major emphasis is typically placed on replacing the adversarial relationship with collaborative, integrative problem solving. Parties may be encouraged to listen to and understand each other's thoughts and feelings about the situation, to generate multiple options, and to work together to locate a mutually agreeable option. Mediation of this sort is often useful in cases of interpersonal conflict, such as divorce or child custody. Effective mediation can bring people closer together.

Narrative Mediation

Mediation specialists generally seek "kinder and gentler" ways of solving conflict than in bargaining and negotiation. One of the most advanced of these practices is represented in narrative mediation (Winslade & Monk, 2001). At the outset, the narrative mediator understands that conflict typically results from people's differing constructions of the world to which they are committed. They come with stories about how they are each deserving and the other is at fault. In effect, the conflict is between narrative constructions, and it is reasoned that narratives can be transformed through dialogue. The mediator thus puts in motion forms of conversation that invite the parties to develop alternative and more mutually beneficial narratives. For example, disputants may be invited to speak about the conflict as if it were external to them, and getting in the way of their negotiations. They might come to see that, "This problem is eating us up; we have to find a way to put it to rest". In this way they abandon the more familiar exercise of mutual blame (for example, "This is all your fault"), and join together against a common threat.

Participants may also be asked to recall times in which their relations were successful. (for example, "Tell me about a time when your relationship was working well"). In telling such stories the participants often find ways of praising each other, and they realize that their past relationship has been a valuable one. The result is not only a softening of the antagonism, but the generation of building material for constructing new narratives. The mediator may also invite others to participate – family, friends, and colleagues. Particularly helpful to the mediation are people who are hurt in some way by the conflict, people who are deeply invested in reaching a resolution. They may spur the participants on, by offering their support and helping them to explore new ways of seeing each other and the situation. The outcome is the development of a new narrative construction of the situation and each other. Especially when their family and friends share this construction, the conflict is replaced by productive coordination.

All of these practices – argumentation, bargaining, negotiation and mediation – can be valuable resources in solving conflicts. From international conflict and labour-management disputes to community and family conflict, these practices have often proved effective. Yet, there is reason to press further. As I mentioned earlier, except for some forms of mediation, such practices are all lodged within a realist and individualist tradition. Things are as they are, and with the application of individual reason there should be an optimal solution. However, from a social constructionist standpoint both the rational and the real are byproducts of communal relations. Constructionists hold that all we take to be real (for example "the problem", "my interests", "the optimal solution") is lodged in traditions of discourse. Thus, to fix "the problem", "my interests", and so on, is to establish fixed limits within which the dialogue must proceed. If we agree that "this is the problem", then by common convention we shall move toward "solution talk". Other kinds of conversation, possibly more useful, are discouraged. If we establish "your interests" as opposed to "mine", we discourage conversation about "duties", "justice", "the spirit", and so on. We also reduce the possibilities for exploring other ways of constructing the situation at hand, ways that might lead to more congenial outcomes. In the same way, constructionists view "good reasons" as cultural creations. To reason is not to engage in some form of superior mental process, but to sustain a tradition. Thus, while traditions are valuable, to limit the conversation to one form of talk, however "reasonable", is to limit the possibilities of what we may now construct. If we engage in rational argument, for example, we create a world of winners and losers. How often have you ever seen anyone "lose" an argument?

The emphasis on individual reason is also a problem, because it constructs a world of fundamentally independent actors, each reasoning to achieve the best outcome for the self. When we define dialogue as a relationship between separate,

DIALOGUE: CONFLICT AND TRANSFORMATION

autonomous individuals, each with private interests, perceptions, and reasons, we create a gap. We imply that, in spite of temporary agreements, the other will always be alien, unknown, and fundamentally untrustworthy. We construct a world in which it is "all against all". In contrast, if we view meaning as a relational achievement, we open doors to new and possibly more useful forms of dialogue.

Toward Transformative Dialogue

If it is necessary to share meaning and share truth,
then we have to do something different.

David Bohm, *On Dialogue*

Let us now approach dialogue as a joint creation of meaning, one in which the parties draw from tradition, but in which they can create new realities and ways of relating. When we have antagonistic traditions, then, we may search for, or create, forms of dialogue that we can call *transformative*. That is, participation in these dialogues would specifically bring the participants into new forms of coordination. These new forms would draw from tradition, but would also enable participants to generate more mutually congenial realities. They would be constructing worlds together, as opposed to separately. Of course, you might say, "well, a nice vision, but how exactly are you going to bring such dialogues about?" As a scholar my first response might be to derive practices from theory. However, an abstract argument never tells you what follows in the concrete circumstance. Thus, in trying to derive practice from theory, one will inevitably favour the kinds of practices that "people like us" prefer, and they will fail to reflect the investments and traditions of those from other backgrounds or cultures. More broadly, it is difficult for any person or group of people to lay out rules or regulations for productive dialogue that are not biased in some way. As critics have shown, even the strict rules of argument and evidence that are used in courts of law – supposedly producing "justice for all" – favour the economically privileged (see, for example, Hunt, 1993; Griggin & Moffat, 1997).

There is another way of proceeding that may offer greater promise. Rather than working "top down" – with authorities laying out the rules or procedures for all – we might better proceed "bottom up". That is, we might move first to the world of action, to cases in which people are wrestling successfully with problems of conflicting realities. By examining these cases we may locate specific actions that often seem to help people in crossing boundaries of meaning. This is not to establish a set of rules for transformative dialogue, but rather a *vocabulary* of relevant actions. On any given occasion we might draw from this vocabulary depending on what is useful for the condition at hand. This is not a vocabulary that can ever be set in stone. For as meanings are transformed over time, and as further voices are added to the mix, the vocabulary itself will grow and change. There are no universal rules for transformative dialogue, because over time, dialogue itself will alter the character of what can usefully be said.

To press forward, let us first consider a single practice, one that has proved successful for many different groups. We can then step back to examine some of its features. What seems to be working here, why is this practice effective, and what might be added? In 1989, Laura and Richard Chasin, Sallyann Roth and their colleagues at the Public Conversations Project in Watertown, Massachusetts, began to apply skills developed in family therapy to heated controversies in the public sphere (see, for example, Chasin & Herzig, 1992).Their practice has evolved over the years and with impressive results. Consider here their attempt to bring together committed activists on opposing sides of the abortion conflict. This is a case in which debate has led nowhere, largely because the opponents construct reality and morality in entirely different ways. What is recognized as a human being for one group is not for the other; what one group considers murder is only a medical procedure for the other. The stakes are high, there is enormous animosity, and the consequences can be lethal.

In the present case, activists who were willing to discuss the issues with their opponents were brought together in small groups. The Project guaranteed that they would not have to participate in any activity that they found uncomfortable. The meeting began with a buffet dinner, in which the participants were asked to share various aspects of their lives *other than* their stand on the abortion issue. After dinner the facilitator invited the participants into "a different kind of conversation". They were asked to speak as unique individuals, about their own experiences and ideas – rather than as representatives of a position – to share their thoughts and feelings, and to ask questions about which they were curious. As the session began, the participants were asked to respond, each in turn and without interruption, to three major questions:

1 How did you get involved with this issue? What's your personal relationship, or personal history with it?
2 We would like to hear about your particular beliefs and perspectives about the issues surrounding abortion. What is at the heart of the matter for you?
3 Many people we've talked to have told us that within their approach to this issue they find some grey areas, some dilemmas about their own beliefs or even some conflicts ... Do you experience any pockets of uncertainty or lesser certainty, any concerns, value conflicts, or mixed feelings that you may have and wish to share?

Answers to the first two questions typically yielded a variety of personal experiences, often stories of great pain, loss and suffering. Participants also revealed many doubts, and found themselves surprised to learn that people on the other side had any uncertainties at all.

After addressing the three questions, participants were given an opportunity to ask questions of each other. They were requested not to pose questions that "are challenges in disguise", but to ask questions "about which you are genuinely curious ... we'd like to learn about your own personal experiences and individual beliefs ...". After discussing a wide range of issues important to the participants, there was a final discussion of what the participants felt they had done to "make the conversation go as it has". Follow-up phone calls a few weeks after each session revealed lasting, positive effects. Participants felt they left with a more complex understanding of the struggle and a significantly more positive view of "the other". No, the participants did not change their fundamental views, but they no longer saw the issues in such black and white terms nor those who disagreed as demons.

The work of the Public Conversations Project is indeed impressive and has led to many additional ventures and variants (www.publicconversations.org). However, the question we must now confront is, what particular features of this kind of dialogue make it so effective? How can we conceptualize these components in such a way that they can be used in other contexts? These exact practices cannot be used in all situations of conflict or difference. But if we can abstract from these practices we have a means of envisioning how we might proceed elsewhere. And also, we should be sensitive to absences within the practice; what might be added to make it more effective? Let us then focus on five important components of special relevance to transformative dialogue.

From Blame to Relational Responsibility

> We have only one person to blame, and that's each other.
>
> Barry Beck, a New York Ranger hockey player, after a brawl at the championship playoffs

In the Western tradition we have a pervasive tendency to hold individuals morally accountable for their actions. We construct persons as sources of their own actions (moral agents), and thus responsible for their misdeeds. There is much about the tradition of individual responsibility that most of us value. Because of a discourse of individual blame we are able to hold persons morally accountable for robbery, rape, murder, and the like. By the same token we are able to praise individuals for singular achievements, humanitarian and heroic acts, etc. Yet, this same discourse of individual blame is divisive. In finding fault with another, we begin to erect a wall between us. In blaming you, I position myself as more intelligent and righteous and you as a flawed being subject to my judgement. You are constructed as an object of scorn, subject to correction, while I remain praiseworthy and powerful. In this way I alienate and antagonize you. The problem is intensified in the case of opposing groups, for each may hold the other responsible: the poor will blame the wealthy for exploitation, while the wealthy will hold the poor responsible for their indolence; the religious conservative will blame the homosexual for corrupting the society, while the homosexual will blame the conservative for intolerance, and so on. Thus, each finds the other guilty, and denies any responsibility. Antagonism is intensified, and the tradition of individual blame sabotages the possibility of transformative dialogue.

It is in this context that we may appreciate the potentials of *relational responsibility* (McNamee & Gergen, 1999). If all that we take to be true and good has its origin in relationships, and specifically the process of jointly constructing meaning, then there is reason for us to honour – to be responsible to – relationships of meaning making themselves. There is value, then, in sustaining processes of communication in which meaning is never frozen or terminated, but remains in a continuous state of becoming. Obviously, mutual blame is an impediment to relational responsibility. How, then, can relational responsibility be achieved in practice? In the case of the Public Conversations Project, the tendency toward blame was simply defined as out of bounds. The conversational tasks didn't permit blame talk, not even disguised as questions. Under normal circumstances, however, we scarcely have control over the rules of conversation. How can one shift from individual blame to a more relationally responsible language in daily life? Although there are no final answers to such a question, we can locate within existing cultural practices several means of shifting the conversation in directions other than individual blame. Consider the following.

Internal others

If I talk too much and too loudly and you are drowned out of the conversation, you have good reason for blaming me. However, if you attack me directly I may counterattack and our relationship may be cooled. One option is to locate within me another voice that is "speaking me" in the situation. If you say, for example, "The way you are talking, I seem to hear your father's dominating voice ...", or "You are really sounding very much like that teacher of yours ...", in effect, you communicate your displeasure, but I am positioned to evaluate my actions as something other than "myself". What we take to be the "core self" is not placed on the defence – the "I" which must be defended at all costs – but rather, you construct me as one who carries many others in my repertoire. It is they who inhabit my undesirable behaviour.

Conjoint relations

If you insult me in the heat of argument, I may justifiably blame you for your abuse and our relationship will suffer. However, I may also be able to locate ways in which it is not you alone who is to blame, but our particular way of relating. It is not you versus me, but *we* who have created the action in question. Remarks such as, "Look what we are now doing to each other ...", "How did we get ourselves into this situation?", or "We are killing ourselves going on like this; why don't we try a different kind of conversation?" all have the effect of replacing guilty individuals with a sense of interdependent relationship.

Group realities

Alice finds Ted so irritating. He is messy, never picks up after himself, thinks only of his needs, and seldom listens to her. Ted can scarcely tolerate Alice's tidiness, her disinterest in his job, and her way of prattling on. They are seething with blame for each other. Yet, there is another vocabulary of possibility here, one that may shift the form and direction of conversation. Specifically, there is a way of seeing ourselves not as singular individuals but as representatives of groups, traditions, families and so on. We may avoid the habit of individual fault finding by considering group differences. For example, if Ted and Alice could speak about gender differences, and trace their undesirable actions to their origin in different gender traditions, they might move into a better space of relating. If we focus on group differences, individual blame recedes in importance.

The systemic swim

When Timothy McVeigh was found guilty of blowing up the Oklahoma City municipal building and taking scores of lives, he was sentenced to death. There was a sense of collective relief; justice was done. Back to work. Yet, consider again the logic of the Militia Movement of which McVeigh was part. From their perspective the national government was destroying the American tradition, trampling on their rights, and forcing them off the land. Justice would be done by revolting against this evil force. In effect, the same logic of blame underlies both McVeigh's crime and our reactions to it. Or to put it another way, there is an important sense in which McVeigh's crime was an extension of the very tradition that most of us support and sustain. This is not to forgive the crime. However, it is to say that the tradition of individual blame is insufficient. We may usefully broaden our vision to consider the ways in which we are all participating in a system that creates outcomes we abhor. It takes more than a single individual to rape, steal, or murder; all of us may contribute to this system from which these actions result.

The Significance of Self-Expression

If we can successfully avoid blame, how can we move dialogue in the direction of change? The Public Conversations work suggests that the sense of self-expression may be vital. Participants in their conversations were each given the opportunity to share views that were important to them. In part, the importance of self-expression can be traced to the Western tradition of individualism. As participants in this tradition we believe that we possess inner thoughts and feelings and that these are essential to who we are; they virtually define us. Thus, if dialogue is to proceed successfully it is critical that the other understands who we are and what we stand for. Moreover, the other must not deny the intelligibility of what is said; the other must listen and comprehend. To paraphrase the logic, "If you do not understand my position – what I think and feel – there can be no dialogue".

Yet, the self-expressions encouraged by the Public Conversations Project were of a very special kind. They asked the participants to speak personally as opposed to using abstract arguments, to tell stories of their own involvement in the issue of abortion. The use of stories is especially significant. There are at least three reasons that *story telling* expressions are desirable for transformative dialogue. First, they are *easily comprehensible:* from our earliest years we are exposed to the story or narrative form, and we are more fully prepared to understand than in the case of abstract arguments. Further, stories can invite *fuller audience engagement* than abstract ideas. In hearing stories we generate images, thrive on the drama, suffer and celebrate with the speaker. One may laugh or cry. Finally, the personal story tends to *generate acceptance* as opposed to resistance. If it is "your story, your experience", then I can scarcely say "you are wrong". However, if you confront me with an abstract principle our common traditions of argument will prepare me for resistance. By flogging me with a principle you set yourself up as a mini-god, issuing commandments from on high. My resentment will trigger a counter attack that you will find equally offensive. "Who are you to tell me that a fertilized egg, detected only microscopically, has a 'right to life?'", "And who are you to tell me that a woman has a right to murder a child in the making?" Stalemate.

It is one thing to express one's feelings or relate life stories; however it is quite another to be affirmed by the listener. Because meaning is born in relationship, an individual's expression alone stands empty. To come into meaning, someone else's affirmation is a required supplement. For example, if you fail to acknowledge what I am saying, or I think you are distorting my story, then I have not truly expressed anything. For you to affirm means treating my words as sensible. Ideally it means locating something within my expression to which you can agree. Such affirmation is important, in part because of the individualist tradition and the belief that thoughts and feelings are individual possessions. As we say, "It is my experience that ...", or "These are *my* beliefs". If you challenge such expressions you *place my being into question*; in contrast, to affirm them is to grant worth to me, to honour the validity of my experience. Further, if one's realities are discounted or discredited so are the relationships from which they derive. If you as reader dismiss social construction-ism as absurd, so are you discrediting an enormous range of relationships in which I am engaged. To embrace an idea is to embrace relationships, and to abandon one's ideas is to undermine one's community.

Of course, you may wonder how affirmation can be achieved when people live in oppositional realities. How can they affirm each other when they do not agree? The work of the Public Conversations Project is informative here. The conversations were effectively staged so as to promote forms of appreciation. Recall that curiosity was invited; to be curious is a signal of affirmation. Similarly, in listening intently to each other's stories the participants expressed affirmation. The stories made sense to them. To "be moved" by another's suffering is a high form of affirmation. The therapist Harlene Anderson speaks to the general importance of affirmation in lis-tening. She proposes that therapy becomes transformative when,

> the therapist enters with a genuine posture and manner characterized by an openness to another person's ideological base – his or her reality, beliefs, and experiences. This listening posture and manner involve showing respect for, having humility toward, and believing that what a client has to say is worth hearing. (1997, p. 153)

Circles for Sharing

The dialogic practices described here are distinctly Western in origin. In working with global differences, ways must be found of incorporating non-Western practices into our vocabularies of relationship. One such practice is the Circle for sharing. Variations on this practice can be found throughout the world, including tribal rela-tions in Africa and Native America.[2] The circle may begin with a ritual that lends value to the event. A prayer, a poem, or silence may all be used. The circular seat-ing of the participants stresses the importance of equality as opposed to hierarchy. To

(Cont'd)

further this emphasis, all participants are invited to speak in turn. Thus, all voices are encouraged to make a contribution to the common consciousness. Although Western dialogic practices emphasize coordination, in circles of sharing each participant may simply "speak the heart". Each is encouraged to express feelings and thoughts around a common concern (for example, tensions in the community, health facilities, a common threat). Often there is an object that is passed from one speaker to another; in some contexts it could be a pipe, in others a walking stick, and so on. When one is holding the object, he or she has the floor; others are invited into a posture of listening and pondering. Throughout the process, there is also an appreciation of silence. A person with the right to speak may speak in silence. If tensions develop between various speakers over the course of sharing, the entire group may be invited into silence. Circles are highly successful in sharing knowledge, ideas, and sentiments. They also invite participants to define themselves as a single unit – we – as opposed to isolated antagonists. And in many cases, the circle process can successfully reduce the intensity of antagonisms.

Coordinating Action: The Challenge of Co-reflecting

In my view one of the most important contributions to the success of the Public Conversations Project stems from the fact that the meetings began with a shared meal. At the outset the participants exchanged greetings, smiles, handshakes. They began to converse in an unplanned and spontaneous way about children, jobs, sports, and so on. They developed rhythms of conversation, eye contact, speaking and listening. In my view transformative dialogue thrives on just such efforts toward mutual coordination. This is primarily because meaning making is a form of coordinated action. Thus, if we are to generate meaning together we must develop smooth and reliable patterns of interchange – a dance in which we move harmoniously together.

Perhaps the most important form of coordination is that of *co-reflecting*. Think here of the participants in dialogue as mirrors. These mirrors may be turned away from each other, or reflect each other. When each reflects the other we have a condition of co-reflection. What does this mean in practice? It does not mean duplicating or agreeing fully with what the other has done or said. Rather, one's words should carry elements or fragments of what the other has said.

If I tell you that I feel we should place a high tax on cars that guzzle gas, and you say, "What's the weather report for tomorrow?" you have failed to include my being in your reply. If you express concern over global warming, you have reflected a theme that is implied in what I have said. You have not necessarily agreed with what I have said, but I can locate "me" in your reply. By reflecting my words, you not only bring us into coordination, but reduce the distance between us. Co-reflection is not only a matter of utterances. On the simplest level, to respond to a smile with a smile (as opposed to a blank stare), to carry the other's tone of voice, to express in one's clothing something of the formality or informality of the other's style, for example, would all contribute to co-reflection. Such moves can be contrasted with actions such as responding to warmth with coldness, to a calm voice with a shrill one, to an informal gesture with formality.

Of course, when differences of opinion are intense, co-reflecting may be more difficult. Most often we tend to find fault with the other's opinions, and in doing so we invite a relationship of *mutual negation*. Under these conditions one of the most useful means of achieving co-reflection is through *linguistic shading*. To shade another's language is to find words that are nearly similar to what the other has said, but slightly change its meaning. Through these slight changes, antagonists can begin to move together. For example, if another says, "you make me angry", a useful shade might be, "I can understand why you are irritated". The latter phrase tends to reduce the hostile intensity of the former. The potentials of shading are enormous, because every substitution of terms also brings with it an array of different associations, new ranges of meaning, and fresh conversational openings. In the midst of conflict to say that there is "tension between us" (as opposed to "hatred") is to reduce the intensity of the difference, and to suggest that harmony can be achieved. There are virtually no limits, other than practical, to the possibilities of shading. At the extreme, any term may possess infinite possibilities for meaning – even to the point of signifying its opposite. For example, "love" can be shaded as "intense attraction", "intense attraction" as an "obsession", and an "obsession" as a "sickness", with the other now serving as "the source of my illness". At the same time, the source of one's illness is "undesirable", and something that is "undesirable" is "not liked"; what is "not liked" is "hated". Thus, when its implications are fully extended, love is hate.

In this light consider again the challenge of coordination. If our statements of opinion contain words that are not fixed in their meaning, then they are open to linguistic shadings that can transform them into something else. Opposing beliefs need not necessarily remain in this condition. Everything that is said could be otherwise, and with appropriate shading could be brought into a state more resembling what is otherwise opposed. On a more practical level, with appropriate shading the most antagonistic arguments can be remoulded in such a way as to allow an exploration of mutual interests. You may oppose someone who favours the death penalty for murderers. However, if "favouring the death penalty" can also mean, for example, a "radical measure against serious crime", chances are you could agree with the other that "radical measures" are sometimes necessary. In such agreement you may locate common ground.

Self-reflection: The Resources of Multi-being

If one's grounding realities are heard and affirmed, and the conversation becomes increasingly coordinated, the stage is set for another significant move toward transformative dialogue: self-reflection. Here recall the earlier discussion of multi-being. One unfortunate outcome of the individualist tradition is that we are defined as *unified egos*. That is, we are constructed as singular, coherent selves. Logical incoherence is subject to ridicule, moral incoherence to scorn. Thus, when we talk with people whose

DIALOGUE: CONFLICT AND TRANSFORMATION

positions differ from ours, we try especially hard to avoid contradicting ourselves. We want our arguments to hang together in a coherent way. Of course, if you do the same, we will soon find ourselves locked in combat. And should the other criticize our position, we may only increase our commitment. As mentioned earlier, no one wishes to lose an argument.

The challenge here is to shift the conversation in the direction of *self-reflection*; toward questioning one's own position. In reflecting on our stand, we can find within ourselves a different voice. We cannot question our statement that "X is true" or "Y is good", unless we can find a voice that questions such positions. Thus, in self-questioning, we relinquish the "stand fast and firm" posture that sustains conflict, and open possibilities for other conversations to take place. Such self-reflection is always possible because we are multi-beings. We carry with us the traces of multiple relationships – in the community, on the job, at leisure, vicariously with television figures. In effect, we have the capacity to speak with many voices. As mentioned earlier, we can find reason to doubt virtually any position we otherwise hold as true, and see limitations in any value we think central to our life. When we are arguing, we suppress these alternative voices. If we could find the means of bringing them to light, we have the means to move beyond our differences and to see new possibilities.

In the case of the Public Conversations Project self-reflection was built in as a conversational requirement. After the opportunity to tell their stories participants were asked about possible "grey areas" in their beliefs, pockets of uncertainty, or mixed feelings. As participants spoke of their doubts, animosities seemed to soften. When a pro-choice advocate expressed doubts in his or her position, the pro-life advocates could hear themselves speaking; and vice versa. Distances were reduced, polarities diminished. Possibilities were opened for other conversations to take place than defending differences.

Extending this line of reasoning, conflict specialists, Pearce and Littlejohn (1997) often employ *third person listening*. When two groups are battling over their differences, a member of one of the groups may be asked to step out of the conversation and to observe the interchange. By moving from the first person position, in which one is arguing for his or her standpoint, to a third person stance, the individual can observe the conflict with other criteria at hand. For example, from the third person position one can ask, is this a productive way of relating, what improvements might be made? In other conflict work, participants have found it useful to introduce opinions or beliefs of groups that differ from both the antagonists. Thus, for example, a conflict between two religious groups (for example, Christians versus Muslims) takes on an entirely different character when many alternative religions are made salient (for example, Judaism or Hinduism).

The Co-creation of New Worlds

Each of the conversational moves outlined above may reduce animosities and open the way to a more mutually appreciative interchange. However, none of them actively promotes the development of new realities. None of them creates a new and mutually shared construction of the real or the good. Needed here are what might be called *imaginary moments* in the dialogue in which participants join in visions of a reality not yet realized by either. These imaginary moments shift the orientation of the participants from combat to cooperation. They move toward a common purpose, and in doing so redefine each other as *us*. Perhaps the simplest way of moving toward a shared reality is through locating a common cause. That is, antagonists temporarily suspend their differences to locate an effort they both support. For example, battling spouses may join together against an intruding do-gooder, or feminist radicals and conservative traditionalists may join in a crusade against pornography. More broadly, there is nothing so unifying for a country than to be threatened by invasion. Social psychologists have long spoken of these commonalities in terms of *superordinate goals*.

Yet, while finding a common cause is often useful, it doesn't necessarily create a new and lasting reality. Some of the most interesting work of this kind has been carried out by Harvard psychologist Herbert Kelman (1997). Kelman's concern is with the Israeli–Palestinian dispute, the origins of which go back to the birth of Political Zionism at the end of the nineteenth century. Violence first erupted in the 1920s, and conditions have been unstable ever since. In the worst case, both sides deny the other's right to identity and to property, and bloodshed results. It was not until 1991 that a concerted peace initiative began, and while sometimes successful, animosities are often resumed.

Beginning in the 1970s, Kelman began a series of workshops that have continued over the years to bring together influential leaders from both sides. The "problem solving workshops", as they are called, are voluntary, private, and unrecorded. Similar to the Public Conversations Project, there is an attempt to curb tendencies for mutual blame and polemic critique. Likewise, there is an emphasis on "here-and-now experiences" – as opposed to abstract principles – as a basis for appreciating the position of the other. Influenced by the negotiation model discussed earlier, participants are challenged to find a win–win solution to the conflict. Most important for present purposes, the participants are encouraged to "work toward a shared vision of a desirable future" (1997, p. 214). Conversation about "who is in the wrong" is thus replaced by joint deliberation on what kind of world they might build together. As Kelman finds, "the process of producing these ideas contributes to building a new relationship between the parties, initially between the negotiators and ultimately between the two societies as wholes" (ibid, p. 218). We shall say more about the practices for building common realities in the following chapter.

Reflection

The idea of transformative dialogue has been very important to me both professionally and personally. In a world in which the globalizing process brings opposing realities into increasingly sharp conflict, new resources for communication seem essential. I have also found these practices very useful in my daily life. Conflict is always immanent in the classroom, and it is virtually endemic to family life, and indeed to any close relationship. Here I have found it especially useful to seek ways of affirming the other, and locate other "selves" within that are not so antagonistic to the other. At the same time, I don't want to be too optimistic about realizing the potentials of transformative dialogue. I find too many cases where a transformative move is possible and desirable, but I simply can't bring it off. For example, I am all too skilled in blaming others if something goes wrong; in this sense I am not relationally responsible. I fail to use an option that would avoid driving a wedge between me and the other. This suggests significant limits to the kinds of academic treatments represented in this book. Analysis is helpful in stimulating ideas about new lines of action; but analysis it is not sufficient. It is one thing to have new resources and another to put them into action. We need to experiment and practise together to become more skilled in dealing with differences, so that we can "just naturally" move toward mutual coordination.

Notes

1   Illustrative of the many social science contributions to understanding inter-group hostility are Brewer, M. (2003). *Intergroup relations*. Buckingham: Open University Press; Ashmore, R.D., Jussim, L., & Wilder, D. (2001). *Social identity, intergroup conflict, and conflict reduction*. New York: Oxford University Press; Levy, S.R, & Melanie, K. (2008). *Intergroup attitudes and relations in childhood through adulthood*. New York: Oxford University Press.
2   For a more complete account of Circle practices, along with many other forms of dialogue, see Bojer, M. Roehl, H. Knuth-Hollsen, M., & Magner, C. (2008). *Mapping dialogue, essential tools for social change*. Chagrin Falls, OH: Taos Institute Publications.

Further Resources

Argumentation, Negotiation, and Mediation

Arrow, K.J., Mnookin, R.H., Ross, L., Tversky, A., & Wilson, R.B. (Eds.). (1995). *Barriers to conflict resolution*. New York: W.W. Norton.

Bercovitch, J., & Rubin, J.Z. (Eds.). (1992). *Mediation in international relations: multiple approaches to conflict management*. New York: St Martin's Press.

Bush, R.A., & Folger, J.P. (1994). *The promise of mediation*. San Francisco, CA: Jossey-Bass.

Dawson, R. (2000). *Secrets of power negotiating*. Franklin Lakes, NJ: Career Press.

Folger, J.P., & Jones, T.S. (Eds.). (1999). *New directions in mediation*. Thousand Oaks, CA: Sage.

Goshgarian, G., & Krueger, K. (2005). *Dialogues: an argument rhetoric and reader*. London: Longman.

Shell, G.R. (2006). *Bargaining for advantage: negotiation strategies for reasonable people*. New York: Penguin.

Winslade, J., & Monk, G. (2001). *Narrative mediation*. San Francisco, CA: Jossey-Bass.

Dialogic practice

Barnett, W.B., & Littlejohn, S.W. (1997). *Moral conflict: when social worlds collide*. Thousand Oaks, CA: Sage.

Baxter, L.A., & Montgomery, B.M. (1996). *Relating, dialogues, and dialectics*. New York: Guilford.

Bojer, M., Roehl, H., Knuth-Hollsen, M., & Magner, C. (2008). *Mapping dialogue, essential tools for social change*. Chagrin Falls, OH: Taos Institute Publications.

Isaacs, W. (1999). *Dialogue: the art of thinking together*. Strawberry Hills, NSW: Currency.

Strauss, D. (2002). *How to make collaboration work*. San Francisco, CA: Berrett Koehler.

Yankelovich, D. (2001). *The magic of dialogue: turning conflict into cooperation*. New York: Touchstone.

6

A PROFUSION OF PRACTICES

The constructionist dialogues now leap from the pages of books and into the practices of society. Not only do practitioners contribute importantly to constructionist ideas, but they also use them in their work. Many constructionist scholars believe that social change should be the major consequence of their work. If language gains its meaning through its use, as outlined in Chapter 1, then the meaning of constructionist theory should be realized in society more generally. In the present chapter I want to expand the range of relevant practices. In particular, l will touch on constructionist practices in four significant areas: education, therapy, organizational change, and scholarly writing. I select these primarily because the activities are fascinating, and in some cases dramatic. At the same time, most of these practices can be adapted to other contexts. I, for one, have found many of the practices discussed in this chapter useful in my relations with family, friends, and colleagues. Perhaps you will as well. With regret, page limitations prevent me from describing many other exciting ventures in practice. However, at the end of the chapter I have included a bibliography earmarking some of these developments.

Education: Collaboration and Community

We frequently speak of "the rewards of a good education". Yet for many people the actual experience of "schooling" is (or was) harrowing. It is replete with fear of failure, anxiety over competition, and excessive boredom. These common experiences are largely owing to two premises that pervade most educational systems: first, it is commonly held that the chief purpose of education is to move students from a condition of ignorance to one of knowledge – replacing mere opinion, mistaken thought, and blind faith with solid fact and logical reasoning. On these grounds experts determine what is true and valid, and thus the curriculum that students must master. Students themselves have no voice in such matters. The second major premise is that education is aimed at improving the minds of individual students. Thus, to ensure that each individual mind properly masters what is true – that each student "possesses knowledge" – frequent assessment is essential. The individual must ultimately "measure up" or be punished. Students are thus confronted with curricula that have little intrinsic interest, and are subjected to frequent examinations of their ability to repeat the truth as determined by the experts.

This orientation toward education has scarcely gone without criticism. One of the harshest critics, Paulo Freire, calls the traditional model *nutritionist* (Friere, 1985). Knowledge is essentially treated as "healthy food", educators are the dispensers of the nutrients, and students are defined as needing food. Ultimate authority in this case lies with those engaged in knowledge production, for example, scientists and scholars. These experts "dispense the truth" that students will ultimately be "fed". Next within the hierarchy are educational experts such as curriculum designers, who package the knowledge into educational units. Following are administrators and bureaucrats who select among these units. Teachers enter only at the end, as instruments to dispense the educational nutrients to the students. Students are like barnyard animals, expected merely to munch the knowledge down. As critics point out, the teacher is disempowered by such an arrangement. When they are required to teach a standardized curriculum, they lose their capacity to reflect on larger educational issues and to create educational experiences tailored to their particular situation. They are *deskilled* (see, for example, Wise, 1979; Apple, 1982). Students have even less power. Their creativity and innovation are stifled (see, for example, Mehan, 1979).

Social constructionist ideas lend support to Freire's critique. As previous chapters have discussed, what we take to be true or rational (knowledge) is an outgrowth of communal relations. There is no truth beyond community. Further, the concept of the individual mind is deeply problematic, both intellectually and politically. If both truth and mind are placed in doubt, then so is the hierarchical structure of education with certain classes determining what is true and rational for all others. What does social constructionism have to offer as an alternative? In general, the emphasis shifts from individual knowers to the collaborative construction of knowledge. Such collaboration should include students as well. The concern with collaboration also draws attention to the quality of relationships, between teachers and students, among students, and between the classroom and the surrounding world. And finally, for the constructionist, the ultimate concern is with the pragmatics and politics of education. That is, what does education equip one to do (other than recite), and who benefits (or loses) as a result of these new capacities? There is much to be said about such issues; the following is but a sample.

Collaborative Classrooms

On the nutritionist view, the teacher possesses the knowledge and students are presumed to be ignorant. Thus, teachers tend to favour monologue (for example, lectures, powerpoint presentations) over dialogue. For the constructionist, however, the advantages of this monologue are highly limited. To be sure there are times when informative lectures are valuable. However, monologues are also impersonal; they speak to no one in particular. Further, the students' skills are not engaged; they simply take notes – or stop paying attention altogether. Finally, there is little opportunity for the students to absorb the subject matter in their own terms. There is little opportunity for them to take what is useful from the material in ways that can speak to their needs and interests; more colloquially, they fail "to own the material".

Many educators now turn from monologue to dialogue as the chief instrument of education (see, for example, Wells, 1999; Verella, 2002; Applebee, 1996; Simon, 2003). This does not mean debate, where there are winners or losers, or Socratic dialogue in which the teacher has the correct answer and simply leads the class to a foregone conclusion. Rather, they emphasize: 1) expanding the domain of participation, and especially of finding ways of preventing a few opinionated students from dominating, 2) reducing control over the direction of a conversation, so that student passions are on a par with those of the teacher, 3) crediting students with respect as opposed to correcting them, and 4) replacing the goal of Truth with the possibility of multiple realities. The dialogic orientation discourages "canned lectures" and lock-step powerpoint presentations, and encourages teachers to risk their status as ultimate knowers. Teachers are invited to thrust themselves into the collective process, and to make whatever they bring to the table relevant to the unfolding conversation.

There are many ways to foster classroom collaboration. In his college English classes, educator Kenneth Brufee establishes *consensus groups*. These groups are challenged with answering in their own terms questions posed by various texts; questions that also invite students to challenge the received opinions of authorities in the field. However, the groups must reach a consensus that they are willing to share with other groups. This means that the group must learn how to deal with internal disagreements – sometimes extreme – in generating an opinion. They must learn how to live together in a world of conflicting realities. In Bruffee's terms, "Being required to arrive at a position that the whole group can 'live with' can hurl students headlong into the knottiest and most sophisticated issues of almost any discipline" (1993: 41). Other scholars have taken a more radical step in establishing collaborative writing practices (Ede & Lunsford, 1990; Forman, 1992; Reagan et al., 1994; Topping, 1995). Rather than viewing students as lone authors, the attempt is to pool the talents and resources. Students participate in brainstorming, information gathering, organizing, drafting, revising, and editing a written work. Where one student may be good at conceptualizing the project, another may have innovative insights, or a fluid writing style. Others may excel at adding visual materials or even keeping the group in good spirits. And through such collaboration, students become models for each other. They teach each other ways of approaching the challenge of writing.

Extending these efforts further, educators also seek ways to bring the classroom into collaboration with the surrounding world. The specific hope is to link the classroom to the world in such a way that education becomes more relevant to societal life. Service learning programmes are among the most popular means of bringing schools and communities together. Here students can gain credit from working within the community, participating for example in a tutoring programme for underprivileged children or apprenticing with a voluntary agency or community service. There are more specialized cases. For example, students in the Foxfire programme work with each other, with their teachers, and with professionals from outside the school to publish magazines and books, and produce radio and TV programmes. For such projects, the classroom materials function as resources to be used in the service of outside projects (see Boyte & Evans, 1986). Barbara Rogoff and her colleagues (2001) developed a programme bringing together students, teachers, and adults from the community. Their belief was that learning occurs most effectively through the interested participation of learners together. Thus, teachers joined with both parents and students to plan the curriculum and classroom activities. Even the youngest students were brought into the discussions. Parents also served periodically as co-teachers. On occasion, students from different grades were brought together for co-learning sessions. The result was the successful creation of a broad community of learners, all drawing from the adventure in collaboration. In other cases, internet communication is established between classrooms around the world; students in far-flung locales talk over problems of global significance (see, for example, Taylor & Saaranen, 1994).

Final Examinations as Dialogue

In my position as a professor, I have never been happy with the practice of giving final exams at the end of term. It was not simply the unfairness of placing so much importance on the student's performance in that brief, stressful, and artificially contrived circumstance.

It was also the way in which examinations so often favoured memorization and regurgitation. As a teacher, the primary question for me was whether students left my courses with increased abilities to engage in educated dialogue about the subject matter. Could they use the course material to do things with others? I thus began to experiment with an alternative to final examinations, namely group dialogue. In one of the most successful experiments, I arranged for small groups of students to work together on a given problem or topic. They were challenged to carry out a weeklong dialogue on e-mail. Prior to the event, the students worked together to generate what they felt were the criteria of good dialogue. Here it is interesting to note that these criteria are quite different from those valued in the individual performance. Where the good essay on an exam is one that is logically coherent and leads to a single best conclusion, the effective dialogue is one that entertains multiple ideas and does not close down voices of possibility. As my students also told me, in a good dialogue the participants care for each other.

The entire transcript of the dialogue is turned in to me at the end of the week. Individual grades (required by the Registrar) are a combination of my evaluation of the dialogue as a whole (based on their criteria), in addition to individual efforts. Upon further enquiry, I learned that most students find these dialogues wonderfully energizing, and intellectually stimulating. They are also enthusiastic about the form of interchange. There is no pecking order; no one dominates the conversation; all contribute. All feel welcome, and at the close of the conversation, they will often congratulate or thank others for their contributions. They are also eager for me to read their work, for they properly sense that I will learn about their interesting ideas. And I do...

Polyvocal Expression: Communicating to All

Consider what it is to "write well". From the early grades to graduate school, one is typically taught to identify the topic, define the key concepts, maintain clarity, make logical links between sentences and paragraphs, illustrate key points with evidence, and so on. In certain respects, these demands stem from the belief that processes of sound reasoning are universal, and that good writing should not only reflect these processes, but also help bring them to fruition. As we find in the Foreword of the *Harper handbook of college composition*, "Learning to think clearly and learning to write correctly, clearly, effectively, appropriately are worthwhile intellectual processes valuable not only in composition classes but in all other our teachings of the mind" (Wykoff, 1969, p. 26). Yet, as constructionist ideas suggest, the idea of universal reason – an inward process manifest in our spoken and written words – is deeply flawed. Moreover, from a political standpoint, why should the standards of "intelligent writing" be set by an elite and privileged minority? And finally, on a pragmatic level we must ask, for whom is this form of educated writing most effective? Given the vast heterogeneity of world peoples, and the increasing move toward globalization, when, where and for whom is the "standard" form of writing ideal? Further, as critics suggest, the standard style prepares one for a subservient role in society, for reporting clearly, economically, and instrumentally

A PROFUSION OF PRACTICES

to one's superiors. This is not the style of an inspiring conversationalist or the agent of social change, but a writer of reports.

It is in the context of such questioning that constructionist educators search for means of facilitating polyvocality, that is, ways in which students can develop multiple voices, forms of expression, or ways of putting things. The move toward polyvocal expression may begin early. Younger students may be encouraged to write about themselves in their "own voice". These autobiographical narratives help students to recognize the validity of their own forms of expression (see, for example, Phillion & Connelly, 2005).

On the university level, Patti Lather (1991) has developed a fascinating innovation. Typically college teachers ask students to write about a subject – to describe, explain, and analyse, for example, prejudice, bird migration, the French Revolution, etc. However, as Lather reasons, this kind of writing is essentially *realist*: that is, it presumes the existence of the subject matter beyond social construction. Thus, after an exercise in realism, Lather asks students to add another form of writing to their report. This time they are asked to write in a *critical* frame, approaching the topic from a politically invested standpoint. They may ask, for example, who benefits when we call something "prejudice"; whose voice is left out of this way of constructing things? Lather then asks for a third writing on the topic, this time *deconstructive*. Here students might explore the multiple interpretations that can be made of the subject matter, the many vantage points from which it might be seen. Further, students might question their own categories of understanding; why these and not others? Finally, Lather asks for a writing that is more personal or *self-reflexive*. Students are asked in this case to write in more innovative, non-linear, expressive ways about the subject and their engagement in it. In the end, Lather believes, by engaging in these different writing forms, students are not only freed from the demands of a realist mode of representation, but that they can also generate multiple perspectives and speak effectively to multiple audiences.

Other teachers achieve polyvocality by having students write to different audiences. A paper on environmental protection, for example, could be written first for fellow students, then for an environmental protection agency, and finally for an opposing group. With each new piece of writing new ways of expression are developed, and new ways of seeing the issues. Many believe that the written word itself is waning in its importance; print technologies are giving way to visual media: film, video, computer graphics, photography and the like. In this case, educators emphasize expanding voice through training in visual media (see, for example, Ulmer, 1989). What would it be to communicate about important issues in art or photography or dance? Could a three-minute segment on YouTube not have greater consequences than a tightly reasoned term paper?

Critical Deliberation

In the nutritionist tradition, knowledge is "cooked up" within the various disciplines – biology, economics, history etc. – and fed to the needy student. As the constructionist points out these "bodies of knowledge" are primarily the vocabularies of particular professional groups. In this sense the student is invited (or forced) by the curriculum into an alien territory. He or she must master its ways, while the aliens sit in judgement. Yet, this process seldom encourages the student to ask questions about the territory from the outside, from other vantage points or value positions. The student *learns history* without being encouraged to ask, for example, "whose history is this?", "why are we talking about kings and wars and wealth, and not the conditions of the people or the treatment of the minorities?" Further, the student is seldom encouraged to "see it another way", to generate alternative histories or alternative views of "what really happened". For the constructionist, then, a premium is placed on the means for increasing critical deliberation. How can students be encouraged to challenge the authoritative discourses from alternative standpoints, to discuss assets and liabilities, and to create alternative interpretations? Toward these ends students may be encouraged to help in planning the curriculum, to bring their own experiences to bear on the classroom material, and to collect materials that might help them to reach their own conclusions.

For many educators, the first important steps toward critical deliberation were taken in discussions of the *hidden curriculum*, a phrase referring to beliefs and values that lie implicitly but unrecognized in the subject matter. For example, if the history of the United States was written as a narrative of progress, i.e. life became better and better, such a history places an unrecognized value on our lives today, while looking at the values, traditions, and investments of the past as somehow inferior. These hidden beliefs and values often reflect the interests of particular classes or ethnic groups, namely those responsible for the curricula. Critics propose, for example, that mainstream curricula systematically prevent members of subordinate groups from achieving academic success, and reinforce and justify the values of dominant groups (see Aronowitz & Giroux, 1993). Working-class students, in particular, are encouraged to be obedient, passive, and unoriginal (Bowles & Gintis, 1976).

Resonating with these concerns, educators have developed *pedagogies of liberation*, educational practices that encourage students to engage in active critique, empowering them to join in determining their futures as opposed to simply swallowing the truth as given. One active exponent of liberation pedagogy, Henry Giroux (1992), points to ways in which teachers can demystify the official curriculum by revealing the evaluative choices implicit in them – the gender, class and racial biases, for example – and then encourages students to explore alternatives to these mainstream beliefs. As Aronowitz and Giroux advocate, we must "make a firm commitment to cultural difference as central to the meaning of schooling and citizenship", and we must, "educate students for the maintenance and defense of the principles and traditions necessary for a democratic society" (1993, p. 12 and p. 34).

Although these are indeed important steps toward critical pedagogy, further development is needed. First, as even the liberation educators acknowledge, there is a danger that the teacher will now simply impose another ideology on the students. For example, how does the liberationist treat those who do not believe in a critical evaluation of their beliefs, for example, orthodox Hindus or Muslims? In effect, a liberation curriculum may run the same risks of hierarchy and suppression as those institutions under attack. The second challenge for liberationist pedagogy is that of going beyond critique. Most liberation curricula emphasize a critique of the dominant traditions, but do little to help students appreciate positive aspects of existing traditions. There is little emphasis on building from dialogue to more positive futures.

These educational developments – in collaboration, polyvocal expression, and critical reflection – are only a few of those favoured by constructionist dialogues. The interested reader may wish to consult some of the resources at the chapter's end. At the same time, you will find many of the constructionist themes in education are amplified as we now turn to therapeutic practice.

Therapy as Social Construction

Kibby frequently visited my yard when I was a child; he seemed anxious to play with my brothers and me; with broad smiles he joined in our games whenever he could. However, we couldn't understand the strange language he seemed to speak, so we couldn't communicate very well. And besides, Kibby was a grown man. My mother encouraged us not to play with him. As everyone said, "Kibby is a bit off". In Gaelic there is a word for people like Kibby, which translates into English as "with God". The modern mental health industry has abandoned all these everyday understandings, and replaced them with a battery of more than 400 terms for "mental illness" (see Chapter 2). Enormous research projects attempt to locate the causes of these "diseases" of the mind, and enormous hours are devoted to testing the efficacy of various therapies in treating the mentally ill. Increasingly the mental health professions will turn to pharmaceuticals as a means for cure.

For the social constructionist these mammoth "scientizing" efforts are not only misguided, but the results are often damaging. Whatever is the case with Kibby and others like him, "illness" is only one of many possible constructions. To presume that he is ill is also to invite practices of "cure". If he was not defined as ill, practices other than "curing" might be set in motion. This *medical model* for treating unusual people also informs most traditional forms of therapy and counselling. People report a problem – depression, violence, fear, incapacity, and the like – and the therapist's job is typically to locate its roots or causes and to remove them, thus bringing relief (cure). In psychoanalysis the causes may be located in the deep recesses of the mind ("repression"); for the Rogerian they may reside in the person's lack of self-regard; the cognitive therapist will trace them to defective thinking. In all cases, it is the individual patient or client who "has the problem", and the therapist who serves as the expert. The therapist is said to be "value neutral", simply doing his or her job of finding the source of the problem and working toward a solution.

Social constructionism challenges these approaches to therapy, along with the medical model on which they are based. Why, it is asked, must we construct the client as "having an illness"; are there useful alternatives; on what grounds can the therapist claim superiority in understanding; and is any form of therapy really value neutral? Thirty years ago therapeutic experts claimed homosexuality to be a form of mental illness, and developed many means of cure. For example, electric shock treatment was used to desensitize men to the nude images of other men. Is this a cure, or a form of political intolerance? And today isn't the very attempt to rid the society of depression based on a vision of an ideal society in which everyone is happy? As it was said in Poland, "If you aren't depressed you must be stupid". How we describe people's problems and what we count as cure are political in consequence (see, for example, Szasz, 1984; Unger & Crawford, 1992).

This is not to condemn the medical model and all traditional therapy. All are exercises in social construction. Rather, it is simply to raise important questions about the taken-for-granted worlds they construct, and to enquire into the potential of alternatives. It is this exploration of alternatives to which many therapists now turn. Informed by constructionist concerns, new practices have emerged. Such constructionist-based therapies generally share the following characteristics.

Focus on meaning Traditional therapy is focused on cause and effect realities – finding the cause of a depression, of marital violence, and so on. In contrast, for the constructionist therapist there are no pre-fixed facts, such as depression and violence, and the assumption of cause and effect is viewed as but one way of looking at things. Nothing must be taken for granted. Rather, the "facts of the case" are inevitably constructed, ways of making the world intelligible by persons in relationship. This does not make "the facts" any less significant. However, it is not essential to "get clear" on what is really happening. Rather, the emphasis is placed on the constructed meanings by which we make our way through life. For example, the psychiatrist will be very curious about a patient's feelings toward her parents; the Rogerian will explore a client's feelings about himself. In contrast, for the constructionist therapist "feelings" are not facts in the world that we must know about; they are conversational objects. Thus, rather than necessarily probing the individual's "mental condition", the constructionist therapist will be more concerned with the individual's particular way of constructing him/herself. Typically the individual is given great latitude to speak, thus possibly revealing preferred constructions. The challenge is then to work with these constructions toward change.

Therapy as co-construction The traditional therapist adopts the stance of expert on such matters as depression and marital conflict. It is this presumption of expert knowledge that allows the therapist to dictate the direction of therapy, often acting as a sleuth who will solve the problem and then guide the patient toward insight. The constructionist therapist realizes, however, that his or her theories of depression, conflict, and so on, are the byproduct of a particular professional community. Not only do these constructions lose their privilege over all others, but it is asked, are they are useful to the client? For example, most professionals view the discourse of romantic love as suspicious, and the discourse of the Holy Spirit as misleading mythology. Yet, for the vast share of the culture these are living and significant ways of constructing the world. As it is said, the constructionist therapist must enter the consultation with a stance of *not knowing* (Anderson & Goolishian, 1992), that is, of avoiding the tendency to impose his or her pre-fixed theories. It is important to remain curious and open to the client's vocabularies of meaning. In this case it is not the therapist's task to "lead the way to knowledge" but to collaborate with the individual (or family) in generative conversations. The therapeutic relationship is thus one of collaborative meaning making.

Focus on relationship Most therapies are preeminently concerned with the mental state of the individual; with emotions, thoughts, motives, the unconscious, and so on. For the constructionist therapist the reality of the mind recedes in importance, and is replaced instead with a concern for relationships. It is from relationships that meaning is generated and patterns of action become reasonable or desirable. Thus, the focus on the interior of the mind is often replaced with an exploration of the networks of relations in which the individual participates. With whom is meaning made, and what are the outcomes? Who are the chief participants – either present or past, actual or fictitional, present or virtual? In family therapy the troubled person is often said to be the *designated patient*, in this way pointing to be the possibilities that the family has selected a scapegoat for problems that are built into the family relationships.

Value sensitivity Unlike the traditional therapists, the constructionist realizes that there is no value neutrality in the therapeutic relationship. Every intervention will favour some form of life, while undermining others. The therapist who favours heterosexuality closes the door on homosexual options; in favouring the client's industrious productivity the joys of hedonism remain unrealized; "empower" the male and the female loses options. Given this sensitivity to the politics of therapy, some therapists establish practices that specifically support a given cause. Feminist, gay, and lesbian therapists are particularly noteworthy. However, most therapists are less singularly committed, and will simply make their values known to their clients when political issues are especially relevant.

Given these orienting attitudes, there is great latitude for practice. Let us consider three of the most popular forms of constructionist therapy.

Solution Focused Therapy: the Power of the Brief Encounter

What if there were no problems? What if all the anguish and hopelessness that bring people into therapy had no basis? There is a sense in which constructionist thought prompts just these kinds of question. It is not that we don't confront difficult problems in our lives, problems that are very real and often very painful. However, the constructionist reminds us, these realities are constructed; problems are not "out there" as realities independent of us, but come to be what they are by virtue of the way we negotiate reality. This insight has prompted many therapists to give up traditional practices of exploring and solving people's problems. More importantly, it is argued, when clients are encouraged to talk at length about their problems, to explore them in detail, to express all their feelings about what is taking place, the results may be harmful to the person. All the problem talk – the exploration of misery – serves to make "the problem" increasingly real, increasingly objective. Why go on endlessly exploring the ravages of early childhood, for example, when this reality is made increasingly salient, vivid, and depressing as a result of its very exploration? Are there other visions of reality, therapists ask, with more promising outcomes?

In this context, many therapists seek ways of refocusing the therapeutic conversation. One widely shared practice is called *solution focused*. One of its central exponents, Steve De Shazer (1994), proposed that it is far more helpful to talk about solutions to problems than the problems themselves. Solution talk is often full of hope and promise. Thus, for example, rather than exploring the depths of a client's depression, it is more helpful to talk about ways the client might "return to school", or "get some day-care help for the children". Further, deShazer proposes, clients are helped when the conversation shifts to their goals and their potential resources for achieving these goals. Talk about depression, for example, creates the reality of depression; to speak of one's aspirations and strengths brings more promising possibilities to light.

One significant means of prompting solution-oriented talk is called *the miracle question*. Here the therapist asks the client, "If a miracle happened tonight and you woke up tomorrow with the problem solved, what would you be doing differently?" The question is intended to provoke discussion of positive courses of action, bringing attention to bear on what might be changed here and now to create a more positive future. The question invites the client to suspend problem language and to focus on "life beyond the problem" (Freedman & Combs, 1993). Through their questions and comments therapists may also help their clients to move away from an *either/or* mentality – in which they frame the world in terms of "either this" action or way of life *or* "that" – for example, heterosexuality *or* homosexuality, career *or* marriage, being firm *or* being compliant. In its place they encourage a *both/and* orientation, where clients are helped to envision multiple and even contradictory ways of living life (Lipchik, 1993). Other therapists make use of a language of *on-track* (Walter & Peller, 1992), in which clients generate a set of goals, and a conception of the steps needed to achieve them. This conceptualizing of life in terms of "a track into the future" can also be facilitated through *scaling questions*, that is queries into "how, on a scale of 1 to 10, do you feel you are doing?" (Berg & deSchazer, 1993).

In contrast to traditional therapies, the emphasis on solutions and positive action often reduces the amount of time clients spend in therapy so much so that the phrase "solution focused therapy" is often used interchangeably with *brief therapy*. Solution focused (or brief) therapy dramatically and refreshingly contrasts with the problem-centred preoccupation of most traditional therapies. The fact that it reduces the number of client hours also makes it desirable for both clients and health care providers. However, such therapy is not without its limitations. For many, it remains too closely cemented to an individualist model in which it is the individual who can simply decide on goals and work to achieve them. The relationships in which the person is embedded seem to play too little a role. Others resist the strong emphasis on goals, arguing that the view of life as a "set of tasks", or accomplishments – complete with measures of progress – does not leave enough room for spontaneous, joyous, and sensual play. Perhaps the most pervasive doubt is in the efficacy of brief therapies with severe problems. A solution focus may be satisfactory for the kinds of day-to-day problems common to life, but what about severe, long-term disturbances? (For a counter-argument, see Duncan et al., 1997.)

A PROFUSION OF PRACTICES

Narrative Therapy

For many constructionist therapists the concept of narrative plays a pivotal role. Recall from Chapter 3 that narrative or story telling is a major means by which we make ourselves intelligible to each other. It is the narratives in which we live that tell us where we have been in our lives, and where we are going. When we suffer, it is reasoned, it is often because of the narrative we have constructed for our life. The anguish of marital break-up is primarily the result of a couple's narrative in which marital happiness was their principal goal; it is when we live in a narrative of becoming successful that we feel remorse when we fail. In this sense, effective therapy enables clients to *re-story* their lives, to conceptualize their life trajectories in new and more livable ways.

How is such change accomplished? In their groundbreaking work *Narrative means to therapeutic ends*, Michael White and David Epston (1990) describe various means by which they help clients to re-story their lives. One of the most interesting innovations is what they call *problem externalization*. For example, it is traditional to view problems as inhering within people, for example, "my depression", "my impotence", or "my hostility". For White and Epston, a major step toward re-storying is taken when the person – along with family members and friends – can separate the problem from the self. The attempt is fundamentally to *externalize* the problem, moving it from "in here" to "out there". To illustrate, a six-year-old boy, Nick, was brought to therapy by his parents. Nick's problem was essentially one of impulsive defecation. Not only was Nick prone to unpredictable "accidents", but he would streak his "poo" on walls, smear it in drawers, roll it into balls and plaster it around the house. The habit seemed uncontrollable and the parents were beside themselves. The challenge was to separate the "poo problem" from Nick himself. A new name was thus developed for the problem, Sneaky Poo. Now the therapist and the family could talk about how Sneaky Poo would try to trick Nick into becoming his playmate, how Sneaky Poo was preventing Nick from having friends, and how the parents could join Nick in resisting Sneaky Poo's tricks.

A second challenge of narrative therapy is to locate *unique outcomes*, that is, events of the case not included in the original story. These unique outcomes can be used as the basis for building a new story. For example, Nick's family entered therapy with a convincing story of "Nick's problem". However, as they began to see the problem as external to Nick, new facts began to emerge. The family began to recall times in which Nick had resisted Sneaky Poo, or they had worked together against Poo's advances. These unique outcomes then became the basis for creating a new story, one in which they were banding together to resist an outside threat, and Nick could be helpful. This new narrative offered a new and more successful direction for the family.

Many narrative therapists are also deeply concerned with the politics of therapy. As they see it, many of the problem-making narratives people bring into therapy are the result of power relations in society more generally. Recall Foucault's critique of the way dominant discourses function to subjugate people (Chapter 2). For example, if I believe I am depressed, and I must find a cure for my depression, I am thus a victim of a story created by the mental health professions; I have swallowed the medical model in which I am the one who requires a cure for my deficiency. For many narrative therapists, a major emphasis is placed on helping people escape the imprisoning grasp of the dominant discourses of the culture, to create "an insurrection" against injurious but prevailing assumptions (White & Epston, 1990, p. 32). For example, in one of Michael White's many letters to his clients, he wrote,

Dear Sue,

Bulimia has required a great deal of you. Its survival has been expensive to you. It has required you to operate upon yourself. It has required you to reject yourself. It has required you to subject yourself to a constant evaluation of your body and your person. It has required docility ...

In this letter, first note how bulimia is externalized. Sue is not bulimic; rather, bulimia is her enemy. Further, White is trying in this letter to help Sue challenge the dominant discourse of the psychiatric profession that looks at bulimia as a disease, and defines the patient as needing a therapist for a cure. He is challenging her to throw off the reins of the widely advertised view that "thin in beautiful", and to explore an alternative conception of self and future that is more uniquely hers.

The focus on narratives has been enormously useful for many therapists. It brings into sharp focus issues of meaning, opens a rich space of exchange between the therapeutic and academic communities, and lends itself to fostering political consciousness. However, many also see opportunities for further development. For example, narrative therapists often focus on the individual's self-narrative – "my story". In this way they lend support to an individualist view of the world in which autonomy and self-direction are privileged over relationship. There is also the question of whether people do indeed live within the structure of single narratives – *a* life story? Do we carry with us only a single story of our lives? Is it not more likely that we harbour multiple narratives, employed on different occasions for different audiences? And what is it to say that we live by or within our narratives? It is perhaps more useful to see narratives not as directing our actions but as forms of action themselves. Or, recalling the Chapter 3 discussion of narrative, that we *use* narratives to carry out relations with people. If this is so then the question shifts from re-storying to how people can mobilize multiple narratives in action.

Polyvocality: Expanding Possibilities

A third focus of constructionist therapy is captured by the term *polyvocality* – or multi-voiced. Here the major emphasis is on expanding the number of interpretations or constructions bearing on the reported problem. The aim is not to locate "the solution" or "the new story", but to generate a range of new options. Rather than a single restricting view of the self or the situation, the client now has many possibilities. Multiple paths to action are thus opened.

For some therapists, the challenge is to release the individual's own potentials for polyvocality. Recall here the discussion of multi-being (Chapter 5), in which the focus is on the many potentials people carry with them, but which are often suppressed in any given relationship. For the therapist the challenge is to give these suppressed voices room for expression. As therapist Karl Tomm (1998) has put it, the attempt is to access the voices of *internalized others*. For example, when a client begins to talk about his problems, the therapist might ask them if he can locate another voice within, a voice that would construct the world in a different light or with different possibilities. If a client suffered from feelings of hatred toward his father, is there a voice that is "not being heard" and might express compassion or admiration? In one variation on this theme, therapists Peggy Penn and Marilyn Frankfurt (1994) have clients write letters to others, living or dead. As they reason, in addressing another – in writing to them so you can be heard – you also address yourself through their anticipated reaction. In writing letters one can thus set in motion new *internal dialogues* that can lead in new life directions. One client, Mary, was furious with her ex-husband; she felt she had been victimized by him and there was nothing good she could say about him. The therapists asked if he had any good qualities at all, and Mary finally admitted that he was a good father to their son. Thus Mary was encouraged to write a letter to him – which might or might not be sent – telling him of her opinion of him as a father. The result of the writing was not only a shift in the way she talked about him, but as well the capacity to see herself in other ways than a victim.

Polyvocality can also be achieved by adding contributors to the conversation. One of the most popular practices, *the reflecting team*, was introduced by Norwegian family therapist Tom Andersen (1991). Families often develop shared constructions of themselves, their members, their problems, and so on. Andersen wished to avoid any radical challenge to these realities; in his view, change is most effectively brought about through a process of comfortable conversation. Thus, while a family talks with an interviewer about its problems, a team of therapists (often three in number) observe the interview. While the interview takes place each team member carries on "a private dialogue" about what is taking place. Later in the session, the team joins in the discussion with the family; together they discuss their views of what took place. To avoid speaking from a dominant position, reflecting team members speak with uncertainty, "I am not sure … maybe … one could think of …", etc. Instead of attempting to rule out competing views, a both/and orientation prevails: "You can see it this way … and another possibility is …". Then, the family members are asked to comment on the discussion of the reflecting team. They are asked, for example, "Is there anything from what you have heard you would like to comment on, talk more about …?" As therapists find, the reflecting team loosens the grip of professional authority, and invites a dialogic, open-ended search for useful meanings. "Therapy becomes both client and therapist focussed, with an emphasis on what fits … at any particular moment in the conversational life of the treatment system" (Lax, 1991, p. 142).

From Diagnosis to Dialogue

Therapy based on the medical model emphasizes expert diagnosis. And it is the therapist who serves as the expert. As we have seen, this orientation not only constructs all problems from a single, disease-oriented perspective, but also eliminates all voices other than the therapist's. A fresh alternative has been developed by Finnish therapist, Jaakko Seikkula, and his colleagues (2006). Here the attempt is to expand the range of voices participating in the construction of the problem and its treatment through a practice of *dialogic meeting*. Dialogic meeting practices were developed in the context of a psychiatric hospital, in which the number of diagnosed schizophrenics had been growing, along with the number of occupied beds in psychiatric hospitals, and prescriptions for medication. Replacing the expert psychiatrist and the singular diagnosis as the beginning of therapy, the Seikkula group developed teams for each case. Teams might be composed of several professionals, representing different points of view, along with family members, close friends, colleagues from work, and other stakeholders. The designated patient also participated in conversations with the team. The meetings encouraged a full expression of opinion and insight, and ultimately a commitment from the group to work together for change. Meetings of the group might be daily in the case of severe episodes, but tapered off over time. The group also remained flexible, with conversations shifting in emphasis as the situation changed. New courses of action could be put in place at any time. There was no attempt to "pin down" the problem, to get to the bottom of it. Rather, the point was to sustain the process of dialogue across shifting circumstances. The results of such dialogic meetings were dramatic: there was a reduction in the number of diagnosed schizophrenics, a decrease in hospitalization, and a lowered number of drug prescriptions.

Collaborative Means to Therapeutic Ends

Therapists have long worked with groups of clients, but group therapy is traditionally used as a means of "healing" the individual participants. The therapist remains in the traditional role of expert, and offers insight and guidance where useful. More recently, however, therapists are exploring the potentials of groups to work together in achieving change. In this way the group participants have a greater say in determining the direction of change, and the therapist acts primarily as a facilitator. The following cases will illustrate the potentials of this movement.

First, a group of family therapists in Houston, Texas brought together homeless women, many of whom suffered from drug abuse and domestic violence.[1] The women were encouraged to talk about their experiences, to share stories about success and failure, and more generally to talk about their lives. Over time, the group grew into a small and caring community. By seeing themselves as a community, they also acquired the ability to look ahead with determination to change their conditions. With the help of the therapists, they ultimately issued a manifesto. As evidenced in the following excerpt, these women collectively drove a stake into future ground:

We the participants of Building Safer Families, agree to be responsible for building better lives for ourselves and our families. We will do this through

(Cont'd)

prioritization, acceptance, and respect for our uniqueness, with unconditional love, lack of judgment or criticism, and living our values for our families and ourselves ... We hope to maintain independence and interdependence through this group.

A second illustration is provided by the London therapist Eia Asen and his colleagues (2002). They take on one of the most difficult problems in contemporary therapy, namely, self-starvation among adolescents (diagnosed as anorexia). Such problems are particularly complex because they often involve anxious parents, and tense relations between them and their children. Rather than focusing on the anorexic individual, Asen and his colleagues have developed a multi-family programme, in which families meet together, and talk over problems, issues, and successes in dealing with eating problems. In this way, both the families and the diagnosed individuals find themselves with others who "understand" and support. Moreover, by exchanging stories of what works and what doesn't, the participants gain new insights into practices they might try in their own families. These meetings are often removed from the antiseptic and largely irrelevant context of the hospital, and take place within family homes. The results of the collaborative work among the families prove far more promising than most individual treatment programs.

Making Meaning in Organizations

> Both organizations and sensemaking processes are cut from the same cloth. To organize is to impose order, counteract deviations, simplify, and connect, and the same holds true when people try to make sense.
>
> *Karl Weick, Sensemaking in Organizations*

As this quote from Karl Weick suggests, the process of generating realities is as central to organizations as it is to personal or family well-being. Without people coming together and determining what they are doing and why it is important, there is no organization. And unless its participants coordinate their actions around a set of specific goals, the organization will fail. Weick also reflects the views of numerous organizational specialists now concerned with the capacities of an organization to navigate within the multiple and ever-changing sea of realities favoured by present-day communication technologies and the press toward globalization. Yet, it is one thing to theorize organizations in social constructionist terms, and another to generate effective practices. Perhaps the first significant move in the direction of practice was developed in Gareth Morgan's revolutionary work, *Images of organization* (1998). Here Morgan made it clear that the way we describe organizations – and thus our ways of living within them – is through metaphors. To say that you work in an organization says little about your life there. If you say that the organization is like a *machine*, we now have an image of your activities. We wouldn't be surprised to find the organization divided into specialty units, in which each person has a specific function (like the parts of an automobile), and responsibilities are clear-cut. In contrast, if you say the organization is like a *team*, we would anticipate more collaborative kinds of relations. There would be more sharing of responsibility and a pulling together. In effect, the social construction of the organization is closely related to its practices.

In recent years constructionist ideas have flourished in organizational studies, and, with them, numerous innovations in organizational life. I focus here on two excellent illustrations, one concerned with decision making and the other with leadership.

Collaborative Decision Making

One of the earliest metaphors of the organization was military in nature. Here large numbers of men were mobilized under conditions of do or die. From the Peloponnesian wars to the present, the primary form of the military organization was, and continues to be, the pyramid. The plans of battle are developed at the peak of the structure, orders are disseminated downward through the various functional units (for example, infantry, supplies, medical), and large numbers of men execute the orders. When there is a failure to follow orders, it is the men who are executed. Information relevant to the success of the plans is conveyed upward through the pyramid to those in command.

The metaphor of the pyramid continues to inform much organizational practice today. Often referred to as "command and control", the view dominated the organizational sphere for much of the twentieth century. However, recent decades have been marked by growing discontent. There is a certain inflexibility in command and control organizations. In the contemporary world, conditions often change very rapidly, and if one is simply waiting for decisions – often from those who know little about the local conditions – opportunities may pass; losses may be inflicted. Even within military circles there are doubts about the practical adequacy of command and control. As they move into the field, ground forces inevitably encounter surprises, and battlefields often border on chaos. In this case, troops must improvize or die.

> I presented a pack of coloured cards to my good friend, Prof. John Rijsman, and asked him to arrange them in such a way that they represented the typical organization of today. The result was the traditional pyramid you see here. However, what makes this especially interesting is the way in which Rijsman demonstrates the full interdependency of all the parts, and the fact that those at the top only remain there by virtue of the strength of those at the bottom.

From a constructionist standpoint, it is useful to view the organization as a *field of conversation*. Wherever people are conversing, they are co-constructing meaning. When decisions are made in the offices of high-ranking managers, they seldom reflect the realities and values shared in the conversations of the average worker. The decisions are imposed on this group from outside. Such announcements as, "the budget must be cut by 10 per cent", "we are closing down the unit", or "the benefits package

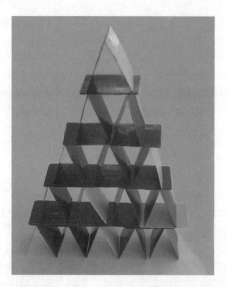

Figure 6.1   Responding to my request to use playing cards to illustrate the modern organization, Professor John Rijsman from Tilburg University created this structure. The hope was to emphasize interdependency.

is going to be different", are often thrust into the workers' conversations as if they had commanding presence. Yet, whatever is communicated from above is always open to interpretation, and those at the top do not control these interpretations. Orders from elsewhere may be accepted as reasonable and desirable; however they may also be constructed as "mindless", "insensitive", "punitive", or "misguided".

The major challenge of decision making, then, is to mobilize collaborative processes in the service of effective action. Establish dialogues that include as many participants as practicable. Facilitate conversation that mobilizes collective meanings, values, and motives. No decision should be an alien arrival into the conversations that make up the organization. They should carry the voices of the participants. When decisions are implemented, they will represent logics and values in which the participants are already invested. Further, by including organizational members in decision making, and affirming their contributions, their investment in the organization may blossom. So decision making will promote the kind of buy-in that is vitalizing for the participants? As Stephen Littlejohn and Kathy Domenici put it, "People support what they create" (2000, p. 53).

A good example of collaborative decision making comes from the CEO of a large subsidiary of an international corporation. He was ordered by his parent organization to reduce the costs of the subsidiary by 15 per cent. He was staggered by the order, and deeply frustrated when he found the demand was non-negotiable. He considered hiring a large consulting firm to advise him on how to make such reductions. Laying off employees was the most obvious solution, but which ones, and when? It was also clear that if he announced a downsizing decision to the organization, he would duplicate the kind of treatment he had received from the parent organization. Such an announcement would foster an atmosphere of fear, anger and dejection.

With his staff, another route to decision making was devised. The organizational members were enlisted into the decision-making process. They would provide inputs into how the organization could be made more cost effective. Thus, 14 discussion groups were created, each composed of members from all sectors and levels of the company. The groups gathered information, conducted interviews, and periodically met with other relevant teams. External consultants were hired only to orchestrate the complex process of communication and scheduling. Ultimately the discussion groups generated a seven-volume summary containing their research and recommendations. The executive board ultimately accepted more than 75 per cent of the teams' recommendations. Down-sizing was minimal; ingenious re-organization was everywhere in evidence; the economic goal was achieved, and enthusiasm was maximal. Virtually all sectors of the company were represented, and when the final policies were announced, broad acceptance and high morale prevailed.

Appreciative Enquiry: From Conflict to Community

Life in organizations is dynamic. Everywhere within the organization – from the mailroom to the boardroom – participants are continuously generating their local sense of the real and the good, who is doing what to whom, and whether it is good or bad. Realities and moralities will necessarily conflict, and with such conflicts often come suspicion, animosity, a loss of morale, and more. These are the daily challenges of organizational life, and when the tensions are high they can deeply hinder organizational functioning. Traditionally, both managers and consultants have approached these problems as realists. That is, the problems are treated as "things", the equivalent, let's say, of an organizational illness. Further, because they are problems they demand solutions – cures for the illness. Certain people are fired, pay is raised or lowered, new positions are created, new training procedures are put in place: all are common treatments for the problems ailing the organization.

Yet, recall from the discussion of therapy, problems exist primarily because of the way reality is negotiated. There are problems if we agree there are problems, and any situation may be defined as problematic or not. Informed by this logic, organizational specialist David Cooperrider and his colleagues at Case Western Reserve University have developed an approach to decision making that is now used throughout the world. It is especially useful in cases of conflict. The approach, called *appreciative enquiry*, sprang from the conception of "the appreciative eye" in art. As it is said, within every piece of art one may locate beauty. Is it possible, Cooperrider (1996) asked, that within every organization – no matter how embroiled in conflict – one can also find beauty? This beauty was defined as "the positive core". And if beauty can be found, can organizational members use it as a basis for envisioning a new future?

The specific means of fostering appreciation draws from the constructionist emphasis on narrative. People carry with them many stories and within this repertoire they can typically locate stories of value, wonderment, and joy. Within an organization these stories are valuable resources, almost like money in the bank. To draw them out and place them in motion, proposed Cooperrider, is to stimulate new visions for the future. In sharing these stories confidence is generated that, indeed, the vision can be realized. In effect, appreciative narratives unleash the powers of creative change.

To illustrate, a world-famous cosmetic company suffered from gender conflict. Women in the company felt poorly treated by the men, seldom acknowledged, sometimes harassed, underpaid, and overworked. At the same time, their male counterparts felt unfairly blamed, and accused the women employees for being unnecessarily touchy and hostile. Distrust was rampant; there was talk of litigation and the company began to falter. The executives then asked Cooperrider and his associates for help. In particular, the executives felt, there should be a code of good conduct, a set of rules specifying appropriate conduct in gender relations, along with penalties for misconduct. Yet, for Cooperrider this orientation simply objectified "the problem", and such a "solution" would still leave a strong residue of distrust.

An appreciative enquiry was thus carried out in which a call went out to all employees. Then, small groups of men and women employees met together; their specific challenge was to recall some of the good experiences shared within the company. Were there cases where men and women worked very well together, had been effective and mutually regarding; were there times when men and women had especially benefited from each other's contributions; what were these experiences like and what did they mean to them as employees? The employees responded enthusiastically to the challenge and numerous stories were recalled about past successes. The groups then shared and compared their stories. As they did so a discernible change began to take place: the animosities began to melt; there was laughter, praise, and mutual regard. In this positive climate, Cooperrider then challenged the employees to begin imagining the future of the company. How could they create together the kind of organization in which the experiences they most valued would be central? How could they make the organization the kind of place that could bring them this kind of joy? As the participants entered this discussion of the future they also began to think of new practices – policies, committees, social planning, and the like. Optimism and a high sense of morale prevailed. "The problem" drifted into obscurity as positive plans were set in motion. The company began to thrive.

From Leadership to Relational Leading

The subject of leadership has a long history. Indeed, there are currently over 200,000 English language books currently treating this subject. Do we not know quite enough; is there anything to add? From a constructionist standpoint, we are barely at the beginning. This is so because the vast bulk of leadership writing locates the source of leadership in the individual as opposed to collaborative relations. From the "great man" theories of yore, to more recent accounts of great leaders' characteristics and the qualities of successful managers, most theories presume that leadership potential resides within the single person. Yet, from a constructionist standpoint, none of the qualities attributed to good leaders stands on its own. Alone, one cannot be inspiring, visionary or insightful. A charismatic leader is only charismatic by virtue of others who treat him or her in this way; remove the glitter in their eyes and there is no charisma. An "intelligent decision" is only intelligent if there are agreeable collaborators. To say anything about the leader as a single human being is to miss the process of relationship responsible for the very idea of "the leader".

The vision of "great leaders" is largely the result of the command and control structures inherited from the past. As we have seen, in a world of rapid flux, such structures are inflexible. Further, there is no individual leader who is equipped to know all there is to know about any particular issue. Anyone who surfs the waters of Google or the blogosphere knows that even for the narrowest topic, there is no end to opinion, pro and con. In this context, new practices of leadership now emerge. Abandoned are the endless and often contradictory lists of what it takes to be a good leader. In their place we find an increasing emphasis on collaboration, empowerment, dialogue, horizontal decision making, sharing, distribution, networking, continuous learning, and connectivity. In effect, there is a deep and pervasive concern with communal process. As a constructionist, it is useful to replace the concept of leadership with that of *relational leading*. While leadership denotes the characteristics of an individual, relational leading refers to the ability of people in the relationship to move with engagement and efficacy into the future. It is not the single individual who is prized, but the process that animates relations and mobilizes people to action. Here we see that leadership is not the task of a specific individual. Rather, it emerges from the way people carry out relationships – the ordinary ways in which we treat each other.

What are the daily practices most important in relational leading? The following are among the top candidates.

Positive Sharing

Mobilizing for the future thrives on a broad sharing of visions, values and insights. Ideally the workplace should be one in which people are free to express their ideas, and there should be ample time for talking about more than the immediate demands of the job. And in addition, the greater the number of voices entering the conversation, the greater the sophistication of the outcome. Each person is a resource of information and value. Thus, more will be known about possibilities and potentials. Further, there will be greater ownership of the outcome by the participants. A senior official may move an organization to action, but members may simply act with wooden conformity. To be treated like a pawn, one behaves like a pawn. Positive sharing means mutual respect for all views.

Adding Value

Engaged activity does not begin with the proposal of a single individual – "I think it would be a good idea to…" – but with others injecting value into the proposal. "That's interesting", "I never thought of that before", "That just might be what we need", "Let's explore that idea". All these inject value into the other's view. Affirmations of this sort are not the only means of adding value. Positive elaboration is also a powerful motivator. "Let's think about what this would mean to…", "I can see where this might help to…". As an idea is elaborated – detailing

A PROFUSION OF PRACTICES

its potential, adding useful information, overcoming possible hurdles – an inviting future takes shape. Frontal critique should be avoided. It is not simply the individual making the proposal who will suffer, but the entire climate of conversation.

Image Building: Metaphor and Narrative

Through positive sharing, a rich and sophisticated range of possibilities can emerge. When value is added, there is motivation. However, there is also a need for organizing the ideas, giving them greater shape and dimension. At this point, two of our old friends are often called into play: *metaphor* and *narrative*. As mentioned earlier, a metaphor can be a powerful tool for integrating diverse ideas and coordinating people's actions. Relational leading importantly depends on the participants locating a guiding metaphor for the future. To seize upon the metaphor of the organization as *family* would have different implications for action from envisioning it as *lean and mean*. It is important that there is broad agreement on the major metaphor. If the members of an organization believe they are participating in a family, and top management decides to downsize the organization, there is trouble ahead. You don't kick out a family member for economic reasons.

Consider the use of narrative: members of an organization are often content with the status quo. At least they know what to do and they are reasonably effective in doing so. Why change? One important reason is because of the lure of a new direction. Yet, moving from one condition to a new and more valued one requires having a story. The story that will explain the significance of this new state, and show the way. "This new plan will help us to serve our customers better, and we can make it work by …", "We are barely getting by in our present situation, and if we move in X direction we can really prosper". Compelling narratives will also situate the present condition in the context of the past. For example, there is the common, "from the ashes' narrative, in which "we came from nothing, but look at us now", or the "rebound" story, in which "we were brought low, but we are resilient". Each story situates the present in terms of past, and in doing so propels us into the future.

These three contributions to leadership – positive sharing, adding value, and image building – are not reserved for any single person or position. Ideally they should be encouraged throughout the organization. This is not to say that all are equal in their potential for contributing. Those occupying senior positions in the traditional organization are often advantaged. Their connections are more numerous, their experiences are richer, and their words may carry more weight. Their skills may be especially useful in affirming, encouraging, creating narrative and metaphor.

Leadership as Empowerment: The Case of Helping Others

We traditionally distinguish between leaders and followers, and in organizational life as elsewhere, it is the leader who counts. Leadership training is a major enterprise; contrastingly, there are no training programmes in "followership". Yet, the turn to collaborative practices in organizations has stimulated many innovations in the concept of leadership. One innovative view defines the leader as one who helps others to bring about valued ends. This empowerment vision is nicely illustrated in the work of Theresa Bertram, the director of a very large and successful gerontology foundation. The foundation was responsible for the well-being of a large community of elders, including the delivery of 800 meals-on-wheels. The organization had reached stagnation point, maintaining an effective programme but with little zest or imagination. Theresa then found herself struck by the views of a consultant who spoke of tapping the latent energies of the staff and board members. As a result she held a retreat in which the staff and board could have a new form of conversation: rather than taking care of business as usual, they told stories and shared dreams of new and better futures. The result was not only an electrifying of their relationships, but as well the realization that the very people to whom they provided care might also harbour such stories. In fact, as Bertram described, the foundation's care taking might actually be draining creative participation from the population they were supposed to be serving.

A further programme was then initiated in which the elderly could share their hopes and dreams for their life in the community. These stories were brimming with innovative ideas. A new policy resulted, one that granted to the community of elders a major voice in how they were to be served. The result was a profound change in the vitality of the retirement community members. They became deeply involved in planning. They developed special events, invited their own speakers, managed their budget, selected menus for social occasions, and more. The bus schedule, formerly arranged by the programme director, was now unscheduled and the bus made available to take the residents wherever they wished to go. Among the selected destinations were the town meetings. Here the elderly became a political voice, expressing their views on basic issues confronting the community at large.

Scholarship: Writing as Relationship

To be able to dance with one's feet, with concepts, with words: need I still add that one must be able to do it with the pen too?

Friedrich Nietzsche, *The Gay Science*

Have constructionist ideas influenced the scholarly practices of scholars themselves? That is the subject of this final section. Of course, this question is partly answered by all the work treated in the preceding chapters. New ideas and research practices have certainly flourished. Yet, the concern here is not with the content of what is written, but with the very practice of writing itself. For the constructionist, scholarly work not only communicates content; it also invites a relationship with the reader. If this is so, our attention is drawn to what our traditional forms of expression do for our relationships. What forms of relationship are welcomed by a given way of putting things, what is discouraged? Or more broadly, what kind of world do we build together through our forms of writing? To illustrate, consider your reactions as you read the following example of sound academic writing:

It is also predicted that when silence (in communication) occurs, it will be differentially assigned, on the basis of the rules as either (i) a gap before subsequent application of Rules 1(b) or 1(c), or (ii) a lapse on the non-application of Rules 1(a), (b) and (c), or (iii) a selected next speaker's significant (or attributable) silence after the application of Rule 1(a). (Levinson, 1983)

By traditional standards this is an example of first-class scholarship. I suspect as well that you found yourself repelled by the excerpt. There are many reasons for this. First, the style of writing tends to create a sense of distance between you and the writer. The writing is formal; it doesn't allow you to glimpse the human behind the formalisms. The writing is flat and emotionless; it is difficult to feel a resonating passion with the author. The style also positions the author as the knower – rational and insightful – and you, the reader, as ignorant. The writing is flawless, thus thrusting the reader into doubt regarding all of his or her own failings. One feels embarrassed to hazard a response. Finally, such writing is elitist. It speaks only to that minority who are educated to take their place in a priviledged community.

The constructionist thus asks, "Why must we sustain the classic tradition of good scholarship?" If we wish to replace alienation with trust, live within communities of care, and share with those outside of these communities, how should we communicate? What alternatives can be created? It is in this context that many are inspired by a new range of scholarship that now blossoms. Consider the following examples.

Embodied Writing

Among the most popular forms of experiment are those attempting to abandon the god's-eye view of traditional scholarship, and to revel within the work of a warm-blooded author, complete with passion, biases and shortcomings. The author may lace his or her writings with "street talk", for example, ethnic idioms or humour. Here is an illustration from a technologies scholar, Rosanne Arquette Stone, writing about the way in which she came into the field of scholarship on technology:

The first time love struck was in 1950. I was hunkered down in the dark late at night, on my bed … helping a friend scratch around the surface of a galena crystal that was part of a primitive radio. We were looking for one of the hot spots, places where the crystal had active sites … and could detect radio waves. There was nothing but silence for a long, long time, and then suddenly the earphones burst into life, and a whole new universe was raging in our heads … I was hooked. Hooked on technology. (1996, p. 3)

One senses the presence of a flesh-and-blood author in the text, someone with whom you might strike up a conversation. She is not "up there" speaking down to you as reader, but speaking "with" you.

The Polyvocal Author: Who am I?

In traditional scholarship the author strives for coherence; it is only by having a fully rational and coherent argument that all critics can be silenced. Embodied writing does bring the reader into a more intimate relationship with the author, but the style still carries traces of the author as a singular, coherent self. More conscious of themselves as multi-beings (Chapter 5), scholars search for the means of inserting multiple voices into the text. After all, such scholars suggest, they have mixed feelings about most issues, shouldn't these be expressed? Thus, at times, the inserted voices may even comment critically on what is being put forward. These additions not only create the sense of a polyvocal author, but invite the audience to have an opinion (or many opinions).

Michael Mulkay's sociological treatise *The word and the world* (1985) is a classic in polyvocal writing. For example, after introducing the volume in a traditional scholarly voice, Mulkay introduces two additional voices, the "reader" and the "private author" behind the scholarly presentation.

The "reader" says, "Well, Author, that's very interesting, but I'm not sure that I properly understood all that the Book has to say. Is it possible for me to ask (the author) some questions?" (p. 7).

The private author responds, "I'm afraid not. That's the trouble with books, research reports and so on; once they've made their statement, that's it. ... There's a built-in rigidity in such texts" (p. 8).

After the private author chastises himself for his rigid control of the text, the reader again interrupts, "*Surely that's your fault, not his! You're the author. The Book will say anything that you want him to*" (p. 9).

Where is Mulkay *himself* in all this? Everywhere of course.

Invocation: Stirring Voices

As we saw, traditional scholarly writing often seems dead, without passion or inspiration. To breathe life into the writing, and thus to move the reader to a richer and more engaged experience, some scholars invoke the voices of non-scholarly traditions of writing – from genres of the novel, poetry, spiritual writing, mysticism and more. Not only are many readers stirred by the writing, but also such genres eradicate the misleading distinction between "straight talk" – objective and rational – and "rhetoric". The reader is continuously reminded of the constructed character of the writing.

To illustrate, consider first a fragment from *The unspeakable*, a work by the iconoclastic anthropologist Stephen Tyler, in which he places the idea of rational systems under attack:

> In the end, the idea of system is only nostalgia for the wholeness analysis has killed and thinks to resuscitate by reinfecting the corpse with the germ that killed it. "System" is another name for the great spider goddess. (1987, p. 54)

Tyler's metaphors are colourful and strong. Adding to such metaphors the cadence of the black ministerial tradition, Afro-American Studies Professor Cornell West writes powerfully on contemporary race relations:

> The accumulated effect of the black wounds and scars suffering in a white-dominated society is a deep-seated anger; a boiling sense of rage, and a passionate pessimism regarding America's will to justice. (1994, p. 28)

A PROFUSION OF PRACTICES

Then arguing against a nihilistic response to such anger,

Nihilism is not overcome by arguments or analyses; it is tamed by love and care. Any disease of the soul must be conquered by a turning of one's soul. (ibid., p. 29)

As West's writing suggests, writers can draw from more than one tradition in their work. They can use different genres that may speak in different ways to different audiences. An excellent example of such combinations is found in *Death at the parasite café*, by the innovative sociologist Steven Pfohl. Throughout the text Pfohl adopts several different personae, including that of the traditional scholar, an editor, a translator, himself as autobiographer, RadaRada, Jack O. Lantern, and Black Madonna Durkheim. Here is Black Madonna responding to Pfohl as a young sociologist seeking help for field research in the southern United States:

Listen Yankee! ... No more closed-circuited white male revolutionaries! No more saviors! No more pimps! We've enough of those already. But some other form of parasite? Perhaps? Maybe in time you'll discover and re-mask yourself in a form that's more power-reflexive. But that's an expensive proposition and (k)not one that will make you feel complete. But ... pack up your belongings and let's dance. (1992, p. 47)

Toward Open Expression

Experiments in representation are scarcely limited to the domain of writing. If "what there is" makes no demands on how we talk about it, there is no strong reason for privileging words above other forms of expression. In large measure the privilege given to words in the academic world derives from the traditional belief that reason (logical thinking) resides in the head of the individual, and that words are its chief expression. Previous chapters have treated the flaws in this belief. More importantly, much is gained by opening the door to the full range of human expression – to art, poetry, music, dance, drama, comedy, film, multi-media, and more (for further appreciation of this work, see Knowles & Cole, 2008). In doing so there is a vital expansion in the audience. For example, in today's culture, film has a much larger audience than academic writing. If so, why should the scholar not use film? In this way, scholars would also avoid the criticism that their work is elitist, speaking only to a privileged few. Further, drama, art, dance, and so on, can invite a fuller form of audience participation. If you are given a crossword puzzle, you simply fill in with words; if the puzzle is also humorous, you are also laughing; if the letters were also in the form of bricks, you might have to carry them to their location. In effect, as the form of communication changes, so does your degree of participation. The challenge, then, is to communicate in ways that invite a full range of participation – visual, auditory, viscoral, and so on.

Increasingly, scholars are rising to the challenge and experimenting with alternatives to traditional reporting. For example, for her dissertation, Deborah Austin interviewed African Americans after the Million Man March in Washington, DC. Then, together

Figure 6.2   Photo representation

In their work with teenage girls marginalized through drug dependency, Marie Hoskins and her colleagues at the University of Victoria, Canada, gave each participant a camera to reflect on their lives in a visual way. This photo above was taken by a 17-year-old girl, B, who was attempting to abandon a life of heavy meth use and street involvement. The photo was taken in response to the overarching question: Who am I at this time in my life? Dialogues that accompanied this image included issues of inclusion/exclusion, isolation and loneliness, and a yearning for the childhood she felt she never had. Note the playground just beyond the fence.

with one of the participants, they wrote a poem to give expression to some of the key sentiments. This is a small excerpt:

> Africans are the same
>
> wherever we are, she says to me
>
> matter-of-factly
>
> I look at her and smile
>
> and ask
>
> like a good researcher should
>
> How so?
>
> I can't explain, she says
>
> with that voice that sounds
>
> like the rush of many rivers. (1996, pp. 207–8)

A PROFUSION OF PRACTICES

And if poetry, why not music? For example, in one innovative case, psychologists Glenda Russell and Janis Bohan were incensed at an amendment to the Colorado state constitution that removed the right of people to sue an organization that discriminated against them on the basis of their sexual orientation. Using themes and statements taken from the transcripts of interviews with those opposed to the legislation, the researchers helped to create a five-part oratorio, *Fire*. The score was written by a professional composer and sung by a choir. This work was so powerful that it was subsequently produced as a television documentary that was aired on public television.

Reflection

Although trained as a traditional social scientist – observing and reporting on the "facts of the matter" through constructionist dialogues – I have come to see the narrowness of such activities. If my scholarly research is not so much truth telling as it is an action in the world, then I have had to ask for whom are my actions significant? Is it enough simply to write books and papers for academics and students? Such questioning has changed my life. Increasingly I find myself working with therapists, organizational consultants, community change specialists, religious groups, and peace builders. One result of this sea-change for me has been to join in the creation of the Taos Institute, a community of scholars and practitioners working at the intersection between social constructionist theory and a range of societal practices.[2] Our special attempt is to enrich social practices, and especially practices that help to overcome barriers and conflict, and to enable people to construct more viable futures. However, even my day-to-day practices of teaching have been dramatically altered as a result of constructionist dialogues. For example, some of my most exciting moments as a teacher in recent years have resulted from abandoning the traditional practice of assigning a term paper. Rather, I have asked my students to use any other means available or interesting to them to give expression to ideas suggested to them by the course. Students have made videos, painted pictures, written short stories, put on photo exhibits, done stand-up comic routines, written and performed theatre pieces, created multi-media presentations, produced musical scores, and, in one case, danced the "term paper". During the final examination period the class meets to share their work, and it is one of the most joyous, intellectually stimulating, and fulfilling experiences of the year.

Notes

1 Feinsilver, D., Murphy, E., & Anderson, H. (2007). Women at a turning point: A transformational feast. In Anderson, H., & Gehart, D. *Collaborative therapy: relationships and conversations that make a difference.* New York: Routledge. Consult this volume for many additional cases of collaborative work outside the therapy room.
2 For additional information see http://www.taosinstitute.net

Further Resources

On Therapy as Social Construction

Anderson, H. (1997). *Conversation, language, and possibilities*. New York: Basic Books.
Anderson, H., & Gehart, D. (Eds.). (2007). *Collaborative therapy, relationships and conversations that make a difference*. New York: Routledge.
Friedman, S. (1993). *The new language of change: constructive collaboration in psychotherapy*. New York: Guilford.
Gergen, K.J. (2005). *Therapeutic realities*. Chagrin Falls, OH: Taos Institute Publications.
Monk, G., Winslade, J., Crockett, K., & Epston, D. (Eds.). (1997). *Narrative therapy in practice*. San Francisco, CA: Jossey-Bass.
O'Hanlon, W.H., & Weiner-Davis, M. (1989). *In search of solutions: a new direction in psychotherapy*. New York: Norton.
Paré, D.A., & Larner, G. (Eds.). (2004). *Collaborative practice in psychology and therapy*. New York: Haworth.
Rosen, H., & Kuehlwein, K.T. (Eds.). (1996). *Constructing realities, meaning-making perspectives for psychotherapists*. San Francisco, CA: Jossey-Bass.

On Organizational Process

Anderson, H., Cooperrider, D., Gergen, K., Gergen, M., McNamee, S., & Whitney, D. (2008). The appreciative organization (2nd ed.). Chagrin Falls, OH: Taos Institute Publications.
Barret, F.J., & Fry, R.E. (2005). *Appreciative inquiry: a positive approach to building cooperative capacity*. Chagrin Falls, OH: Taos Institute Publications.
Boje, D.M., Gephart, R.P., & Thatchenkery, T.J. (Eds.). (1996). *Postmodern management and organization theory*. Thousand Oaks, CA: Sage.
Brown, J.S., Denning, S., Groh, K., & Prusak, L. (2004). *Storytelling in organizations*. London: Butterworth Heinemann.
Gergen, K.J., & Thatchenkery, T.J. (1997). Organizational science in a postmodern context. *Journal of Applied Behavioral Science*, 32, 356–77.
Grant, D., Oswick, C., Hardy, C., Putham, L. (Eds.). (2004). *Handbook of organizational discourse*. London: Sage.
Weick, K. (1995). *Sensemaking in organizations*. Thousand Oaks, CA: Sage.

On Education

Barkley, E., Cross, K.P., & Major, C.H. (2004). *Collaborative learning techniques: a handbook for college faculty*. San Francisco, CA: Jossey-Bass.
Bruner, J. (1996). *The culture of education*. Cambridge: Harvard University Press.
Cumings, R. (Ed.). (2008). *Wiki writing: collaborative learning in the college classroom*. Ann Arbor: University of Michigan Press.
Freire, P. (1978). *The pedagogy of the oppressed*. Harmondsworth: Penguin.
Jennings, T.E. (Ed.). (1997). *Restructuring for integrative education*. Westport, CT: Greenwood.
Walkerdine, V. (1990). *Schoolgirl fictions*. London: Verso.

Other Practices in a Constructionist Frame

Best, J. (Ed.). (1995). *Images of issues: typifying contemporary social problems*. New York: Aldine de Gruyter.
Fox, C.J., & Miller, H.T. (1995). *Postmodern public administration*. Thousand Oaks, CA: Sage.

Lorber, J. (2002). *Gender and the social construction of illness.* Thousand Oaks, CA: Alta Mira.

Mank, G., Winslade, J., & Sinclair, S. (2008). *New horizons in multicultural counseling.* Thousand Oaks, CA: Sage.

Neimeyer, R. (2001). *Meaning reconstruction and the experience of loss.* Washington, DC: APA Publications.

Newman, F. (1996). *Performance of a lifetime.* New York: Castillo International.

Paré, D.A., & Larner, G. (Eds.). (2004). *Collaborative practice in psychology and psychotherapy.* London: Routledge.

Payne, M. (2005). *Modern social work theory* (3rd Ed.). Chicago, IL: Lyceum Books.

7

SOCIAL CONSTRUCTION
IN QUESTION

REALISM: "BUT THERE IS A WORLD OUT THERE!"

••••

THE QUESTION OF MENTAL STATES: NEUROSCIENCE TO
THE RESCUE

••••

IS CONSTRUCTIONISM SELF-DEFEATING?

••••

THE CHALLENGE OF MORAL RELATIVISM

••••

WHAT IS WORTH DOING: THE QUESTION OF
A NOURISHING LIFE

••••

SOCIAL CONSTRUCTION AND SCIENTIFIC PROGRESS

••••

REFLECTION

••••

FURTHER RESOURCES

I raise the question of whether social constructionism
has become a main cultural danger today.

Swend Brinkmann, University of Aarhus

In his classic work *The discourse on method*, René Descartes raised questions that
continue to challenge us today. We all make claims to knowledge, but how can we
ever be certain we know anything? Perhaps we are living in illusions; on what solid
base can we rest our beliefs? Authorities claim knowledge, proposed Descartes, but
how can we trust authority? Nor can we trust our senses (they are often misleading), and certainly we should not count on the opinions of the crowds around us.
How can we, then, make solid claims to knowledge? The painful question now
posed, Descartes moved on to furnish a voice of resounding reassurance. We begin,
says Descartes, with the recognition of doubt itself. Although our reason may lead
us to doubt all that we survey, we cannot doubt that we are reasoning. It is this
process of reasoning, then, that guarantees that we exist at all: *Cogito ergo sum*.

The celebration of the individual mind continues until the present day. We prize the individual who doesn't "follow the crowd", but "makes up his own mind", demonstrates "sound decision making", and shows "integrity of moral choice". And we trust that individual scientists, endowed with powers of reason and attentive to the contours of the objective world, can improve our lives and help move society toward prosperity for all.

Yet, as we found in Chapter 4, Descartes' dictum is deeply flawed. Why should we believe that "doubting" is a process of individual reasoning? We use our common language to tell someone, "I doubt that is correct". But how do we know that behind the language there is something in the head called "doubt?" As we asked, how did Descartes know that he was thinking at all? Isn't it more reasonable that in doing what he called thinking Descartes was silently engaged in public conversation? And when he raised questions concerning the trustworthiness of authorities, our senses, community opinion, and the like wasn't he also using the common language? As we have seen, language is not the possession of the single individual. The creation of meaningful language requires social coordination; there is nothing we call language that is born within the private mind. If there were no relationships there would be no meaningful discourse; and without discourse there would be no way of deliberating, in public or in private, about "doubt" or "reason". We may properly replace Descartes' dictum with, *Communicamus ergo sum*: we communicate, therefore I am!

Yet, while social constructionism traces our sense of the rational, the true and the good to communal relationships, this is not a final resting place. It would be a serious mistake to close this book and declare, "Now I know". Yes, constructionist proposals open new and exciting vistas of understanding and action. At the same time, many find these ideas deeply troubling, if not repugnant. Terms such as "nihilist", "anti-rational", "anti-scientific", and "morally bankrupt" are not uncommon. What reply can be made to such criticism? I could respond in the traditional scholarly way, and try to defeat or silence those who disagree. But this is a tradition in which there is competition for the Truth. Within this tradition, there is no room for detractors; all critique must be eradicated. In contrast, constructionists are not playing the truth game. There are no claims here that the arguments are true, objective or rational. Rather, constructionist ideas are offered as possible resources for living. The question is not whether they are objectively true, but what happens to our lives when these ideas enter into our relationships? It is for this reason that much of the present work has been devoted to practice. And, for constructionists it is imperative to open spaces for those who find problems in constructionist ideas. We should welcome critical reflection; no voice should go unheard.

The present chapter gives voice to major lines of critique and questioning about social construction. Indeed, you may find your own voice as reader among those who find problems in constructionist proposals. Differing groups – philosophers, scientists, humanists, religious thinkers, practitioners and more – raise these various concerns. For the present chapter I have selected six of the most common questions, and will proceed in each case to develop a constructionist rejoinder. In particular, I shall treat each of the following questions:

1. Does constructionism deny the material world and its very real problems of life and death?
2. Does constructionism deny the importance of personal experience and other mental states?
3. Doesn't constructionism deconstruct itself?
4. Does constructionism have a moral or political position; does it advocate moral relativism?
5. If all that we take to be real and good is constructed, what is worth doing? Or, why should we not just do anything we please?
6. What account can constructionists give of the obvious gains made by the natural sciences?

Realism: "But There is a World Out There!"

My Grandmother always told me to make friends with those who search for the truth, but to run for the hills when you meet those who have found it.

Karen Dawson

A frequent reaction to constructionist ideas is a frustrated cry of disbelief. "Are you trying to say that pollution is not real, or poverty, or death? Are you saying that there isn't a world out there, that we are just making it up? Absurd!" Yes, it does seem absurd. As Woody Allan once quipped, "The one thing you can say about reality, is that it's the only place you can get a good steak". And for me, pollution, poverty, and death are also very real. However, as reasonable as they are, such objections are based on a misunderstanding of constructionist arguments. Constructionism makes no denials concerning pollution, poverty, or death. Constructionists don't say, "death is not real", for example; nor do they make any affirmations. As noted in earlier chapters, constructionism doesn't try to rule on what is or is not fundamentally real. Whatever is, simply is. However, the moment we begin to articulate what there is – what is truly or objectively the case – we enter a world of discourse, and thus a tradition, a way of life, and a set of value preferences. Even to ask whether there is a real world "out there" is already to presume the Western view of the person, with a subjective world "inside" the head and an "objective" world somewhere outside. As we speak so earnestly about the world's problems we often forget that we are functioning from within a particular tradition. To be sure, realist talk is essential to carrying out life within these traditions. We must treat talk about our families, our work, our health, and so on, as real to function within everyday life. Constructionists do not argue against such usages. Rather, they propose, be careful of treating these daily realities as unquestionably the Real. We do so at our peril. Consider the following.

Whenever we are certain about what is real, we seal ourselves off from other possibilities. In this sense, what is most obvious to us – most fully compelling at any given time – is also the most limiting. If the earth *simply is flat*, a once obvious fact, there is no room for those who wish to explore the potentials of "round"; for those who believe the grass truly is green, there is little room for research showing that the experience of colour is produced by light reflected on the retina; or for those who believe that stones are solid, there is no reason to suspect that they might also be composed of molecular particles, the position of a contemporary physicist. Nor is this to give the advocates of the round earth, the retina, and molecular particles the inside track on the real. Such scientific views are surely useful, but for certain ends and not others. If I am sailing across a lake, or looking for signs that my grass is parched, or propping up a door with a stone, the good old realities are perfect. In effect, a commitment to the Real eliminates a rich sea of alternatives, and by quieting alternative discourses we limit possibilities of action.

This is also to say that we should be cautious when people make strong claims to understand "more" and "better" than previous generations. The effects of such claims may be numbing. With every thrill of "breakthrough" – the sense of "now we truly know" – there is a simultaneous silencing and a loss. For example, in earlier centuries people commonly believed that nature had a spiritual essence; to explore the beauties of nature was to be closer to God. Of course, now we "know better". The world is simply material, minute particles of matter. Spirit has nothing to do with it. As we become satisfied with the "really real" of the material world, the early appreciation of the spiritual dimension is cast away. When committed to a language of the "material world" we lose a precious voice of enchantment, awe, and wonderment. As many believe, it is this loss that has lead to the disregard of nature and the degradation of the earth (Eliade, 1971). The same erasure takes place as the sciences tell us that love is merely hormonal arousal, religious worship a brain state, and a mother's care for her children a genetic disposition. As we redefine human actions as "mere biology", they become flat and meaningless. "You stimulate my hormones" is no substitute for "I love you". Do we truly wish to give up the discourse of mystery, awe, and deep significance?

As we make declarations of the real – what is true, what really happened, what must be the case – we also close off options for dialogue. Declarations of the real operate as conversation stoppers; they establish the limits of what others can say, who can be heard. Consider, for example, the discourse of medicine. Who could doubt the reality of breast cancer, heart disease, or cystic fibrosis? Of course, these are all daily realities in society, and the point here is to eliminate neither the words nor the research and treatment practices in which they are embedded. However, as these terms of the medical profession expand into the culture, and become the "really real", so are competing voices eliminated from dialogue. Consider the reality of AIDS. There have been active attempts by many groups to bring this reality home to the public at large. One of them, an exhibition of Nicholas Nixon's photographs, called "Pictures of People", toured widely in the United States. The exhibition, depicting AIDS victims as they slowly wasted away toward death, was a powerful statement of the horrors of the disease. The Museum of Modern Art described the exhibit as, "telling the story of AIDS: showing what this disease truly is, how it affects those who have it, their lovers, families and friends ..." (quoted in Crimp, 1992). Yet, in all their photographic clarity, are we informed about what the disease "truly is"? Not according to a group of AIDS activists demonstrating against the exhibition. They handed out fliers accusing the exhibition of perpetuating misconceptions, and failing to "address the realities of those of us living every day with this crisis". As their flier proclaimed, "We demand the visibility of persons with AIDS who are vibrant, angry, loving, sexy, beautiful, acting up and fighting back" (Crimp, 1992, p. 118). Would this additional set of images finally depict the real? Not

Figure 7.1

according to many others. Some point to the way in which such depictions reduce the full, complex individual to a disease; others argue that depictions of persons with AIDS are essentially acts of exploitation used to feed the public spectacle. And as still others point out, the focus on the victim circumscribes our concerns, blinds us to the context of the disease, to governmental neglect, funding deficiencies, and failures in health care. Are not all these voices – and still others – needed in deliberation about the reality of AIDS? And in this case should we not be wary of attempts to terminate the discussion by appeals to "the true" and "the real?"

In the final analysis, claims to what is truly True or really Real set us against each other. They are denials of others' traditions and eradications of their values. How many thousands have been slaughtered in the name of Truth?

The Question of Mental States: Neuroscience to the Rescue

How did we ever come to use such an expression as "I believe ...?"
Did we at some time become aware of a phenomenon of belief?

Ludwig Wittgenstein, *Philosophical Investigations*

Consider the many times each day we use such words as "think", "hope", "want", "need", and "remember". And consider how important it is to our relationships to speak of our "love", "sadness", and "joy". Yet, as the preceding chapters propose, the discourse of the mind is socially constructed. The case for social construction was particularly powerful in this case, because mental terms have no obvious referent. The word "tree" is also a social construction. However, in this case we can point to something, and if the two of us agree to call it a tree, and not a bush, then for us there is an observable world of trees. In the case of mental discourse, however, we have no observable referent. There is no means of penetrating the "surface of the skin" to observe the state in itself. As proposed in the earlier discussion of social understanding, there is no means of getting behind the words to discover what the speaker "truly intended" (Chapter 5). So, it could be said, our words for mental life are free floating constructions, open to the imaginations of the times.

Here the critics begin to recoil. Doesn't this mean that social constructionism argues for the abandonment of mental language? Isn't such language misleading, based on a fallacious tradition of understanding? Wouldn't constructionists eradicate such "folk talk" from our daily lives? What about the fields of psychology and psychiatry, both of which place "the mind" in the centre of concern? Shouldn't the constructionist call these disciplines into question? By the same token, are all clinical practices in which therapists probe the "interior life" or "lived experience" of their clients just futile exercises? And what about personal agency? Do we want to abandon the belief that we are free to make choices, that we are personally responsible for what we do? Is all this eradicated as well?

At this point in history, the defenders of mental reality often resort to the rapidly accumulating findings from the field of neuroscience. Neuroscience is currently one of the most exciting fields of science. Why? Because brain scanning technology (e.g. MRI, PET, EEG, MEG) now seems to give us direct access to human minds. As subjects are engaged in various activities – problem solving, remembering, bargaining, watching films, meditating, and so on – measures are taken of heightened neuro/chemical activity in various areas of the brain. If a certain area of the brain is active when one is working on mathematical problems we now have evidence for the neural basis of reason; if another area is activated when one is viewing a sad movie, there is evidence for the neural foundation of emotion. The guesswork is finished. On this basis, neuroscientists now claim to reveal the cortical basis not only for reason and emotion, but also for social understanding, aggression, leadership, and moral behaviour.

But let us consider such proposals more carefully. Do brain states truly reveal the existence of mental states? Consider again the problem of how we can identify a psychological condition from what we can observe. For example, if psychologists want to know if a person is in a mental state of depression, they will typically use a checklist of behavioural indicators. Does the person sleep too much, eat too little, feel fatigued, and so on. However, none of the indicators tell us for sure that the person is depressed. An individual may feel suicidal precisely because he is so exhausted from lack of sleep that he cannot cope. Depression may be irrelevant. Any interpretation remains suspended, then, on a network of other interpretations.

Do brain scan data now solve this notorious problem of knowing what's in the mind? Using brain scans, we now observe the neural condition of the person we have shakily diagnosed as depressed. We succeed in locating a neural condition unique to people who make high scores on the depression checklist. Yet, we may ask, how can we determine that the observed state of the brain is in fact "depression?" Why is it not simply a neural correlate of sleeplessness, appetite loss, or feelings of fatigue?" Or for that matter, how could we determine that the neural state is not an indicator of "spiritual malaise", "anger", "withdrawal from oppressive conditions", or "cognitive integration and regrouping?" In effect, brain scan data do not open the mind to inspection. They simply replace one site of speculation to another. Brain scans do not speak for themselves. To read them as evidence of depression, deceit, trust, empathy, morality, and so on, is little more than an exercise in extending one's cultural beliefs.

Let us then return to the common complaint: constructionism leads to an eradication of our belief in the mind. In response, it should be clear by now that constructionism does not argue for the eradication of any reality claims. To recognize that a favoured reality is constructed is no reason for its abandonment. If we abandoned all constructions we would simply be mute. For the constructionist, the question is not whether the mind is Real. Whether thought, emotion, or agency are real, for example, is an unanswerable question. They are real for those living within specific traditions, but not others. Beyond all traditions of understanding there is nothing to say. The more important question for the constructionist concerns the consequences in cultural life of placing such terms in action. Herein lies a fertile ground for dialogue.

When we ask about the practical implications of mental terms, we first realize that they are of inestimable importance. The language of the mind plays a pivotal role in Western cultural life. For example, without a language of the passions, of love, desire, needs and wants, it would be difficult to engage in the tradition of romantic love; the language is an essential part of carrying out love, just as much as gazing, holding hands, or caressing. Similarly, without terms objectifying "reason", "memory", and "attention", educational institutions would falter; similarly if we lacked the words "intention", "conscious choice", "knowledge of right and wrong", our system of justice would deteriorate. Without prizing a language of "individual reason" and "free choice" the very idea of democracy makes little sense. Psychological discourse is an essential ingredient of Western cultural tradition. I can also assure you that although I write extensively about constructionism, I will continue to use these words in most of my relationships. Yet, I am also invited by the constructionist dialogues to explore the possible ways in which such traditions bring injury to people, and to consider how we might generate new alternatives.

It also follows that while disciplines using mental explanations can make an important contribution to society, we should not embrace them as final authorities. In using mental discourse, disciplines such as psychology, anthropology, history, and the like, carry the culture's traditions on their shoulders. They keep the language of the mind alive, and thus the forms of relationship in which these languages are embedded. The same argument holds for mental health professions such as psychiatry and clinical psychology. Such professions do work with a potent vocabulary of human change. People will change the course of their lives for what they index as their "unconscious desires", "hidden yearnings", and feelings of self-revelation and psychological growth. Yet, constructionism also asks us to be aware that we are, in each case, working within traditions. These traditions can and do oppress many people; they dismiss their realities and leave them outside the dialogues that affect their future. And, as argued in Chapter 4, because of the ways in which the language of mind lends itself to an ideology of individualism – with all its invitations to alienation, narcissism, and exploitation – we should be open to more relational alternatives.

Is Constructionism Self-Defeating?

The point is not a set of answers, but making possible a different practice.

Susanne Kappeler, *The Pornography of Representation*

Over the centuries many philosophers have critically examined the concepts of objectivity, truth, and empirical knowledge. Perhaps the most frequently resounding response to these various forms of skepticism was first posed in Plato's *Theatetus*. In brief, the message buried there is: "If there is no truth, objectivity, or empirical knowledge, as skeptics claim, then on what grounds should skepticism be accepted? By its own account, the skeptic's proposal cannot be true, objective, or empirically based. Skepticism is thus incoherent; it asks us to accept the truth of its position while simultaneously proclaiming that there is no truth". It would appear that constructionist arguments fall heir to this form of critical reaction. If all realities are socially constructed, then how can constructionism be true? Isn't constructionism itself a construction?

To this latter question, the constructionist replies in the affirmative. At the outset, constructionists do not claim constructionist propositions and arguments to be True, objective, or empirically grounded. Constructionist ideas are resources for use, not maps or mirrors of the world. So, constructionists are quite willing to recognize that their arguments are tied together by metaphor and narrative, they are historically and culturally bounded, and are rational only within particular traditions. However, consider two matters of special note. First, on the clever side, realize that by claiming that constructionism is itself a construction, such critics have themselves become constructionists. That is, the attempt to undo constructionism uses constructionist arguments to do its work. More important and more positively, the constructionist welcomes such criticism. It is just such questioning that enables us to step out of the discourse of constructionism, to avoid its hardening as a dogma, and to prevent it from becoming "the New Truth". In this kind of critique we may begin to ask about the effects of constructionist discourse in various situations, its gains and its losses, its potentials and shortcomings. In effect, constructionism does not itself seek to be a *final word*, but a form of discourse that will help us to avoid building worlds in which claims to Truth put an end to dialogue.

There are numerous ways which the world's peoples have found to ensure that certain ways of talking are the only way. Authorities have variously claimed divine inspiration, reason, empirical fact, and self-evidence to establish the foundations for what amounts to a way of life. Many significant battles – both in the intellectual world and the world more generally – are fought on the grounds of claims to fundamentals. Yet, these attempts are ultimately futile, because there is no the way to establish a foundation for the foundations. It is common for scientists to say, for example, that a theory approximates Truth when all the empirical evidence confirms it and there is no evidence that is falsifying. However, on what grounds can such a foundation for truth be justified? It would scarcely be appropriate to go out and test the proposition by gathering data. The very attempt to prove the theory empirically is already committed to the theory. It would be circular to test the empirical view of truth empirically. And to use any other grounds, such as "we know this theory to be true by virtue of logic", would subtly undermine the proposal. If you proved empiricism true by reasoning alone, then it is reasoning that tells us what is true and not empirical data. In effect, there are no claims to truth that can justify themselves. In addition to the futility of this conflict, there is also the silencing discussed above. Once the foundations are laid, they create barricades between people. In this context, it should be recognized that constructionism is unique in its avoidance of claims to fundamental justification. Constructionism is not a set of beliefs to which one must be committed, forsaking all others. Rather, it is more like a poem, a melody, or a gymnastic move. The primary question is, what kind of world can we create together when we place it into action?

The Challenge of Moral Relativism

[Deconstruction] ... is mischievously radical in respect to everyone else's opinions, able to unmask the most solemn declarations as mere disheveled plays of signs, while utterly conservative in every other way. Since it commits you to affirming nothing, it is as injurious as blank ammunition.

Terry Eagleton, *The Illusions of Postmodernism*

The saints are gathering at the real places, trying tough skin on sharp conscience ... you can hear them yelping.

A.R. Arnmons, *The Confirmers*

Perhaps the most heated attack against constructionist views is directed against its moral and political posture. As it is said, constructionism has no values; it seems to tolerate everything and stand for nothing. Worse, it discourages a commitment to any set of values or ideals; all values are "just constructions". Constructionism fails to offer any social criticism or directions for change. I first became aware of the bitterness of this critique during a lunch with a Jewish philosopher friend. As I tried to explain constructionist ideas to him, he responded with anger, and announced he could no longer eat with me. My constructionist ideas, he said, did not condemn the Holocaust. In effect, constructionists would simply go along the Nazis. Such tolerance is morally repugnant. Another hour of dialogue was needed to re-cement our friendship.

How can a constructionist respond to my companion? First, it is important to realize that constructionism has served as a powerful friend to dialogues on good and evil. Increasingly over the past century the scientific world-view has come to represent the road to Truth. It is through scientific research, we have believed, we can come to understand the world as it is. And with such understanding in place, we can control the future. Thus we have witnessed a vast expansion in the natural sciences, and an explosion of social sciences. Yet, with the expansion of the scientific perspective, issues of good and evil have largely been pushed to the side. Science is about using rationality and observation in discovering the truth. Science does not attempt to tell us what "ought to be" but what is the case. Or, as commonly put, we must distinguish between facts and values. The realm of values is separate from science, and scientists make no claims to expertise in such matters. At worst, if scientific knowledge is driven by values (what we would *like* to believe), it is likely to be biased. It may be politically desirable to say that "all persons are born equal", but from the scientific perspective, when all the evidence argues for the inheritance of differences in basic intelligence, it would corrupt the science to report otherwise.

Yet, during the 1960s, this view of scientific neutrality began to wear thin. Scientific knowledge seemed so often used in the service of domination. Military forces, industries, and governments used scientific information to increase their control over others. Whether it was whites over blacks, the haves over the have-nots, the US over North Vietnam, government over the people, men over women, educational institutions over the students, the science establishment was almost invariably found on the side of domination. Scientists seemed unflinchingly to supply the technologies of domination, control, and exploitation; claims to neutrality seemed naive if not absurd. Although constructionist ideas were then in their infancy, they began to flourish precisely because they furnished intellectual ammunition for piercing the armour of scientific neutrality – objectivity beyond ideology. As outlined in previous chapters, the languages used by scientists to describe and explain are not required by whatever is the case. We have enormous latitude in our accounts of the world. Further, because scientific discourses enter social life as a means of sorting people into categories, giving credit, and laying blame, this language is never value-free in its effects. If certain data are called "indicators of inherited intelligence", and used to privilege certain groups ("the intelligent") and penalize others (those low in IQ), then scientific descriptions are scarcely neutral. They enter society with all the impact of a police force. On this account, all scientific propositions should be open to question on moral and political grounds. Thus we find that the constructionist critique of the distinction between fact and value invites scientists – indeed, all of us – to speak out on issues of the good. This is not because we are trained experts, but because we participate in the cultural generation of meaning, and thus the creation of our ways of life – today and in the future.

Yet, while constructionist arguments do open the way to moral and political deliberation, they do not champion one ideal over another. Constructionism furnishes a mandate for feminists, ethnic minorities, Marxists, gays and lesbians, the elderly, the poor, and indeed all of us to challenge the "truth" and "the facts" of the dominant order. There is reason to include all traditions of value – religious and spiritual, political, social – in matters of policy making. However, constructionism does not select a victor among the competing voices. In this sense one might say that it is relativistic; all moral positions are legitimate in their own terms. However, one should not make the error here of saying that constructionists believe that "all moral values are equal". To say that everything is equal is itself a value judgment. All evaluations, deliberations, or comparisons of competing positions will necessarily carry with them presumptions of the real and the good, including the view that "no position is better than any other". I know of no constructionists who adopt such a view. Rather, most of my constructionist colleagues are very much like me. We all champion certain ways of life as opposed to others; we feel good about the values we hold, and hope that others can come to see the world in the way we do. However, the chief difference between constructionists and most of those committed to a value position, is that constructionists will not claim their values to be fundamentally superior to others. They will try to avoid knockdown competition, the kind that so often leads to bloodshed, and to replace such competition with mutual exploration.

With this said, let us consider a contrasting possibility: what if constructionists listened to the voice of the critics and offered a slate of values? Constructionism is for Christianity, or Marxism, or Islam, or Liberalism, or ... . Would you truly wish constructionists to establish the nature of the good, a universal slate of values, or the way of life to be followed by all people? Chances are you would not. And, typically those who criticize the moral shallowness of constructionism are seldom interested in establishing just any value commitment. It is not simply a moral posture of some kind that is being demanded, but typically a commitment to their particular values. Do we wish any group, religious, governmental, academic, or other, to legislate the good for all? There is no single value, moral ideal, or political good that, when fully pursued, will not work toward the obliteration of some alternative value – even those we might especially wish to sustain. Pursue individual freedom to its limits and we lose community; favour honesty above all and personal security is threatened; champion community well-being and individual initiative may be destroyed. Again, do we truly wish to establish ethical codes against which all people at all times can be judged?

It is at just this point that the constructionist "failure of moral commitment" begins to open new vistas on problems of ethical and political value. First, consider the account of ethical value emerging from the preceding pages. As proposed, in coordinating ourselves with each other, we typically develop patterns of action that we favour, what we do and prefer. This is so for the mother and the infant, friends out camping, strangers on a train, and even man and dog. We develop a way of life that we prefer over others. Moral rules or laws are not essential to establishing these patterns of preference; when there is perfect harmony there is little need to declare what is good as opposed to evil. We seldom "do good" because there are rules, laws, principles, a bill of rights, and the like. Most of us do not rob banks because there is a law against it; it just never occurs to us in our way of life that this could be a good idea. Moral rules become important when there is disharmony, when someone is violating the preferred way of life. Such rules are used to reinforce the tradition. "This is wrong; don't do it again!" Or, when there is a threat to a way of life, we use moral principles to credit or praise those who punish deviants. Hence our tales of heroism, from Robin Hood to contemporary whistle-blowers. They fought for good over evil.

If this seems reasonable, then we find that neither constructionism nor any other credo can dictate a way of life. Rather, there will be tendencies toward creating the good wherever there is successful coordination among people (Chapter 5). Or, in effect, some form of local morality will grow into being. We can scarcely anticipate a single good, but rather a virtual infinity of local goods, coming into being at all times when people are relating closely with each other. The challenge, then, is not that of creating ethical or political commitments; ethics and politics are always already under creation.

If each community of the good lived in total separation from all others, we would have little problem about political or moral stands. Each community could live by its own standards without interference, which is to say, no challenge to its values or ways of life. But of course, this is seldom the case, and as the world rapidly shrinks and its peoples increasingly collide, so are value conflicts increasingly in evidence. Consider the explosion of ethnic, political, and religious conflicts of recent decades. The major challenge, then, is how we are to manage in a world of increasing value conflict. It is at just this point that we find constructionist resources particularly useful: the constructionist will recognize the legitimacy of the competing value investments, each within its own tradition. The constructionist may even share in one or more traditions. However, there is also the recognition that strong commitments lend themselves to eradicating the other, to eliminating any voice antithetical to one's own. If we do not wish to see a world of escalating violence, terror and genocide, we might wish to consider alternatives.

It is in just this context that many constructionist scholars and practitioners find their work most meaningful. As previous chapters demonstrate, there is keen interest among constructionists in the problem of working across conflicting realities. Recall, for example, the work of the Public Conversations Project, and the relevant discussion of transformative dialogue (Chapter 5). This discussion was precisely concerned with sustaining processes of making meaning in otherwise hostile conditions. Also prominent is the practice of appreciative enquiry (Chapter 6), used broadly in organizations to help antagonistic groups build a mutually viable future. Do these offerings imply that constructionists are, then, committed to a foundational value – namely that of sustaining meaning and thus value itself? No, it simply means that constructionists are also participants in cultural history, and act within traditions. Thus, to offer such dialogic practices is an expression of a tradition. However, it does not follow that such values are presumed to be universal. Yet, if it were a choice between conflicting traditions fighting it out, as opposed to participating in collaborative future building, what would you choose?

What is Worth Doing?: the Question of a Nourishing Life

If I took all your arguments to heart, I wouldn't
have anything to do on Monday morning.

Personal communication from a colleague

Many critics feel constructionist arguments are disillusioning. As it is said, people desire solid reasons for their actions, values they can believe in. If they find that what seem to be solid grounds are "only constructions" they will lose their desire to act. If resisting injustice has no intrinsic merit, if it is only a cultural construction, then why bother? If we learn that the mind is a social construction, then how can we take seriously the study of psychology or the education of minds? If love is something we make up, then doesn't this undermine our most committed relations? If intentions are culturally constructed, then why should we hold anyone responsible for what they do? What is worth doing at all?

In reply, it is first necessary to carefully inspect the line of critique. What is assumed in making such arguments? One major assumption is that unless a way of life depends on some sort of foundation, or is grounded in good reasons, it is not worth living. But why do we ask for such justifications? How did we come to believe that foundations were essential to a meaningful life? Isn't it likely that such a belief grew from our relationships with others? As children we scarcely had such justifications or foundations. Yet, as children we were fully engaged in our projects. For hours we could build sand castles, play with a dollhouse, dress up in adult clothes, or kick a ball back and forth without any justification whatsoever. We didn't ask, "am I wasting my time?" or "is this justified?" The demand for solid reasons for action derives from a social tradition. And if this is so, we are free to ask whether this is a tradition we wish to sustain.

More promisingly, the constructionist inquires into the source of commitment, the sense of worth, and the nourishment of action. What gives champagne a kick? As the preceding chapters suggest, life acquires its zest from relationships. It is through our participation in relationships that we acquire the sense of value, justice, and joy. To use the metaphor of the game, we thrill at the goal or feel anguish in loss not because the game is based on a fundamental truth or morality. When we are in the midst of the game, it *is* the real and the good – for that moment. Yet, the game is a social construction; wins or losses have no significance outside a history of relationship. Or in Hans Georg Gadamer's words, "The game is what holds the player in its spell, draws him into play, and keeps him there" (Gadamer, 1976, pp. 75–76).

What are the implications of approaching the meaning of life in this way? For one, we are invited to be open to others, to welcome their world-views, and to explore their sources of value and pleasure. In these relationships we expand our own potentials for finding nourishment and joy in life. Think for a moment about the activities you most value and you will find that unless you had been open to relationship, these activities would be empty. This orientation also underscores the emptiness of materialism in itself. New clothes, new cars, a big house, and so on, are not worth anything in themselves. Whatever value they have results from the relationships in which we participate. Caring for relationships is essential. Here we also find implications for approaching those who suffer from a sense of a meaningless life, who are depressed or suicidal. Pharmacology may provide a band-aid for such problems, but the path to a meaningful life is through relationships. Finally, this constructionist orientation offers a way out of life – ways that are enjoyable and nourishing, but ultimately strangulating. Drugs and alcohol, along with gambling, videogame playing, and the like, all give pleasure, but in the long run are harmful to the person and disrupt relationships. If such pleasures owe their genesis to relationships, then the exit may be found through the development of new relationships. The success of Alcoholics Anonymous has far-reaching implications.

Social Construction and Scientific Progress

Constructionist arguments seem most powerful when you aren't certain about what is real or good. For example, few are shocked to learn that terms such as "social structure", "the unconscious", and "neurosis" are socially constructed. Most of us were never quite convinced that these words reflected real things in the first place. However, suspicion mounts when we turn to the work of sciences such as biology, chemistry, and physics. Scientific terms for the physical world are virtually taken for granted. We just know that DNA, dopamine, chemical elements, gravity, atomic particles, and so on, truly exist. It is partly for this reason that the early pages of the book took great pains to look at the socially constructed character of natural science. Yet, even with these arguments in place, you may resist. One of the most important sources of this resistance is the commonly shared belief that somehow natural science research has yielded increases in knowledge. Regardless of constructionist contentions, who can deny that scientific research has not generated a harvest of resources for human benefit – the electric light, cures for smallpox and typhoid fever, jet propulsion, atomic power, and more? If science does create socially constructed worlds, how can we account for these estimable advances? Don't these advances reflect the fact that scientific methods, unlike any other, really do help us to know what is true?

There are several points of reply. First we must be careful about what constructionism is arguing here. There is no attempt to deny that "something is happening" when the scientific community is at work. However, the significant question is whether the scientist's terms for naming or describing this "something" can reflect what is actually the case. To be sure, we have a language of atomic properties, chemical elements, and neuro-transmission. The danger is in concluding that these words are somehow privileged in "reflecting" or "mapping" what exists, that these terms tell or inform us about the nature of the real. From a constructionist perspective, for example, all that we call "chemical elements" could be given the names of Greek gods. Or, with no loss in accuracy, in physics we could substitute the term Neptune for the neutron and Zeus for the proton. Let us not mistake the word for the "world".

Yet, you might rejoin, it is not simply words we are talking about here. Scientific formulations make predictions; our scientific theorizing leads us to conclude that a rocket can be sent to Mars, and lo, we witness the success of the prediction. Doesn't the fact of good predictions tell us something about the nature of reality? When we can predict well, don't we approach the truth of the matter? In reply, it is a mistake to hold that effective predictions are indicators of the truth. If I propose that God makes the sun rise every day and set every night, does the fact that my proposal is verified make it true? Does the fact that intelligence test scores can predict academic achievement make the concept of intelligence true? Does the fact that people who take anti-depressant drugs are less depressed make it true that drugs reduce depression? People everywhere seek to make reliable predictions, and when they do so they use the language available to them to make sense of the predictions. The success of the predictions says nothing about the Truth of these particular ways of making sense. The words may be more or less useful in the community engaged in the predictions. But we shouldn't mistake utility for Truth.

We must also consider as well the value attached to the word "progress". Progress is about improvement; something becomes better and better. Yet, constructionists ask, "better for whom?" Values are created within various communities, and what is better for one may actually worse for another. "Progress" may depend on which side of the fence you are standing. This is easy enough to see in the case of mental illness. As discussed in Chapter 2, terms for mental illness carry values; they define "the good person". Thus, as the concepts of mental illness have multiplied, so are there more ways to find people deficient. The result is an increasing demand for therapeutic and pharmacological cures. We are now very good at "curing illnesses" that we never knew we had. This may seem less obvious in the case of medical science. However, we must also realize that physical deficits too are value-saturated constructions. And, just as the homosexual population ultimately rejected psychiatry's labeling them "mentally ill", so are the blind now rejecting society's view of them as debilitated. The National Federation of the Blind now brings together the force of over 50,000 people to establish blindness as simply a difference, not a deficit. And with respect to science in general, there are many who view with alarm the "progress" represented in our capacities to destroy each other and the environment. The concern with environmental destruction now moves thousands to seek ways of replacing "progress" in our world with "sustainability". Whenever the banner of progress is flown, one must also look about carefully for the destruction.

Reflection

This book now draws to a close, and with its completion comes a certain sense of sadness. This writing carries with it the remnants of a thousand conversations. At the same time, I have also carried out an imaginary conversation with you, my reader. And as I imagine it, you have been caring in your attention, curious in your questions, willing to follow the strange twists of logic into exotic lands, and indulgent of my passions and prejudices. So, as I complete the writing, this projected relationship sadly comes to an end. Every disconnection is a small death, and this one is not trivial. So what can I now hope? Perhaps it is that your relationship with me – as reader and writer – has sparked an internal conversation for you. More importantly, perhaps this conversation can move outward into your life, entering your own relationships, giving them vitality. As the dialogues go on, remnants of our relationship may spread beyond. And in this case, there is hope that we shall meet again.

Further Resources

Critical Deliberations

Cromby, J., & Nightengale, D.J. (1999). *Social constructionist psychology: a critical analysis.* Buckingham: Open University Press.

Gross, B., & Levitt, N. (1994). *Higher superstition: the academic left and its quarrels with science.* Baltimore, MD: Johns Hopkins University Press.

Held, B. (1996). *Back to reality, a critique of postmodern psychotherapy.* New York: Norton.

Hibberd, F. (2005). *Unfolding social constructionism.* New York: Springer.

Nagel, T. (1997). *The last word.* New York: Oxford University Press.

Parker, I. (Ed.). (1998). *Social constructionism, discourse and realism.* London: Sage.

Phillips, D. (1997). Coming to grips with radical social constructivisms. *Science and Education,* 6, 85–104.

Constructionist Reflections

Edwards, D., Ashmore, M., & Potter, J. (1995). Death and furniture: the rhetoric and politics and theology of bottom line arguments against relativism. *History of the Human Sciences,* 8, 25–49.

Gergen, K.J. (1994). *Realities and relationships.* Cambridge, MA: Harvard University Press.

Gergen, K.J. (2002). *Social construction in context.* London: Sage.

Hacking, I. (1999). *The social construction of what?* Cambridge, MA: Harvard University Press.

Hosking, D.M. (2007). Can constructionism be critical? In J.A. Holtstein & J.F. Gubrium (Eds.), *Handbook of constructionist research.* New York: Guilford.

Ruse, M. (1999). *Mystery of mysteries: is evolution a social construction?* Cambridge, MA: Harvard University Press.

Simons, H.W., & Billig, M. (Eds.). (1994). *After postmodernism.* London: Sage.

Smith, B.H. (1997). *Belief and resistance.* Cambridge, MA: Harvard University Press.

Squires, J. (Ed.). (1993). *Principled positions: postmodernism and the rediscovery of value.* London: Lawrence & Wishart.

REFERENCES

Andersen, T. (Ed.). (1991). *The Reflecting Team.* New York: Norton.

Anderson, H. (1997). *Conversation, Language, and Possibilities.* New York: Basic Books.

Anderson, H., & Goolishian, H. (1992). The client is the expert: a not-knowing approach to therapy. In S. McNamee & K. Gergen (Eds.). *Therapy as Social Construction.* London: Sage.

Apple, M. (1982). *Education and Power.* Boston, MA: Routledge & Kegan Paul.

Applebee, A. (1996). *Curriculum as conversation: Transforming traditions of teaching and learning.* Chicago: University of Chicago Press.

Argyris, C. (1980). *Inner Contradictions of Rigorous Research.* New York: Academic Press.

Aronowitz, S., & Giroux, H.A. (1993). *Postmodern Education: Politics, Culture and Social Criticism.* Minneapolis, MN: University of Minnesota Press.

Asen, E., Dawson, N. and McHugh, B. (2002). *Multiple family therapy: The Marlborough model and its wider applications.* London: Carnac.

Ashmore, R.D., Jussim, L. and Wilder, D. (2001). *Social identity, intergroup conflict, and conflict reduction.* New York: Oxford University Press.

Austin, D. (1996). Kaleidoscope: The same and different. In C. Ellis & A. Bochner (Eds.). *Composing ethnography: Alternative forms of qualitative writing* (pp. 207–208). Walnut Creek, CA: AltaMira Press.

Averill, J.R. (1990). Inner feelings. In D. Leary (Ed.). *Metaphors in the history of psychology.* New York: Cambridge University Press.

Avramides, A. (2001). *Other minds.* London: Routledge.

Bad Object-Choices (Ed.) (1991). *How do I look? Queer film and video.* Seattle: Bay Press.

Bakhtin, M. (1986). *Speech genres and other essays* (Eds. M. Holquist and C. Emerson). Austin, TX: University of Texas Press.

Barnes, B. (1974). *Scientific knowledge and sociological theory.* London: Routledge & Kegan Paul.

Belenky, M., Clinchy, B.M., Goldberger, J.N.R., & Tarule, J.M. (1986). *Women's ways of knowing.* New York: Basic Books.

Bellah, R.N., Madsen, R., Sullivan, W.M., Swidler, A., & Tipton, S.M. (1985). *Habits of the heart.* Berkeley, CA: University of California Press.

Bennett, L.W., & Feldman, M.S. (1981). *Reconstructing reality in the courtroom.* New Brunswick, NJ: Rutgers University Press.

Berg, I.K., & deShazer, S. (1993). Making numbers talk: language in therapy. In S. Friedman (Ed.). *The new language of change.* New York: Guilford.

Berger, P., & Luckmann, T. (1966). *The social construction of reality.* New York: Doubleday.

Bertaux, D. (1981). *Biography and society.* Beverly Hills, CA: Sage.

Bial, H. (2003). *The performance studies reader.* London: Routledge.

Billig, M. (1996). *Arguing and thinking* (2nd Ed.). Cambridge: Cambridge University Press.

Bloor, D. (1976). *Knowledge and social imagery.* London: Routledge & Kegan Paul.

Bojer, M., Roehl, H. Knuth-Hollsen, M., & Magner, C. (2008). *Mapping dialogue, essential tools for social change.* Chagrin Falls, OH: Taos Institute Publications.

Bowles, S., & Gintis, J. (1976). *Schools in capitalist America.* New York: Basic Books.

Boyte, H.C., & Evans, S.M. (1986). *Free spaces, the sources of democracy in America.* New York: Harper & Row.

Brewer, M. (2003). *Intergroup relations.* Buckingham: Open University Press.

Bruffee, K.A. (1993). *Collaborative learning, higher education, interdependence, and the authority of knowledge.* Cambridge: Harvard University Press.

Bruner, J. (1990). *Acts of meaning.* Cambridge, MA: Harvard University Press.

Bruner, J., & Feldman, C.F. (1990). Metaphors of consciousness and cognition in the history of psychology. In D. Leary (Ed.). *Metaphors in the history of psychology.* New York: Cambridge University Press.

Bush, R.A., & Folger, J.P. (1994). *The promise of mediation.* San Francisco, CA: Jossey-Bass.

Butler, J. (1990). *Gender trouble: feminism and the subversion of identity.* New York: Routledge.

Carr, C. (1993). *On edge, performance at the end of the twentieth century.* Hanover, NH: University Press of New England.

Chasin, R., & Herzig, M. (1992). Creating systemic interventions for the sociopolitical arena. In B. Berger-Could & D.H. DeMuth (Eds.). *The global family therapist: integrating the personal, professional, and political.* Needham, MA: Allyn & Bacon.

Cohen, E. (2000). The animated pain of the body. *American Historical Review,* 105, 36–68.

Cooperrider, D.L. (1996). Resources for getting appreciative inquiry started. *OD Practitioner,* 28, 23–34.

Crawford, J., Kippax, S., Onyx, J., Gault, U., & Benton, P. (1992). *Emotion and gender: constructing meaning from memory.* London: Sage.

Crimp, D. (1992). Portraits of people with AIDS. In L. Grossberg, C. Nelson & P. Treichler (Eds.). *Cultural studies.* New York: Routledge.

Daston, L., & Galison, P. (2007). *Objectivity.* Zone Books.

Davis, N.Z. (1983). *The return of Martin Guerre.* Cambridge: Harvard University Press.

de Roux, G. (1991). Together against the computer: PAR and the struggle of Afro-Colombians for public services. In O. Fals-Borda & M.A. Rahman (Eds.). *Action and knowledge.* New York: Apex.

Deleuze, G., & Guattari, E. (1986). *A thousand plateaus.* Minneapolis, MN: University of Minnesota Press.

Derrida, J. (1981). *Positions.* Chicago: University of Chicago Press.

Derrida, J. (1997). *Of grammatology.* Baltimore, MD: Johns Hopkins University Press.

De Shazer, S. (1994). *Words were originally magic.* New York: Norton.

Douglas, M. (1986). *How institutions think.* London: Routledge & Kegan Paul.

Duncan, B.L., Hubble, M.A., & Miller, S. (1997). *Psychotherapy with impossible cases: the efficient treatment of therapy veterans.* New York: W.W. Norton.

Ede, L., & Lunsford, A. (1990). *Singular texts/plural authors: perspectives on collaborative writing.* Carbondale: Southern Illinois University Press.

Eliade, M. (1971). *The quest: history and meaning in religion.* Chicago: University of Chicago Press

Ellis, C. (1995). *Final negotiations: A story of love, loss, and chronic illness.* Philadelphia, PA: Temple University Press.

Engestrom, Y., & Middleton, D. (Eds.). (1996). *Cognition and communication at work.* Cambridge: Cambridge University Press.

Fals-Borda, O. (1991). Some basic ingredients. In O. Fals-Borda & M.A. Rahman (Eds.). *Action and knowledge.* New York: Apex.

Feinsilver, D. Murphy, E., & Anderson, H. (2007). Women at a turning point: A transformational feast. In H. Anderson & D. Gehart (Eds.). *Collaborative therapy: relationships and conversations that make a difference.* New York: Routledge.

Fisher, R., Ury, W., & Patton, B. (1992). *Getting to yes: negotiating agreement without giving in.* New York: Penguin Books.

Flax, J. (1993). *Multiples.* New York: Routledge

Fleck, L. (1935/1979). *Genesis and development of a scientific fact.* Chicago: University of Chicago Press.

Forman, J. (Ed.). (1992). *New visions of collaborative writing.* Portsmouth: Boynton/Cook.

Foucault, M. (1978). *The history of sexuality, vol. 1.* New York: Pantheon.

Foucault, M. (1979). *Discipline and punish.* New York: Vintage.

Frank, A.W. (1997). *The wounded storyteller: body illness and ethics.* Chicago: University of Chicago Press.

Freedman, J., & Combs, G. (1993). Invitation to new stories: using questions to suggest alterna-tive possibilities. In S. Gilligan & R. Price (Eds.). *Therapeutic conversations*. New York: Norton.

Freire, P. (1985). *The politics of education*. South Hadley, MA: Bergin and Garvey.

Gadamer, H.G. (1975). *Truth and method*, ed. C.Barden & J. Cumming. New York: Seabury. Original German.

Gadamar, H.G. (1976). *Truth and method*. New York: Seabury.

Gagnon, J., & Simon, W. (1973). *Sexual conduct*. Chicago: Aldine.

Garfinkel, H. (1967). *Studies in ethnomethodology*. Englewood Cliffs, NJ: Prentice-Hall.

Gergen, K.J. (1993). *Toward transformation in social knowledge* (2nd Ed.). London: Sage.

Gergen, K.J. (1994). *Realities and relationships*. Cambridge, MA: Harvard University Press.

Gergen, K.J. (1995). Metaphor and monophony in the twentieth-century psychology of emo-tions. *History of the Human Sciences*, 8, 1–23.

Gergen, K.J. (2006). *Therapeutic realities, collaboration, oppression and relational flow*. Chagrin Falls, OH: Taos Institute Publications.

Gergen, K.J. (2008). *Relational being, beyond the individual and community*. New York: Oxford University Press.

Gergen, K.J., & Hoskins, D.M. (2006). If you meet social construction along the road, a dia-logue with Buddhism. In M. Kwee, K.J. Gergen, & F. Koshikawa (Eds.). *Horizons in bud-dhist psychology*. Chagrin Falls, OH: Taos Institute Publications.

Gergen, K.J., Gloger-Tippelt, G., & Berkowitz, P. (1990). The cultural construction of the devel-oping child. In G. Semin & K.J. Gergen (Eds.). *Everyday understanding*. London: Sage.

Gergen, M.M. (1992). Life stories: pieces of a dream. In G. Rosenwald & R. Ochberg (Eds.). *Storied lives*. New Haven, CT: Yale University Press.

Gergen, M. (1999). *Impious improvisations: feminist reconstructions in psychology*. Thousand Oaks, CA: Sage.

Gergen, M. (2001). *Feminist reconstructions in psychology*. Thousand Oaks, CA: Sage.

Gilligan, C. (1982). *In a different voice*. Cambridge, MA: Harvard University Press.

Giroux, H. (1992). *Border crossings*. New York: Routledge.

Gitlin, T. (1995). *The twilight of common dreams*. New York: Henry Holt.

Goffman, E. (1959). *The presentation of self in everyday life*. Garden City, NY: Doubleday.

Gordon, C. (Ed.). (1980). *Power/knowledge: selected interviews and other writings by Michel Foucault, 1972–1977*. New York: Pantheon.

Griggin, S.M., & Moffat, R.C. (Eds.). (1997). *Radical critiques of the law*. Lawrence, KA: University of Kansas Press.

Habermas, J. (1971). *Knowledge and human interests*. Boston, MA: Beacon Press.

Hall, S. (1996). New ethnicities. In D. Morley & K. Chen (Eds.). *Stuart Hall: critical dialogues in cultural studies*. London: Routledge.

Hardy, B. (1968). Towards a poetics of fiction: an approach through narrative. *Novel*, 2, 5–14.

Harré, R. (1979). *Social being*. Oxford: Blackwell.

Harré, R., & van Langenhove, L. (Eds.). (1999). *Positioning theory: Moral contexts of inten-tional action*. Malden: Blackwell.

Hermanns, H.J.M., & Kempen, H.J.G. (1993). *The dialogical self, meaning as movement*. New York: Academic Press.

Hill Collins, P. (1990). *Black feminist thought*. New York: Routledge.

Hochschild, A. (1983). *The managed heart: commercialization of human feeling*. Berkeley, CA: University of California Press.

Holstein, J.A., & Gubrium, J.F. (Eds.). (2008). *Handbook of constructionist research*. Thousand Oaks, CA: Sage.

hooks, b. (1989). *Talking back*. Boston, MA: South End Press.

hooks, b. (1990). *Yearning, race, gender, and cultural politics*. Boston, MA: South End Press.

Hunt, A. (1993). *Explorations in law and society*. New York: Routledge.

Hunter, J.D. (1991). *Culture wars: the struggle to define America*. New York: Basic Books.

Hunter, J.D. (1994). *Before the shooting begins*. New York: Free Press.

Iniguez, L., Valencia, J., & Vasquez, F. (1997). The construction of remembering and forgetfulness: memories and histories of the Spanish civil war. In D. Pennebaker, D. Paez, & B. Rime (Eds.). *Collective memory of political events*. Mahwah, NJ: Erlbaum.

Josselson, R. (1995). *Exploring identity and gender: the narrative study of lives*. Thousand Oaks, CA: Sage.

Karl, Cynthia, Andrew & Vanessa (1992). Therapeutic distinctions in an on-going therapy. In S. McNamee, & K.J. Gergen (Eds.). *Therapy as social construction*. London: Sage.

Kelman, J.C. (1997). Group processes in the resolution of international conflicts. *American Psychologist*, 52, 212–30.

Kingwell, M. (1995). *A civil tongue: justice, dialogue, and the politics of pluralism*. University Park: Pennsylvania State University Press.

Knowles, J.G., & Cole, A.L. (2008). *Handbook of the arts in qualitative research*. London: Sage.

Kuhn, T.S. (1962). *The structure of scientific revolutions*. Chicago: University of Chicago Press.

Kuhn, T.S. (1970). *The structure of scientific revolutions* (2nd Ed.). Chicago: University of Chicago Press.

Kuhn, T.S. (1977). *The essential tension*. Chicago: University of Chicago Press.

Lakoff, G., & Johnson, M. (1980). *Metaphors we live by*. Chicago: University of Chicago Press.

Lasch, C. (1979). *The culture of narcissism*. New York: Norton.

Lassiter, L.E. (2005). *The Chicago guide to collaborative ethnography*. Chicago: University of Chicago Press.

Lather, P. (1991). *Getting smart*. London: Routledge.

Lather, P., & Smithies, C. (1997). *Troubling the angels: women living with HIV/AIDS*. Boulder, CO: Westview Press.

Latour, B., & Woolgar, S. (1979). *Laboratory life: the social construction of scientific facts*. London: Sage.

Lauclau, E. (1990). *New reflections on the revolution of our time*. London: Verso.

Lawson-Te Aho (1993). The socially constructed nature of psychology and the abnormalisation of Maori. *New Zealand Psychological Society Bulletin*, 76, 25–30.

Lax, W. (1991). The reflecting team and the initial consultation. In T. Andersen (Ed.). *The reflecting team*. New York: Norton.

Lebow, R.N. (1996). *The art of bargaining*. Baltimore, MD: Johns Hopkins University Press.

Levinson, S.C. (1983). *Pragmatics*. New York: Cambridge University Press.

Levy, S.R., & Klein, M. (2008). *Intergroup attitudes and relations in childhood through adulthood*. New York: Oxford University Press.

Lillard, A. (1998). Ethnopsychologies: cultural variations in theories of mind. *Psychological Bulletin*, 123, 3–32.

Lipchik, E. (1993). Both/and solutions. In S. Friedman (Ed.). *The new language of change: constructive collaboration in psychotherapy*. New York: Guilford.

Linda B., as quoted in P. Lather & C. Smithies (1997). *Troubling the angels: women living with HIV/AIDS*. Boulder, CO: Westview Press. p. xxvi.

Link, B.G., & Phelan, J.C. (1999). The labeling theory of mental disorder. In A.V. Horwitz & T.L. Scheid (Eds.). *Handbook for the study of mental health*. Cambridge: Cambridge University Press.

Littlejohn, S., & Domenici, K. (2000). *Engaging communication in conflict: systemic practice*. Thousand Oaks, CA: Sage.

Lutz, C. (1988). *Unnatural emotions*. Chicago: University of Chicago Press.

Mannheim, K. (1951). *Ideology and utopia*. New York: Harcourt Brace.

Martin, E. (1987). *The woman in the body: a cultural analysis of reproduction*. Boston, MA: Beacon.

Maruna, S. (1997). Going straight: Disistance from crime and life narratives of reform. In Lieblich, A., & Josselson, R. (Eds.) *The narrative study of lives*. V.5. Thousand Oaks, CA: Sage.

Matza, D. (1969). *Becoming deviant*. Englewood Cliffs, NJ: Prentice-Hall.

McAdams, D. (2005). *The redemptive self*. New York: Oxford University Press.

McLuhan, M., & Powers, B.R. (1989). *The global village: transformation in world life and media in the 21st Century*. New York: Oxford University Press.

McNamee, S., & Gergen, K.J. (1992) *Therapy as social construction*. London: Sage.

McNamee, S., & Gergen, K.J. (1999). *Relational responsibility*. Thousand Oaks, CA: Sage.

Mead, G.H. (1934). *Mind, self and society*. Chicago: University of Chicago Press.

Meadows, D.H., Meadows, D.L., & Raners, J. (1992). *Beyond the limits: confronting global collapse, envisioning a sustainable future*. Post Mills, VT: Chelsea Green.

Mehan, H. (1979). *Learning lessons, social organization in the classroom*. Cambridge, MA: Harvard University Press.

Middleton, D., & Edwards, D. (1990). Conversational remembering: a social psychological approach. In D. Middleton & D. Edwards (Eds.). *Collective remembering*. London: Sage.

Milgram, S. (1974). *Obedience to authority*. New York: Harper & Row.

Moll, L.C. (1990). (Ed.). *Vygotsky and education*. Cambridge: Cambridge University Press.

Morgan, G. (1998). *Images of the organization*. Thousand Oaks, CA: Sage.

Morris, D. (1993). *The culture of pain*. Berkeley: University of California Press.

Morris, E. (2000). *Dutch: A memoir of Ronald Reagan*. New York: Modern Library.

Mulkay, M. (1985). *The word and the world*. London: George Allen & Unwin.

Myerson, G. (1994). *Rhetoric, reason and society: rationality as dialogue*. London: Sage.

Nagel, T. (1997). *The last word*. New York: Oxford University Press.

Naylor, A. (1991). *Exploring African American history*. New York: Heart of Lakes.

Naylor, G. (1982). *The women of Brewster Place*. New York: Viking.

Overton, W.R., & Reese, H.W. (1973). Models of development: methodological implications. In J.R. Nesselroade & H.W. Reese (Eds.). *Life-span development psychology: methodological issues*. New York: Academic Press.

Penn, P., & Frankfurt, M. (1994). Creating a participant text: writing, multiple voices, narrative multiplicity. *Family Process*, 33, 217–31.

Pearce, W.B., & Littlejohn, S.W. (1997). *Moral conflict: when social worlds collide*. Thousand Oaks, CA: Sage.

Pfohl, S. (1992). *Death at the parasite cafe*. New York: St Martins.

Phillion, J., He, M.F., & Connelly, F.M. (2005). *Narrative and experience in multicultural education*. Thousand Oaks, CA: Sage.

Potter, J. (1996). *Representing reality*. London: Sage.

Queneau, R. (1981). *Exercises in style*. New York: New Directions.

Reagan, S.,B., Fox, T., & Bleich, D. (1994). *Writing with: New directions in collaborative teaching, learning, and research*. Albany: State University of New York Press.

Ricoeur, P. (1981). *Hermeneutics and the human sciences*. New York: Cambridge University Press, p. 278.

Rodina, K.A. (In press). *Vygotsky's social constructionist view on disability: A methodology for inclusive education*.

Rogoff, B., Turkanis, C.G., & Bartlett, L. (Eds.). (2001). *Learning together, children and adults in a school community*. Oxford: Oxford University Press.

Rosenblatt, P.C., Karis, T.A., & Powell, R.D. (1995). *Multiracial couples: black and white voices*. Thousand Oaks, CA: Sage.

Ross, G., & Sinding, C. (2002). *Standing ovation: performing social science research*. Walnut Creek, CA: Alta Mira.

Ryle, G. (1949). *The concept of mind*. London: Hutchinson.

Said, E.W. (1978) *Orientalism*. New york: Vintage.

Sansom, W. (1956). *A contest of ladies*. London: Hogarth.

Saussure, E de ([1916]1974). *Course in general linguistics*. London: Fontana.

Schaeffer, R. (1976). *A new language for psychoanalysis*. New Haven, CT: Yale University Press.

Schudson, M. (1992). *Watergate in American memory*. New York: Basic Books.

Seikkula, J., & Arnkil, T.E. (2006). *Dialogic meetings in social networks*. London: Karnac.

Shapin, S. (1995). *A social history of truth: civility and science in seventeenth-century England*. Chicago: University of Chicago Press.

Shotter, J. (1985). *Social accountability and selfhood*. Oxford: Blackwell.

Shotter, J. (1990). The social construction of remembering and forgetting. In D. Middleton & D. Edwards (Eds.). *Collective remembering*. London: Sage.

Shotter, J., & Cunliffe, A.L. (2003). The manager as practical author II: conversations for action. In D. Holman & R. Thorpe (Eds.). *Management and language: the manager as practical author*. London: Sage.

Simon, K. (2003). *Moral questions in the classroom*. New Haven: Yale University Press.

Slife, B.D., & Williams, R.N. (1995). *What's behind the research, discovering hidden assumptions in the behavioral sciences*. Thousand Oaks, CA: Sage.

Spence, D. (1982). *Narrative truth and historical truth*. New York: Norton.

Spence, D. (1987). *The Freudian metaphor*. New York: Norton.

Squire, C. (1994). Empowering women? The Oprah Winfrey Show. In K. Bhavnani & A. Phoenix (Eds.). *Shifting identities, shifting racisms*. London: Sage.

Stone, A.R. (1996). *The war of desire and technology at the close of the mechanical age*. Cambridge: MIT Press.

Susskind, L., & Cruikshank, J. (1987). *Breaking the impasse: consensual approaches to resolving public disputes*. New York: Basic Books.

Szasz, T. (1984). *The therapeutic state*. Buffalo, NY: Prometheus.

Taylor, M.C., & Saaranen, E. (1994). *Imagologies: media philosophy*. London: Routledge.

Tillman-Healy, L.M. (1996). *A secret life in a culture of thinness: reflections an body, food, and bulimia*. In C. Ellis and A. Bochner (Eds). *Composing ethnography*. Walnut Creek, CA: Alta Mira.

Tomm, K. (1998). Co-constructing responsibility. In S. McNamee & K.J. Gergen (Eds). *Relational responsibilty*. Thousand Oaks, CA: Sage.

Topping, K.J. (1995). *Paired reading, spelling and writing: the handbook for teachers and parents*. London: Cassell.

Turner, R.H. (1978). The role and the person. *American Journal of Sociology*, 84, 1–23.

Tyler, S. (1987). *The unspeakable*. Madison, WI: University of Wisconsin Press.

Ulmer, G. (1989). *Applied grammatology, post-pedagogy from Jacques Derrida to Joseph Beuys*. Baltimore, MD: Johns Hopkins University Press.

Unger, R., & Crawford, M. (1992). *Women and gender: a feminist psychology*. Toronto: McGraw-Hill.

Ury, W. (1993). *Getting past no*. New York: Bantam.

van Eemeren, F., & Grootendorst, R. (1983). *Speech acts in argumentative discussions*. Dordrecht: Forris.

Verella, J.K. (2002). *Learning to listen, learning to teach: the power of dialogue in educating adults*. San Francisco, CA: Jossey-Bass.

Vygotsky, L. (1981). The genesis of higher mental functions. In J.V. Wertsch (Ed.). *The concept of activity in Soviet psychology*. Amronk, NY: M.E. Sharpe.

Wallach, M., & Wallach, L. (1983). *Psychology's sanction for selfishness*. San Francisco, CA: Freeman.

Walter, J., & Peller, J. (1992). *Becoming solution-focused in brief therapy*. New York: Brunner/Mazel.

Weisbord, M.R., & Janoff, S. (1995). *Future search*. San Francisco, CA: Barrett-Koehler.

Weisstein, N. (1993). Power, resistance and science: a call for a revitalized feminist psychology. *Feminism and Psychology*, 3, 239–245.

Wells, G. (1999). *Dialogic inquiry, towards a sociocultural practice and theory of education*. Cambridge: Cambridge University Press.

West, C. (1994). *Race matters*. New York: Vintage.

White, H. (1975). *Metahistory: historical imagination in nineteenth-century Europe*. Baltimore: Johns Hopkins University Press.

White, M., & Epston, D. (1990). *Narrative means to therapeutic ends*. New York: Norton.

Willis, P. (1977). *Learning to labour*. Westmead: Saxon House.

Winch, P. (1946). *The idea of a social science*. London: Routledge & Kegan Paul.

Winslade, J., & Monk, G. (2001). *Narrative mediation*. San Francisco, CA: Jossey-Bass.

Wise, A. (1979). *Legislated learning*. Berkeley, CA: University of California Press.

Wittgenstein, L. (1953). *Philosophical investigations*. Oxford: Blackwell.

Wykoff, G.S. (1969). *Harper handbook of college composition*. New York: Harper & Row.

INDEX

Cole, A.L. 108, 154
collaborative
    classroom 131–2
    decision making 145–7
    enquiry 73–4, 77
collective remembering 102–3
Collins, P.H. 51
Combs, G. 139
community 170
    functioning 44
    learning 132
    research 71
    retirement 151
    scientific 172
    as langage 143
Connelly, F.M. 134
Connolly, W.E. 56
consensus groups 131
Cooperrider, D. 147
co-reflecting 124
    mutual negotiation 125
    linguistic shading 125
Crawford, J. 73
Crawford, M. 137
Crenshaw, K. 30
Crimp, D. 162
critical theory 16, 49
    race theory 16
    reflexivity 13
Cromby, J. 174
Cruikshank, J. 116
Culler, J. 30
cultural imperialism 27
cultural psychology 94, 108
culture wars 53
Cumings, R. 157
Curthoys, A. 78

Danziger, K. 30, 78
Darwin, C. 81
Daston, L. 25
Dawson, K. 161
Dawson, R. 128
Davis, N.Z. 64
deconstruction 19
Deleuze, G. 54
democracy 20–1, 82
Denzin, N.K. 71, 79, 108
depression 96, 106, 137, 164–5
Derrida, J. 19–21
de Roux, N. 75
Desai, G.D. 30
Descartes, R. 47, 100–1, 159–60
De Shazer, S. 139
dialogue 110–15, 117–28, 132, 166, 168
    joint creation of meaning 118
    imaginary moments 126

dialogue cont.
    internal 142
    transformative 115, 118, 125–7
differentiating appraisal 50
discourse 120
    constructionism 166
    content studies 64
    function of 64, 69
    knowledge 48
    medicine 162
    mental 98, 100, 164
    mind 164
    psychological 165
    study/research 64–5, 79
disciplinary regimes 48
Domenici, K. 146
double helix 35
dramaturgy 90–1
Duncan, B.L. 139

Eagleton, T. 167
Ede, L. 132
education 157
    collaboration and community 130–6
Edwards, D. 55, 108, 174
Eliade, M. 162
Eliot, G. 33
Elliot, J. 79
Ellis, C. 72, 79
Einstein, A. 81
empiricism
    research 58–62, 74
    science 167
    tradition 63
emotional scenarios 103
emotions 35, 43, 65, 99–100, 102–5
Enlightenment 27–8
Epston, D. 140–1
ethnography 62–3
    collaborative 63, 73
ethnomethods 44
Evans, S. 132

Fals-Borda, O. 75
Fish, S. 30
Flax, J. 54, 88
Fleck, L. 23
Frank, A. 105
Feldman, B. 38
Feldman, C.F. 35
Fischer, R. 116
Folger, J.P. 116, 128
Forman, J. 132
forms of life 9
Foucault, M. 47, 49, 87
Fox, C.J. 157
Fox, D. 30

Fox, T. 132
Francis, D. 55
Frankfurt, M. 142
Freedman, J. 139
freedom 49, 85
Freud, S. 34, 81
Friedman, S. 157
Freire, P. 130, 157

Gadamer, H.G. 171
Gagnon, J.H. 104
Galison, P. 25
Garfinkel, H. 44
Gault, U. 73
gender 15
  conflict 148
  differences 36
  imbalance 68
  of words 65
generative theory 12, 81–8
Gergen, K. 30, 78, 104, 108, 120, 157, 174
Gergen, M. 30, 68, 73, 79
Gilligan, C. 66
Gintis, H. 135
Giroux, H. 135
Gitlin, T. 54
global village 26
Gloger-Tippelt, G. 104
Goffman, E. 90–1
Goodman, N. 2
Goolishian, H. 137
Gordon, C. 48
Goshgarian, G. 128
Grant, D. 157
Gregg, G.S. 56
Griffin, S. M. 118
Grootendorst, R. 115
Gross, B. 174
Grudin, R. 110
Guattari, F. 54
Gubrium, J.F. 65
Guerre, M. 64

Habermas, J. 15
Hacking, I. 174
Hall, S. 53
Hardy, R.L. 38
Harre, R. 70
Healy, L.T. 72
Held, B. 174
Heine, S.J. 108
Hepburn, A. 30
Hermans, H.J.M. 108
Hermanns, C. 101
hermeneutic studies 96
Herzig, M. 119
Hewitt, J.P. 108

Hibberd, F. 174
hidden curriculum 135
Hinchman, L.P. 55
Hobbes, T. 86
Hochschild, A. 108
Holstein, J.A. 30, 65
Holocaust 167
Hosking, D.M. 174
Hoskins, M. 155
Hubble, S.D. 139
Hunker, P.J. 54
Hunt, C. 118
Hunter, J.D. 53

Ibanez, T. 30
identity
  activism 51
  politics of 50–4, 56
ideological critique 15–17
individualism 45–6, 70, 83–91, 107, 122, 160
instrumentalist orientation 84
internal others 121, 142
Issacs, W. 128

Janson, P.O. 91
Jenkins, K. 78
Jennings, T.E. 157
Johnson, M. 34
Josselson, R. 66, 79

Kappeler, S. 166
Karpov, J. 108
Karis, T. 66
Kelman, H. 127
Kempen, H. 101
Kingwell, B.A. 54
Kippax, S. 73
Knowles, J.G. 79, 154
knowledge, scientific 21–5
Kuhn, T. 24
Kvale, S. 79

labeling theory 23
Laclau, E. 50
Lakoff, G. 34, 55
language 11
  see also discourse
  differences and deferral 20
  language game 9
  mental 164
  mind 165
  picture theory 6
  psychological 165
  social utility 9–11
  statistical 60
  structure 32–40, 44–50
  system of differences 19

Taylor, H. 132
therapy
  brief 139
  collaborative 143
  contemporary 144
  group 143
  medical model 142
  narrative 140–1
  historical 40
  as social construction 136–8, 157
  solution focused 138–9
Tomm, K. 142
totalitarianism 27–8, 113
transformative dialogue 118–27
truth 10–11, 18, 160, 166
  being in style 18
  beyond tradition 22
  universal 27

understanding as relational achievement 111–12
Unger, R. 137
Ury, W. 116

value
  added 149
  neutrality 14–16, 30
van Eemeren, F.H. 115
van Langenhove, L. 70

Verella, J.K. 131
Vygotsky, L. 92–3

Wallach, L. 85
Wallach, M.A. 85
Walkerdine, V. 157
Walter, J.L. 139
Wells, G. 131
Weick, K. 144, 157
Weisstein, N. 54
Wertsch, J.V. 108
Wetherell, M. 79
West, C. 54
White, M. 140–1
Willis, P. 45–6
Winch, P. 23
Winslade, J. 116, 128
Wise, M.R. 130
Wittgenstein, L. 6, 8, 9, 24, 32, 111, 163
Woofit, R. 55
Woolgar, S. 25, 42
writing
  as relationship 151–6
  embodied 152
Wykoff, G.S. 133

Yankelovich, D. 128
Yeats, W. 5

Supporting researchers for more than forty years

Research methods have always been at the core of SAGE's publishing. Sara Miller McCune founded SAGE in 1965 and soon after, she published SAGE's first methods book, Public Policy Evaluation. A few years later, she launched the Quantitative Applications in the Social Sciences series – affectionately known as the "little green books".

Always at the forefront of developing and supporting new approaches in methods, SAGE published early groundbreaking texts and journals in the fields of qualitative methods and evaluation.

Today, more than forty years and two million little green books later, SAGE continues to push the boundaries with a growing list of more than 1,200 research methods books, journals, and reference works across the social, behavioral, and health sciences.

From qualitative, quantitative, mixed methods to evaluation, SAGE is the essential resource for academics and practitioners looking for the latest methods by leading scholars.

www.sagepublications.com

Research Methods Books from SAGE

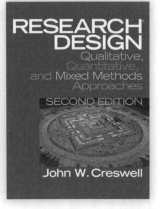